NJ DOL LIBRARY P O ROX 043

P9-DGK-557

CHILDREN, YOUTH AND FAMILY ISSUES

1999 State Legislative Summary

A Publication of the
Children and Families Program

RECEIVED

MAR 0 9 2000

Dept. of Labor Library

National Conference of State Legislatures
William T. Pound, Executive Director

1560 Broadway, Suite 700
Denver, Colorado 80202

444 North Capitol Street, Suite 515
Washington, D.C. 20001
www.ncsl.org/public.cfh.htm

January 2000

The National Conference of State Legislatures serves the legislators and staffs of the nation's 50 states, its commonwealths, and territories. NCSL is a bipartisan organization with three objectives:

- To improve the quality and effectiveness of state legislatures,
- To foster interstate communication and cooperation,
- To ensure states a strong cohesive voice in the federal system.

The Conference operates from offices in Denver, Colorado, and Washington, D.C.

Cover photos courtesy of Harry Cutting.

Printed on recycled paper

©2000 by the National Conference of State Legislatures. All rights reserved.
ISBN 1-58024-077-1

CONTENTS

FOREWORD

The Children and Families Program within the National Conference of State Legislatures (NCSL) is dedicated to providing policymakers with information that is critical to bettering the lives of America's families. The *Children, Youth and Family Issues: 1999 State Legislative Summary* is one of the many products and services the program offers.

Published annually since 1983, this book is a compilation of summaries of newly enacted state legislation that affects children and families. It documents legislative activity, emerging trends and innovative policies in the states, the District of Columbia and Puerto Rico—information that is essential to effective policymaking.

As public concern heightens regarding the nation's primary domestic problems—child abuse, juvenile delinquency and poverty—lawmakers are recognizing that families play a key role in ameliorating and preventing some of these societal ills. They are examining ways to shape public policy to strengthen and support families and protect all children, particularly our most vulnerable.

To assist legislators and legislative staff who are working in these policy areas, this publication provides necessary citations for further, more in-depth research.

In addition to the annual legislative summary, the Children and Families Program offers a variety of other publications, research and technical assistance to state legislators and their staff. We encourage constituents to contact the Denver office staff at (303) 830-2200 for a publications list or additional information.

Toby Goodman
Chair
Children, Families and Health Committee
Assembly on State Issues

Luci Hadi
Staff Chair
Children, Families and Health Committee
Assembly on State Issues

ACKNOWLEDGMENTS

The *1999 Legislative Summary* is a cooperative effort of the states and the Children and Families Program at the National Conference of State Legislatures (NCSL). The program staff gratefully acknowledge and appreciate the assistance of all legislative staff contacts, for without their efforts and thoroughness, this compilation of enacted legislation would not be possible.

The publication of this book is supported by the Annie E. Casey Foundation, the Ford Foundation, the Charles Stewart Mott Foundation, the Office of Child Support Enforcement and the Children's Bureau, U.S. Department of Health and Human Services, the A.L. Mailman Family Foundation, the Edna McConnell Clark Foundation, the U.S. Office of Juvenile Justice and Delinquency Prevention, the W.K. Kellogg Foundation, the David and Lucile Packard Foundation, The Pew Charitable Trusts, and NCSL.

The following Children and Families Program staff worked on the publication: Stephanie Bedi, Jessie Bullock, Steve Christian, Jenna Davis, Lisa Ekman, Mary Fairchild, Angela Garcia, Scott Groginsky, Barbara Houlik, Shanae Leffall, Mari Lucero, Teresa Myers, Julie Poppe, Kyle Ramirez-Fry, Dana Reichert, Bethany Robinson, Julie Thomerson, Julie Trosvig, Jack Tweedie, Stephanie Walton and Nina Williams-Mbengue. Scott Groginsky served as project coordinator. Jay Kroshus served as a consultant.

The cover was designed by Bruce Holdeman. The cover photos were taken by Harry Cutting. The publication was edited by Leann Stelzer. Scott Liddell provided formatting assistance.

The NCSL Children and Families Program

NCSL's Children and Families Program provides services to legislators and staff who are working to improve state policies that affect children and their families. The program tracks legislation, provides research and offers policy analysis, consultation and technical assistance specifically geared to the legislative audience. Whether you have worked on these issues for 20 years or are newly-elected, program staff can provide comprehensive, thorough, timely and in-depth information about critical family and children's state policy issues. The following services are available at no cost to legislators and staff:

- Research assistance
- Information
- On-line information

- Technical assistance
- Publications
- Human Services Discussion Group

Technical assistance includes testimony at committee hearings, briefing sessions for state legislators and their staffs, and bill drafting and analysis. Resources and expertise are provided by program staff, national experts and legislators through the following projects.

An e-mail discussion list—focused on human services issues—provides State and Federal policy updates and is available to help communicate with NCSL staff and colleagues in other states. After signing up, you can ask questions or provide information from your state to NCSL staff and other legislators and staff who also have subscribed to the list—humser-l@ncsl.org. Messages are sent and delivered to you via your Internet e-mail address. Remember that all messages are available to all other subscribers and participation is limited to legislators, legislative staff and NCSL staff. To subscribe, send an e-mail to dana.reichert@ncsl.org. Give your name, position, voice phone number and e-mail address. The service normally will be available to you within two working days of your request.

PROJECT AREAS

Child Care and Early Education—It is more evident today than ever before that providing quality early care and education affects children's development and adjustment from the early years into their adult years. Research shows that investing in quality early childhood care and education significantly improves school success and employment rates, and reduces future involvement with the criminal justice system. NCSL staff can provide current policy and program information about early childhood education as well as child care as a critical component of effective welfare reform. Visit the child care website at: www.ncsl.org/programs/cyf/cc.htm

Child Welfare—State legislators play a critical role in oversight of the child welfare system, which is charged with protecting children from abuse and neglect and ensuring that they are raised in safe, permanent families. NCSL can provide technical assistance to state legislatures on a variety of policy issues that affect child welfare, including child abuse investigations, coordination and financing of services to troubled families, permanency planning, foster care and adoption. Visit the child welfare website at: www.ncsl.org/programs/cyf/cw.htm

Child Support—With nearly one quarter of America's children living in single-parent families, child support is more relevant than ever. As states struggle to adequately serve this population and meet federal program requirements, NCSL staff is on hand to provide technical assistance and the most current research information. Visit the child support website at: www.ncsl.org/programs/cyf/cs.htm

Human Service Reorganization—During the past decade, state legislators have become increasingly concerned about the failure of children and family service systems and their complex and uncoordinated array of services. NCSL staff can help legislatures examine how other states have responded to these problems by reorganizing state agencies and increasing flexibility and control of resources for local governments and communities.

Juvenile Justice—Spurred by public fear of crime and concern that juveniles are disproportionately responsible for violent crime, legislatures are engaged in a full-fledged movement to reinvent juvenile justice. NCSL staff provide information and technical assistance to help legislators explore causes of juvenile crime and delinquency, craft comprehensive responses to youth crime, and examine model approaches in such a strategy. The project focuses on how legislatures can effectively and cross-jurisdictionally develop a policy framework for more effective juvenile justice. Visit the juvenile justice website at: www.ncsl.org/programs/cyf/jj.htm.

Nurturing Responsible Families—Recent findings on the importance of good parenting, especially during the early years of a child's life, indicate that a father's involvement can contribute to better child development and long-term outcomes. Although states initially focused on welfare and child support changes in requirements and supports for mothers, many policymakers have begun to examine the effect of the absence of the father as a regular participant in the financial and emotional support of his family. Through information resources, policy analysis and technical assistance, project activities are designed to educate legislatures about the opportunities for investment in programs targeted at low-income, noncustodial parents and their children. Activities include widespread distribution of information about existing fatherhood programs and on-site assistance to legislators and staff in particular states to help them craft programs for their states.

Welfare Reform—State legislatures continue the transformation of welfare into a work-based system—strengthening efforts in job training, child care and transportation and developing new programs that help recipients who have multiple barriers find jobs and help former recipients stay in their jobs. The welfare project works with legislators and staff to learn about program innovations in other states and how they can adapt them for circumstances in their own states. The project also helps legislators understand the flexibility of block grant financing and establish studies to track families that leave welfare and evaluate their reforms. Visit the welfare reform website at: www.ncsl.org/statefed/welfare/welfare.htm

For more information, call or write program staff at the National Conference of State Legislatures, 1560 Broadway, Suite 700, Denver, Colorado, 80202; (303) 830 2200; Fax (303) 863-8003. Visit the Human Services Home Page at http://www.ncsl.org/programs/cyf/hswelfare.htm

- Jack Tweedie, program director—general children and families, welfare
- Jessie Bullock—welfare
- Steve Christian—child welfare
- Jenna Davis—human services reform, welfare
- Mary Fairchild—juvenile justice, youth at risk
- Scott Groginsky—child care, early childhood education
- Barbara Houlik—child care, general children and families
- Shanae Leffall—welfare
- Mari Lucero—child support, juvenile justice
- Teresa Myers—child support
- Nina Williams-Mbengue—child welfare
- Julie Poppe—child care, early childhood education
- Dana Reichert—welfare, low-income fathers
- Kyle Ramirez-Fry—child welfare
- Julie Thomerson—juvenile justice
- Stephanie Walton—child support

Abbreviations and Acronyms

ASFA	Adoption and Safe Families Act
CAPTA	Child Abuse Prevention and Treatment Act
CASA	Court Appointed Special Advocate
CHINS	Children In Need of Supervision
CINA	Child In Need Of Assistance
CPS	Child Protective Services
CPR	Cardio Pulmonary Resuscitation
CRC	Crisis Residential Center
DCF	Department of Children and Families
DCTED	Department of Community, Trade, and Economic Development
DHS	Department of Human Services
DNA	Deoxyribonucleic Acid
DPRS	Department of Protective and Regulatory Services
DUI	Driving Under the Influence
DWI	Driving While Intoxicated
ESL	English as a Second Language
FINS	Families In Need of Supervision
FPL	Federal Poverty Level
FPS	Family Preservation Services
FWSN	Family With Service Needs
FY	Fiscal Year
GAL	Guardian Ad Litem
GED	General Equivalency Diploma
HCR	House Concurrent Resolution
HIV	Human Immunodeficiency Virus
HJR	House Joint Resolution
HR	House Resolution
ICWA	Indian Child Welfare Act
IDA	Individual Development Account
IV-D	State Child Support Agency
JOBS	Job Opportunity and Basic Skills
MOE	Maintenance Of Effort
OAG	Office of Attorney General
PINS	Person In Need of Supervision
PRWORA	Personal Responsibility and Work Opportunity Reconciliation Act
RFP	Request For Proposal
SCR	Senate Concurrent Resolution
SDU	State Disbursement Unit
SJR	Senate Joint Resolution
SMI	State Median Income
SOS	Support Our Students
SR	Senate Resolution
SSI	Supplementary Security Income
TANF	Temporary Assistance to Needy Families
TEA	Transportation Equity Act
Title IV-D	Child Support Section of the Social Security Act
UCCJA	Uniform Child Custody Jurisdiction Act
UCCJEA	Uniform Child Custody Jurisdiction Enforcement Act
UIFSA	Uniform Interstate Family Support Act
URESA	Uniform Reciprocal Enforcement of Support Act

INTRODUCTION

In an ongoing effort to document and track legislative activity on issues critical to children and families, the Children and Families Program of the National Conference of State Legislatures has published an annual state legislative summary for the past 16 years.

This publication is a joint effort between the program and the states. Every year, key legislative staff contacts provide NCSL with the latest enactments affecting children and families and assist in editing the completed summaries. The publication is available for legislative constituents on NCSLnet and to others, in hard copy, through NCSL's marketing department.

For the majority of states the publication includes all current year enactments. However, 10 legislatures—California, Illinois, Massachusetts, Michigan, New Jersey, New York, Ohio, Pennsylvania, Wisconsin and the District of Columbia—hold year-long sessions. Enactments for these legislatures included those signed into law between July 1, 1998, and June 30, 1999.

Kentucky did not hold a regular session in 1999. Oregon's session ended too late for most of its bills to be included in this publication.

NCSL appreciates any suggestions regarding this effort to provide a complete and comprehensive legislative summary. To comment, please call or write to NCSL's Children and Families Program in the NCSL Denver office.

ABUSE AND NEGLECT

Background Checks/Screening

AL   *1999 Ala. Acts, Act 361*
Establishes a comprehensive system for criminal background checks on current and prospective employees of public and private schools.

AR   *1999 Ark. Acts, Act 328*
Requires criminal history records checks for prospective adoptive and foster parents, in accordance with Adoption and Safe Families Act (ASFA).

CO   *1999 Colo. Sess. Laws, Chap. 293*
Adds certain convictions to grounds for denying licenses to family child care homes and certification of family foster homes. Requires all child care applicants, owners and employees to obtain a criminal background record check. Exempts certain providers, but requires them to sign a statement affirming no convictions. Criminalizes a false statement by applicants and requires a notice to be put on the application.

Sec. 10 Authorizes and funds a pilot study in three counties on background checks and requires a report to the legislature.

FL   *1999 Fla. Laws, Chap. 193*
Allows the department to place a child in a foster home that otherwise meets licensing requirements if the state and local records checks do not disqualify the home and the department is awaiting results from the federal criminal records check.

MS   *1999 Miss. Laws, Chap. 330*
Provides that the Department of Public Safety is responsible for releasing information relating to criminal history record checks to certain child residential facilities.

MO   *1999 Mo. Laws, Chap. 210*
Establishes the Family Care Safety Registry for child care providers and requires the registry to be publicly accessible with a toll-free number in 2001. Requires any provider or worker in a licensed or license-exempt child care home or center or receiving state or federal funds to submit to a background check. Provides a penalty. Excludes certain child care providers. Requires the registry to contain certain background information. Requires license-exempt child care facilities, such as religiously-operated centers, to conduct background checks on employees. Limits the state fee for conducting a background check. Allows for an appeal process. Requires an annual report to the legislature.

NV   *1999 Nev. Stats., Chap. 440*
Establishes a revolving account within the state general fund to investigate the backgrounds of volunteers who work with children.

NH   *1999 N.H. Laws, Chap. 326*
Requires that individuals who have regular contact with children in a child care program submit background information to the state. Outlines compliance licensing and enforcement process for convictions of crimes that could pose a threat to a child.

NY   *1999 N.Y. Laws, Chap. 7*
Secs. 7, 54 Specifies requirements for criminal history records checks on prospective foster and adoptive parents, in accordance with ASFA.

ND   *1999 N.D. Sess. Laws, Chap. 282*
      Secs. 21-24   Adopts requirements for fingerprinting and background screening of foster parents, legal guardians and adoptive parents.

OK   *1999 Okla. Sess. Laws, Chap. 2*
      Secs. 1-3   Replaces "criminal history investigation" with "criminal history records search." Authorizes department and child placement agencies to place a child in a home pending the completion of a background search under certain conditions. Authorizes the department to make an exception to fingerprinting requirement if a severe physical condition of the applicant prevents it.

UT   *1999 Utah Laws, Chap. 77*
      Requires a family child care provider caring for more than five but fewer than eight children to obtain a state certificate to screen for child abuse or neglect.

Court Procedures and Considerations

AR   *1999 Ark. Acts, Act 1363*
      Sec. 2   Specifies contents of adjudication orders in cases of medical neglect for religious reasons.

DE   *Vol. 70 Del. Laws, Chap. 212*
      Sec. 2   Clarifies that the hearsay exception applies to child victims as well as child witnesses who testify in criminal cases.

      Sec. 3   Adds certain violent felonies to the list of those in which children may testify via out-of-court statements.

      Vol. 70 Del. Laws, Chap. 173
      Sec. 6   Grants the state authority to request an order to compel from the family court, when able to show need for such an order. Defines "need" for the purposes of this section.

FL   *1999 Fla. Laws, Chap. 168*
      Allows the court to designate a community-based agency under contract with the state to provide protective services as a participant in proceedings involving the child.

LA   *1999 La. Acts, Act 1215*
      Requires that a local child protection unit provide notice to parents of a continued custody hearing.

MA   *1998 Mass. Acts, Chap. 179*
      Requires the court to consider evidence of domestic violence and child abuse when issuing a custody order, creates a rebuttable presumption against awarding custody to abusive parent, and outlines factors in setting visitation with abusive parent.

MI   *1999 Mich. Pub. Acts, Act 325*
      Allows special accommodations for testimony in juvenile proceedings for certain witnesses under age 16 and other developmentally disabled witnesses over age 16.

      1999 Mich. Pub. Acts, Act 530
      Extends family court jurisdiction in abuse and neglect cases to include authority over nonparent adults in family service plans and termination of parental rights. Defines "nonparent" adult.

MN   *1999 Minn. Laws, Chap. 245*
      Art. 8, Sec. 46   Requires that a petition be filed within 90 days of a voluntary placement. Requires that a petition be filed within six months of a voluntary placement of a handicapped child. Requires petition to state the reason for the placement, the progress on the case plan, and the statutory basis for the petition.

      Art. 8, Sec. 47   Clarifies that a court has jurisdiction over a domestic child abuse matter even if a parent is willing to accept services.

Art. 8, Sec. 48 Simplifies procedures regarding petitions and temporary orders in domestic child abuse proceedings.

Art. 8, Sec. 49 Lists people who are to be notified that a "child in need of protection or services" petition is pending.

Art. 8, Sec. 53 Requires that a case plan be filed within 30 days of the filing of a petition. Allows the court to approve or modify the case plan before ordering parent to comply.

Art. 8, Sec. 54 Adds dispositions the court may order when a child is found to be in need of protection or services.

Art 8, Sec. 56 Allows the agency to be dismissed as a party in cases of domestic abuse of a child, if the remaining parent can adequately enforce an order excluding the abusing party from the home.

Art. 8, Sec. 57 Requires the court to order a disposition when a child is not returned home.

Art. 8, Sec. 63 Clarifies when prior judicial findings are required for proceedings involving termination of parental rights.

MT   *1999 Mont. Laws, Chap. 566*
Secs. 7-8 Provides that information contained in a report filed by the guardian ad litem is not hearsay when it is used to form the basis of the guardian's opinion as to the best interests of the child. Requires that abuse and neglect petitions be accompanied by an affidavit by the department alleging abuse, neglect or abandonment. See also *Legal Representation/Ad Litems/Special Advocates* section.

NV   *1999 Nev. Stats., Chap. 435*
Secs. 24, 28 Requires courts to ensure that a person with a special interest in a child is allowed to make recommendations regarding placement. Adopts notice provisions of ASFA.

NH   *1999 N.H. Laws, Chap. 199*
Requires that a person having custody or control of a child and who is served with a summons in a child protection proceeding appear with the child not less than 24 hours after service.

NC   *1999 N.C. Sess. Laws, Chap. 318*
Sec. 5 Requires the court to consider the results of a mental health evaluation in custody determinations where there are allegations of physical abuse.

Secs. 6, 8 Requires the court to consider the results of the perpetrator's mental health evaluation in making custody determinations where the perpetrator has a history of violent behavior and the juvenile has been found to suffer physical abuse.

SC   *1999 S.C. Acts, Act 104*
Secs. 4, 19-20 Expands the applicability of the hearsay exception to children who function developmentally under the age of 12.

Provides that the pendency of an appeal concerning a child in foster care does not deprive the court of jurisdiction.

Requires court administration to use a separate code to identify child protection cases and to conduct a study of the feasibility of collecting additional data to ensure compliance with statutory time frames for hearings. Requires report to chief justice by July 1, 2000.

TN   *1999 Tenn. Pub. Acts, Chap. 164*
Expands circumstances and time frames under which the advisory review board on foster care may make a direct referral to the judge with findings or recommendations.

TX   *1999 Tex. Gen. Laws, Chap. 787*
Sec. 3   Requires the court to deny a parent access to child when the parent has a history of family violence, except in specific circumstances.

1999 Tex. Gen. Laws, Chap. 1150
Sec. 26   Specifies situations in which a status hearing is not required.

1999 Tex. Gen. Laws, Chap. 1302
Adds a subchapter to Family Code regarding the appointment of associate judges for substitute care and child protective services cases.

UT   *1999 Utah Laws, Chap. 67*
Clarifies venue requirements in child abuse proceedings.

1999 Utah Laws, Chap. 164
Permits a finding of abuse to be supported by a child's reliable out-of-court statement. Adds to circumstances in which a finding of abuse may be challenged.

VA   *1999 Va. Acts, Chap. 668*
Increases the age at which a child victim can request to testify via closed-circuit television.

1999 Va. Acts, Chap. 807
Requires the issuance of an emergency protective order when a warrant is issued for assault and battery against a family or household member to make the issuance of a protective order discretionary when the defendant is a minor.

WY   *1999 Wyo. Sess. Laws, Chap. 4*
Requires the child's safety to be considered at annual placement reviews.

Definitions/Offenses/Penalties

AK   *1999 Alaska Sess. Laws, Chap. 62*
Creates crime of failure to report a violent crime committed against a child.

CO   *1999 Colo. Sess. Laws, Chap. 216*
Creates crime of female genital mutilation of a minor. Authorizes outreach and education concerning such abuse. Requires district attorney to report to immigration and naturalization service when there is reasonable belief that any person arrested for said offense is not a U.S. citizen or national. See also *Sexual Abuse and Exploitation* section.

DE   *Vol. 70 Del. Laws, Chap. 173*
Prohibits the defense of not knowing the victim's age, by those accused of assault in the second degree.

Sec. 1   States that anyone 18 years or older who recklessly or intentionally harms a child who under the age six is guilty of assault in the second degree, a Class D felony.

FL   *1999 Fla. Laws, Chap. 168*
Amends the definition of "harm" to include those situations in which a parent or caregiver makes a child unavailable in order to avoid or impede an investigation.

Increases the penalties for knowingly failing to report child abuse. Creates a penalty for those over age 18 living in the same house as a child abuse victim who knowingly fail to report the abuse. Makes an exception for those individuals the court determines to be victims of domestic violence.

Defines as an accessory after the fact those who aid or assist a child abuse offender, regardless of the person's relationship to the offender. Makes an exception for victims of domestic violence. Increases penalties for aggravated child abuse.

HI   *1999 Hawaii Sess. Laws, Act 153*
Defines "abandoned infant," as required by ASFA.

IN   *1999 Ind. Acts, PL 197*
Increases penalties for neglect of a dependent.

LA   *1999 La. Acts, Act 769*
Replaces "willful" failure of care with "unreasonable" failure of care in the statutory definition of neglect.

1999 La. Acts, Act 784
Adds to grounds for determining that a family is in need of services that a child is found in possession of a handgun under circumstances that reasonably tend to exclude any lawful purpose.

1999 La. Acts, Act 1178
Adds to grounds for child abuse or neglect that the child is a victim of abuse perpetrated by a person who is dating or engaged to a parent or by a person living in the same residence with the parent.

1999 La. Acts, Act 1356
Provides for a temporary restraining order to protect a child from neglect as well as from abuse.

MI   *1998 Mich. Pub. Acts, Act 531*
Includes a nonparent adult who has a close personal relationship with a child's parent in the definition of "person responsible for the child's health or welfare." Defines "nonparent adult."

MN   *1999 Minn. Laws, Chap. 245*
Art 8 Sec. 43   Modifies definition of term "child in need of protection or services" to include a child in voluntary placement under certain circumstances.

MT   *1999 Mont. Laws, Chap. 541*
Replaces the phrase "detrimental to the best interest of the child" with "endangers the child's physical, mental or emotional health" that petitioner must establish in affidavit requesting an interim parenting plan.

1999 Mont. Laws, Chap. 566
Sec. 2   Defines "abandonment." Amends definition of "physical abuse" to add references to intent and gross negligence. Defines "psychological abuse or neglect" and "unfounded."

NV   *1999 Nev. Stats., Chap. 157*
Requires that a child be placed in protective custody if the death of a parent resulted from domestic violence.

NY   *1998 N.Y. Laws, Chap. 600*
Creates the crime of misrepresentation by a child care provider and defines reckless assault of a child.

1999 N.Y. Laws, Chap. 7
Secs. 12-13   Amends definitions of "severely abused" and "repeatedly abused."

NC   *1999 N.C. Sess. Laws, Chap. 190*
Sec. 1   Expands the definition of "caretaker" to include any employee or volunteer of a division, institution or school operated by the state institution.

1999 N.C. Sess. Laws, Chap. 451
Increases the penalty for certain child abuse offenses from a Class E felony to a Class C felony.

ND   *1999 N.D. Sess. Laws, Chap. 282*
Sec. 1   Defines "abandon," "abandoned infant" and "aggravated circumstances" in accordance with ASFA.

1999 N.D. Sess. Laws, Chap. 123
Increases class of crimes of assault and aggravated assault one degree when victim is under age 12. Increases class of crime of child abuse one degree when child is under age 6.

OH   *1999 Ohio Laws, HB 484*
Provides that a child is presumed abandoned when the parents have failed to contact the child for more than 90 days.

PA   *1998 Pa. Laws, Act 126*
Adds "aggravated circumstances" and "aggravated physical neglect" to definition of dependent child and clarifies how these situations affect revocation of parental rights. Defines sexual violence and rape to include use of child's likeness for photographing, videotaping, depicting on computer or filming. Provides for release of a minor's substance abuse treatment records under certain circumstances.

TX   *1999 Tex. Gen. Laws, Chap. 787*
Sec. 2   Clarifies definition of "safe environment" for a child.

      1999 Tex. Gen. Laws, Chap. 1087
Sec. 3   Makes voluntarily delivering a child to an emergency medical service provider an affirmative defense to a charge of abandonment of a child.

VA   *1999 Va. Acts, Chap. 665*
Broadens the definition of "family abuse" to apply to situations beyond "acts of violence," as previously defined.

      1999 Va. Acts, Chap. 721
Revises definition of family or household members to include parents, stepparents, children, stepchildren, brothers, sisters, grandparents and grandchildren, regardless of whether they reside in the same household. Broadens the applicability of protective orders and family assault statutes.

Financing

CA   *1998 Cal. Stats., Chap. 329*
Sec. 39-41   Reallocates funds for child abuse prevention to provide for oversight functions. Establishes the California Families and Children Home Visit Program. Requires participating counties to submit plans for implementing home visit programs. Authorizes the state to award program operation grants and evaluate program implementation. Establishes a task force to identify and recommend funding sources for the home visit program.

MN   *1999 Minn. Laws, Chap. 245*
Art. 8, Secs. 10-18   Expands the availability of claiming federal child welfare targeted case management funds to include contract staff and Indian tribes.

MT   *1999 Mont. Laws, Chap. 394*
Sec. 2   Authorizes courts to access district court reimbursement fund to cover certain expenses incurred in proceedings involving abused and neglected children. Eliminates requirement that excess funds in district court reimbursement fund be used for youth court and probation foster placements.

Legal Representation/Ad Litems/Special Advocates

AR   *1999 Ark. Acts, Act 708*
Requires the state Supreme Court to adopt standards of practice and qualifications for service for attorneys providing legal representation to children. Charges the Administrative Office of the Courts with responsibility for establishing a system of representation that equitably serves all areas of the state. Requires the office to publish requests for proposals. Deletes language regarding representation of parents.

CA   *1998 Cal. Stats., Chap. 706*
Permits minors age 12 or older to appear in court without guardian or counsel to request or oppose a protective or restraining order. Permits persons under age 12 to appear with guardian in same situations.

ID   *1999 Idaho Sess. Laws, Chap. 123*
Secs. 1, 2   Allows court to appoint a guardian for any child abused, neglected, abandoned or lacking a stable home environment. Defines "abandonment." Requires court to consider the best interest of the child as the primary factor in considering whether to appoint a guardian. Prohibits the court from using advanced age as criteria to determine the suitability of a potential guardian. See also *Definitions/Offenses/Penalties* section.

Deletes language that requires courts to consider whether a custodian is unable to provide a stable home environment by reason of immaturity or disability.

IA   *1999 Iowa Acts, Chap. 164*
Sec. 1   Clarifies that a guardian ad litem (GAL) is not required to interview child if child is not age appropriate. Requires GAL to obtain authorization from parent's counsel prior to interviewing parents. Expands duties of GAL. Requires court order to specify duties of GAL and authorize access to certain information.

LA   *1999 La. Acts, H Con. Res. 242*
Requests the state supreme Court to adopt rules governing the appointment of counsel for children in child in need of care proceedings.

ME   *1999 Me. Public Laws, Chap. 303*
Clarifies procedures for appointment of a guardian by probate courts.

MI   *1998 Mich. Pub. Acts, Act 480*
Defines the duties and responsibilities of a lawyer-guardian ad litem. Requires the appointment of a lawyer-guardian ad litem in certain proceedings. Defines duties of an attorney for a child. Provides for assessment of costs. Requires court to consider information from a child's lawyer-guardian ad litem or attorney.

1998 Mich. Pub. Acts, Act 483
Requires the appointment of a lawyer-guardian ad litem in proceedings under the child protection law.

MN   *1999 Minn. Laws, Chap. 245*
Art. 8, Secs. 50-51   Requires that a guardian ad litem be appointed in cases of abuse or neglect.

NV   *1999 Nev. Stats., Act 584*
Sec. 15   Appropriates $200,000 for a pilot program to provide guardians ad litem for abused and neglected children.

1999 Nev. Stats., Chap. 435
Secs. 16, 25   Specifies training requirements and duties for guardians ad litem.

NH   *1999 N.H. Laws, Chap. 30*
Authorizes a study of issues concerning procedure and standards for appointment and supervision of guardians ad litem.

NC   *1999 N.C. Sess. Laws, Chap. 432*
Extends guardian ad litem appointment from two years to until a permanent plan has been achieved for the juvenile. Expands the duties and authority of a guardian ad litem.

PA   *1998 Pa. Laws, Act 128*
Outlines standards, expectations and liabilities of court-appointed special advocates.

TX   *1999 Tex. Gen. Laws, Chap. 1515*
Requires an attorney ad litem to interview a child's foster parents in certain circumstances.

VA   *1999 Va. Acts, Chap. 606*
Adds court-appointed special advocates to the list of those mandated to report suspected cases of child abuse and neglect.

WV   *1999 W. Va. Acts, Chap. 10 - 2nd Special Session*
Sec. 48-11-302   Allows the court to appoint an attorney or guardian ad litem to represent the child, and requires the court to order an investigation when substantial allegations of domestic abuse have been made. Also allows the court to require the parents to provide necessary information to the investigator, and specifies that both the guardian ad litem and an investigator are subject to cross-examination. Directs that these services will be provided at no cost to the parties.

Organization/Oversight

AR   *1999 Ark. Acts, Act 36*
Sec. 1   Clarifies that the child abuse hotline and the central intake unit of the Department of Human Services are the same entity.

CA   *1998 Cal. Stats., Chap. 329*
Secs. 39-41   Reallocates funds for child abuse prevention to provide for oversight functions. Establishes the California Families and Children Home Visit Program. Requires participating counties to submit plans for implementing home visit programs. Authorizes the state to award program operation grants and evaluate program implementation. Establishes a task force to identify and recommend funding sources for the home visit program.

HI   *1999 Hawaii Sess. Laws, Act 116*
Permits the director of human services, rather than the governor, to appoint members to the Blueprint Pilot Project, to expand the size of the child protective services reform coordinating committee to include two line staff of the child protective services unit, and to extend the project through June 30, 2002.

IL   *1999 Ill. Laws, PA 60*
Requires the establishment of at least three citizen review panels, as required by CAPTA.

IA   *1999 Iowa Acts, Chap. 203*
Sec. 45   Requires that the independent evaluation of the child protection system be completed in the fiscal year that begins July 1, 2000.

KS   *1999 Kan. Sess. Laws, Chap. 172*
Creates Kansas Children's Cabinet. Changes oversight of Family and Children Trust Account for the prevention of abuse and neglect to the cabinet. Defines duties, membership and functions of cabinet.

MD   *1999 Md. Laws, Chaps. 355, 356*
Renames the existing state Citizen Board of Review of Foster Care for Children to be the State Citizens' Review Board for Children. Authorizes the creation of local citizen review panels. Creates a state Child Fatality Review Team and requires the creation of child fatality review teams in each county. Codifies the Governor's Council on Child Abuse and Neglect and renames it the State Council on Child Abuse and Neglect.

MN   *1999 Minn. Laws, Chap. 245*
Art. 8, Sec. 80   Requires that a member of a county multidisciplinary child protection team be designated as a lead person responsible for the planning process to develop standards for battered women's programs and services.

Art. 8, Sec. 81   Requires that chemical dependency assessment criteria address issues related to parents who have open child protection cases. Requires the commissioner to amend the chemical dependency rules to address pregnancy as a risk factor in determining the need for treatment.

MO   *1999 Mo. Laws, Chaps. 210, 660*
        Lists the regional child assessment centers to be funded by the state. Requires the director of the Department of Social Services to develop caseload standards. Requires that such standards shall be used as the basis of the department's budget request. Requires the director to convene a caseload standards committee.

NV   *1999 Nev. Stats., Chap. 435*
        Sec. 17   Requires the state to establish a panel of volunteers to evaluate the effectiveness of protective services.

NC   *1999 N.C. Sess. Laws, Chap. 237*
        Sec. 11.28   Requires the Division of Social Services and the Department of Health and Human Services to report semiannually to the state legislature on the activities of the state Child Fatality Review Team, providing a final report that includes recommendations for changes in the statewide child protection system.

TX   *1999 Tex. Gen. Laws, Chap. 1490*
        Establishes the position of "investigations coordinator" within child protective services. Outlines job responsibilities and duties.

Prevention/Treatment/Training

AR   *1999 Ark. Acts, Act 1240*
        Sec. 1   Requires department to provide informational materials regarding parenting, abuse and family planning to parents of children in state custody.

CA   *1998 Cal. Stats., Chap. 329*
        Sec. 39-41   Reallocates funds for child abuse prevention to provide for oversight functions. Establishes the California Families and Children Home Visit Program. Requires participating counties to submit plans for implementing home visit programs. Authorizes the state to award program operation grants and evaluate program implementation. Establishes a task force to identify and recommend funding sources for the home visit program.

CO   *1999 Colo. Sess. Laws, Chap. 216*
        Creates crime of female genital mutilation of a minor. Authorizes outreach and education concerning such abuse. Requires district attorney to report to immigration and naturalization service when there is reasonable belief that any person arrested for said offense is not a U.S. citizen or national.

DE   *Vol. 70 Del. Laws, Chap. 173*
        Sec. 3   Requires that all public and private early childhood education providers contracting with the Department of Education ensure that every employee receive a minimum of one hour of training every year in the detection and reporting of child abuse.

GA   *1999 Ga. Laws, Act 316*
        Extends the Children's Trust Fund and the Children's Trust Fund Commission until 2010.

IN   *1999 Ind. Acts, PL 101*
        Expands the shaken baby syndrome education program to include other childhood hazards. Requires state to implement a program on awareness and prevention of childhood hazards.

KS   *1999 Kan. Sess. Laws, Chap. 172*
        Creates Kansas children's cabinet. Changes oversight of Family and Children Trust Account for the prevention of abuse and neglect to the cabinet. Defines duties, membership and functions of cabinet.

ME *1999 Me. Public Laws, Chap. 515*
Expands home visiting services to include parents of all newborn children in the state, contingent upon sufficient funds.

  1999 Me. Public Laws, Chap. 529
Includes quality child care as part of the state's overall statewide goal to prevent child abuse and expands the definition of prevention programs to include the promotion of high quality child care. Requires applicants to the Maine Children's Trust be made public, with applicants' permission.

MI *1998 Mich. Pub. Acts, Act 479*
Requires the state to review a child's case with his or her physician if it involves certain diagnoses. Requires the court to allow the physician to testify regarding the service plan in certain cases.

MN *1999 Minn. Laws, Chap. 245*
Art. 8, Secs. 3-4 Requires experimentation with different chemical dependency service models for parents with children who are found to be in need of treatment.

  Art. 8, Sec. 5 Expands medical assistance to cover certain services for children in residential facilities for severe emotional disturbance.

  Art. 8, Sec. 71 Requires the local welfare agency to collect information on the existence of substance abuse discovered during assessments of reported abuse or neglect. Requires that, if the assessment indicates a potential for substance abuse, a chemical use assessment be conducted, and the determination, recommendations and referrals for treatment be reported to the state authority on alcohol and drug abuse.

  Art. 8, Sec. 74 Eliminates language referencing the Maltreatment of Minors Advisory Committee.

MO *1999 Mo. Laws, Chaps. 210, 660*
Expands membership on the Children's Trust Fund Board.

MT *1999 Mont. Laws, Chap. 566*
Sec. 15 Specifies contents of required treatment plans.

NJ *1999 N.J. Laws, Chap. 127*
Secs. 1-3 Requires a substance abuse assessment for all adults residing in the home of a child under the custody of the division, when necessary. Requires the parent or adult whose assessment is positive for substance abuse to prove he or she is receiving and cooperating with their treatment before a child can be returned home. Requires commissioner to adopt regulations to implement this act. Makes appropriation.

  Requires the Department of Human Services to prepare and distribute to the general public a pamphlet providing information on child abuse and neglect.

NC *1999 N.C. Sess. Laws, Chap. 237*
Sec. 11.28 Allows accredited social work master's or bachelor's degree program curricula to substitute for preservice training for child welfare workers.

OH *1999 Ohio Laws, HB 484*
Requires that addicted parents of children identified as being at risk of abuse or neglect be referred for treatment. Specifies services required to be provided by drug and alcohol addiction programs. Requires that such services be given a priority and that the public children's services agency and the addiction program share necessary information. Requires courts to order addicted parents of adjudicated children to obtain an assessment and treatment. Allows court to order drug testing.

VA *1999 Va. Acts, Chap. 868*
Grants localities the authority to establish a team to examine fatal family violence incidents and to create a clearinghouse of information to help prevent future family violence fatalities.

WA   *1999 Wash. Laws, Chap. 389*
Sec. 2   Establishes a statewide training program for persons responsible for investigating child sexual abuse.

Sec. 5   Adds specialized training in child sexual abuse investigations to the minimum training standards for caseworkers.

Registries and Records

CO   *1999 Colo. Sess. Laws, Chap. 259*
Requires an adoption investigation to include a check of the central child abuse registry.

IN   *1999 Ind. Acts, PL 197*
Sec. 4   Requires that medical records relating to child abuse be sent, upon request, to law enforcement agencies.

IA   *1999 Iowa Acts, Chap. 111*
Sec. 8   Authorizes the central registry to release information on specific cases of child abuse that resulted in a child fatality or near fatality.

LA   *1999 La. Acts, Act 750*
Requires release of limited information from child abuse or neglect case reports upon written request. Specifies when and to whom such limited information can be released.

        1999 La. Acts, Act 1217
Requires the state, upon request by a caregiver, to release to an employer or prospective employer information regarding whether a report has been received regarding the caregiver.

ME   *1999 Me. Public Laws, Chap. 305*
Allows certain state agencies to provide to the state child welfare agency records for use in the investigation of suspected child abuse.

MD   *1999 Md. Laws, Chap. 214*
Establishes hearing procedures for individuals who challenge child abuse or neglect findings and sets forth requirements for the maintenance of data regarding abuse and neglect investigations in the computerized data base operated by the state Department of Human Resources. Clarifies that the release of information regarding abuse and neglect is required under court order or order of an administrative law judge. Specifies that information may be disclosed on request to foster care and adoption workers of the department.

Defines "central registry" and "identifying information." Requires the department to notify an individual who has been found responsible for abuse or neglect that he or she may be listed on the central registry. Authorizes individuals in cases where allegations are unsubstantiated to request a conference with department and outlines procedures. Authorizes individuals to contest the outcome of the conference through a contested case hearing and establishes procedures for hearings. Authorizes individuals to request a contested case hearing in cases where allegations are indicated.

Specifies cases in which identifying information can be included on the central registry and cases where inclusion of such information is prohibited. Specifies circumstances under which an individual may be identified as responsible for abuse or neglect from the central registry. Establishes a time line for the removal of names from the registry. Requires the secretary of the department to adopt regulations.

MI   *1998 Mich. Pub. Acts, Act 485*
Requires that information in the central registry be maintained until the perpetrator dies. Requires notification to perpetrators that a report is being classified as a central registry case and that information may be released to authorized persons.

MO   *1999 Mo. Laws, Chaps. 210, 660*
Requires the state to destroy child abuse records two years from the date of a finding of insufficient evidence of abuse.

NV   *1999 Nev. Stats., Chap. 26*
Requires that photographs and certain medical records made in connection with a child abuse investigation be provided to the prosecuting attorney.

      1999 Nev. Stats., Chap. 435
Secs. 20-21 Makes records available to rural advisory boards to expedite placement proceedings and to the panel created to evaluate protective services.

      1999 Nev. Stats., Chap. 557
Requires expunction of records relating to incidents involving reasonable exercise of parental discipline.

PA   *1998 Pa. Laws, Act 126*
Provides for release of a minor's substance abuse treatment records under certain circumstances.

      1998 Pa. Laws, Act 127
Sec. 9 Requires that the information concerning a report of suspected child abuse be maintained for a period of one year after the date the report was received.

SC   *1999 S.C. Acts, Act 104*
Sec. 14 Raises the age at which a child named in a report of abuse may receive information regarding the report. Authorizes the state to disclose certain information to participants in a family group conference.

SD   *1999 S.D. Sess. Laws, Chap. 134*
Sec. 1 Allows department to release information, excluding the child's identity, to the media regarding cases of abuse or neglect involving a fatality or near fatality under certain conditions. Defines "near fatality." See also *Definitions/Offenses/Penalties* section.

TN   *1999 Tenn. Pub. Acts, Chap. 453*
Requires the establishment of a procedure and format for child protective services investigation data collection. Allows child advocacy center staff access to confidential child abuse information.

      1999 Tenn. Pub. Acts, Chap. 522
Makes it unlawful for anyone, except for purposes directly connected to the administration of child protective services, to disclose information on reports of harm to a child. Allows information to be disclosed to department employees, medical professionals, contract or other agency service providers, child advocacy staff, and attorney or guardian ad litem for a child. See also *Legal Representation/Ad Litem/Special Advocates* section.

TX   *1999 Tex. Gen. Laws, Chap. 1150*
Sec. 3 Adds child care providers to the list of those the court may order to disclose information regarding reported child abuse and neglect.

UT   *1999 Utah Laws, Chap. 164*
Specifies when unsubstantiated reports of child abuse must be removed from the child welfare database.

WA   *1999 Wash. Laws, Chap. 339*
Mandates disclosure of information by Department of Social and Health Services (DSHS) where child is a victim of a near-fatal act.

      1999 Wash. Laws, Chap. 389
Sec. 7 Requires employees of the department who conduct interviews while investigating allegations of abuse and neglect to retain an original written record of the interview. Requires that written records be, at a minimum, a near verbatim record of the interview.

Reporting/Investigations

AR   *1999 Ark. Acts, Act 214*
Sec. 1   Clarifies that all reports of suspected abuse or neglect should be made to child abuse hotline. Requires investigating agency to notify law enforcement agency immediately of all reports of severe maltreatment.

            1999 Ark. Acts, Act 626
Sec. 1   Clarifies that notification of the prosecuting attorney's office concerning initial child maltreatment reports is at the discretion of the individual prosecutor.

CT   *1999 Conn. Acts, PA 85*
Requires the department to notify parents of a substantiated complaint of child abuse when the child is in the department's custody. Requires notification within a specified amount of time, and in English or the principal language of the recipient.

DE   *Vol. 70 Del. Laws, Chap. 173*
Sec. 4   Requires that the state investigate all reports that, if true, would constitute violations against a child by a person responsible for his or her care, custody or control. Requires the state to contact an appropriate law enforcement agency. Requires that the assisting law enforcement agency conduct its own criminal investigation and keep the division informed of its findings.

            Sec. 7   Gives the division investigator authority to exercise temporary emergency protective custody, provided that the child in question is located at a school or child care facility.

DE   *Vol. 70 Del. Laws, Chap. 179*
Clarifies immunity for those reporting child abuse and neglect, by adding definition of "good faith." Provides immunity form any liability, civil or criminal, for anyone who notifies police officers of child abuse. See also *Definitions/Offenses/Penalties* section.

DC   *1999 Ark. Acts, Act 1580*
Secs. 1-5   Creates Juvenile Ombudsman Division. Outlines duties, including investigation of complaints of abuse of juveniles in state custody. See also *Organization/Oversight* section.

FL   *1999 Fla. Laws, Chap. 168*
Amends the definition of "harm" to include those situations in which a parent or caregiver makes a child unavailable in order to avoid or impede an investigation.

            Increases the penalties for knowingly failing to report child abuse. Creates a penalty for those over age 18 living in the same house as a child abuse victim who knowingly fail to report the abuse. Makes an exception for those individuals the court determines to be victims of domestic violence.

            Creates the Kayla McKean Child Protection Act to address statutory gaps in the child protection system. Adds judges to the list of people required to provide their names when reporting child abuse. Requires the department to accept for investigation any child abuse report from a judge, teacher or other professional school official. Requires the department to voice record all incoming or outgoing calls received or placed by the central child abuse hotline and consider the recording confidential. Requires the department's quality assurance program to review reports to the child abuse hotline that involve three or more unaccepted reports on a single child to detect harassment or the need for an investigation because of the frequency of the reports. Requires the department to provide mandatory reporters with a written summary of the outcome of the investigation. Requires the department to contract with an independent entity to evaluate the central child abuse hotline.

            Requires the department to immediately notify law enforcement agencies in the county in which the abuse is believed to have occurred to determine if a criminal investigation is warranted and, if so, to take the lead in such investigation.

Requires the department to maintain a master file for each child accepted for an investigation and make the file available to any department staff or agent conducting a protective investigation. Requires that all protective investigations for a child be conducted, as much as possible, by the same worker or at least supervised by the same supervisor and that the department conduct a multidisciplinary staffing when a new investigator is assigned to investigate a second and subsequent report involving a child.

Requires that the assessment of risk and needs of the child and family must include an unannounced face-to-face interview with the child, siblings, parents and other adults in the household and an on-site assessment of the child's residence.

Changes the time frame to within three days, instead of as soon as possible, for the department to send written abuse reports to the local state attorney or law enforcement agency. Requires law enforcement agency participating in an investigation to take photographs of the child's living environment. Authorizes law enforcement agency to share criminal history information with the department in child protective investigations.

Requires any child with bruises, burns, fractures or injuries to the head who is the subject of a report to be referred to the child protection team rather than only those children under age three. Adds school district representatives to the child protection team.

Clarifies procedures and the relationship between the department and community-based agencies providing services.

Establishes a state Child Abuse Death Review Committee within the Department of Health and also establishes local child abuse death review committees.

HI   *1999 Hawaii Sess. Laws, Act 271*
Allows law enforcement to assume protective custody of a child victim of abuse without a court order, with conditions.

IA   *1999 Iowa Acts, Chap. 192*
Requires the state to notify parents of a child who is the victim of confirmed child abuse in a child care facility. Requires notification about the type of abuse, but prohibits identification of the victim, perpetrator or circumstances of the abuse.

LA   *1999 La. Acts, Act 593*
Creates an "inconclusive" category when local protection units determine that evidence tends to support a finding of abuse or neglect, but not enough evidence exists to confirm a justified report. Sets that Department of Social Services (DSS) is responsible for filing and safeguarding inconclusive reports and how those can be used in establishing a pattern of behavior if there are ensuing abuse or neglect investigations. See also *Organization/Oversight* section.

      1999 La. Acts, Act 1178
Requires reporting of abuse caused by a person who is dating or engaged to a parent or who lives in the same residence with the parent.

      1999 La. Acts, Act 1355
Authorizes assessment of families rather than investigation in response to certain low risk reports of abuse.

ME   *1999 Me. Public Laws, Chap. 300*
Expands the list of mandatory reporters of child abuse to include administrators and counselors at summer camps.

MI   *1998 Mich. Pub. Acts, Act 484*
Establishes five categories and corresponding state responses for investigations of child abuse and neglect reports, ranging from "no services needed" to "court petition required." Requires a report to the Legislature regarding cases categorized as requiring no services. Requires that mandatory reporters be notified of

the categorization of the report. Requires that schools or other institutions cooperate with the state during a child abuse investigation.

MN   *1999 Minn. Laws, Chap. 245*
Art. 8, Sec. 65   Creates a program of alternative responses to reports of child abuse and neglect.

Authorizes counties to establish programs that use alternative responses to child abuse reports. Clarifies that families are voluntary participants in the program.

Outlines general framework for determining how to respond to a report. Lists circumstances under which an investigation must be conducted based on the allegations in the report.

Specifies documentation requirements regarding the outcome of cases in which an alternative response is used.

Requires that counties using the alternative response program include it in their community social service plan and program evaluation.

Authorizes the state to develop guidelines and procedures for the alternative response program.

Art. 8, Sec. 67   Adds the term "agency responsible for assessing or investigating the report" to the list of agencies authorized to receive child abuse reports.

Art. 8, Sec. 68   Lists the agencies that are responsible for assessing or investigating reports of alleged child maltreatment.

Art. 8, Sec. 69   Adds to the lists of people who are immune from civil and criminal liability in making a voluntary or mandated report or assisting in the assessment of an alleged report of child abuse or neglect.

Art. 8, Sec. 70   Requires the local child welfare agency, if requested, to inform the person who made the report of maltreatment or abuse within 10 days, as to whether the report was accepted for assessment or investigation.

Art 8 Sec. 73   Clarifies the notification requirements regarding neglect or abuse in a facility.

Art. 8, Sec. 76   Specifies who is considered to be a mandated reporter. Clarifies that information social services releases to mandated reporters about the child must be limited to data pertinent to the individual's responsibility for caring for the child, and be released with the best interests of the child in mind.

MT   *1999 Mont. Laws, Chap. 566*
Sec. 5   Removes immunity from liability for those who knowingly make false reports of child abuse.

NV   *1999 Nev. Stats., Chap. 26*
Expands civil and criminal immunity granted to persons who investigate reports of child abuse to include performance of medical tests and provision of medical test reports to certain agencies.

1999 Nev. Stats., Chap. 435
Sec. 20-21   Requires child protective agencies to disclose the identity of a person who reports child abuse if the person knowingly made a false report.

1999 Nev. Stats., Chap. 557
Provides that an investigation is not warranted if the reported incident was the result of the reasonable exercise of parental discipline involving corporal punishment.

NH   *1999 N.H. Laws, Chap. 223*
Conforms to federal CAPTA requirements by authorizing the department to release information to the public in fatality or near- fatality child abuse cases. Defines near fatality and specifies type of information to be released.

NC   *1999 N.C. Sess. Laws, Chap. 190*
Sec. 2   Specifies the responsibilities of the director of the Department of Social Services when there is a juvenile death in an institutional facility.

Sec. 4   Makes findings of the state Child Fatality Review Team inadmissable as evidence in a proceeding against a participant in a clinical fatality review.

1999 N.C. Sess. Laws, Chap. 237
Sec. 11.27   Mandates that the Division of Social Services work with local departments to develop and implement a dual response system of child protection in a limited number of pilot demonstration state-wide. Requires that local child protective services and law enforcement agencies work together to coinvestigate cases of serious abuse while the local department of social services provides a family assessment and services approach to cases of child abuse and neglect. Requires an assessment of the effect of these pilots on 1) child safety, 2) timeliness of response, 3) timeliness of services, 4) coordination of local human services, 5) cost-effectiveness, and any other related issues. States that the Department of Health and Human Services may proceed to implement the pilots if non-state funds are identified for this purpose.

1999 N.C. Sess. Laws, Chap. 318
Secs. 1, 4   Requires the Department of Health and Human Services to conduct a thorough investigation of the caregiver's background whenever a juvenile is removed from a caretaker's home due to physical abuse. Requires the department to review the caretaker's criminal history and any available mental health records.

OH   *1998 Ohio Laws, SB 212*
Adds administrators and employees of child day camps and residential camps to the list of people required to report suspected abuse or neglect.

OK   *1999 Okla. Sess. Laws, Chap. 44*
Sec. 1   Requires the department to assist with abuse or neglect investigations after referral to law enforcement agency when person under investigation is not the parent or responsible for the child.

SC   *1999 S.C. Acts, Act 104*
Secs. 7, 26-30   Requires mandatory reporters to report to law enforcement agencies abuse or neglect allegedly perpetrated by a person other than a parent or guardian. Allows any person to report suspected abuse. Requires that the identity of a reporter of abuse remain confidential. Requires the child welfare agency to disclose such identity to a law enforcement agency to which a report is referred. Extends civil immunity to people who participate in an investigation. Clarifies when child fatalities investigated by law enforcement agencies be investigated by the child welfare agency.

Amends the legislative authorization for a family assessment track pilot project. Clarifies requirements regarding performance evaluations and deadlines for completion of assessments. Extends the pilot program for an additional year. Clarifies how records of assessment cases are to be maintained.

SD   *1999 S.D. Sess. Laws, Chap. 135*
Sec. 1   Allows photographs, videotapes and electronic images of children to be taken during investigations of suspected abuse or neglect. Requires that such images be taken by law enforcement and department officials or their designees.

TX   *1999 Tex. Gen. Laws, Chap. 1490*
Establishes the position of "investigations coordinator" within child protective services. Outlines job responsibilities and duties.

1999 Tex. Gen. Laws, Chap. 1150
Sec. 2   Allows a person making a report of child abuse and neglect to waive his or her right to confidentiality.

Sec. 4   Establishes guidelines for conducting investigations of child abuse and neglect in department operated facilities.

Sec. 5   Gives courts the authority, upon good cause, to order release of a child's prior medical, psychological or psychiatric records to the department.

Sec. 18   Outlines the actions to be taken by the department when taking emergency custody of a child.

Sec. 29   Makes all participants of an alternative dispute resolution proceeding subject to the child abuse reporting statute.

UT   *1999 Utah Laws, Chap. 164*
Specifies procedures for informing someone making a report of abuse of the penalties for knowingly making a false report.

VA   *1999 Va. Acts, Chap. 606*
Adds court-appointed special advocates to the list of those mandated to report suspected cases of child abuse and neglect.

1999 Va. Acts, Chap. 828
Increases from a misdemeanor to a felony the penalty for the first offense of knowingly making a false report of child abuse. See also *Definitions/Offenses/Penalties* section.

1999 Va. Acts, Chap. 868
Grants localities the authority to establish a team to examine fatal family violence incidents and to create a clearinghouse of information to help prevent future family violence fatalities.

WA   *1999 Wash. Laws, Chap. 389*
Sec. 8   States that parents, guardians and foster parents whose child is being investigated for possible abuse and neglect may be made a party to later court proceedings and may be subject to examination by a physician, psychologist or psychiatrist.

Sec. 9   Prohibits law enforcement officers from investigating alleged abuse and neglect cases involving a child to whom they are or have been a parent, guardian or foster parent.

Sexual Abuse and Exploitation

AR   *1999 Ark. Acts, Act 1575*
Sec. 1   Expresses legislative intent to establish a pilot program of specialized centers for investigation of child sexual abuse cases. Authorizes state police to contract with private child advocacy centers to establish program using state police maintenance and general operation funds. Outlines services centers are required to provide.

IL   *1999 Ill. Laws, PA 223*
Adds to the definition of child sexual exploitation to include enticing a child to remove clothing for sexual gratification and sets penalty.

1999 Ill. Laws, PA 225
Allows the attorney general to seek a statewide grand jury to investigate and prosecute child solicitation, exploitation or prostitution using the Internet, other electronic devices and/or a computer.

1999 Ill. Laws, PA 226
Expands solicitation of a child to include solicitation of anyone under age 17. Increases penalties.

1999 Ill. Laws, PA 238
Requires a life sentence for predatory criminal sexual assault against two or more children.

1999 Ill. Laws, PA 279
Requires that those on parole or in mandatory supervised release for repeat sexual assault or abuse against a victim under age 18 serve the first two years in electronic home detention.

1999 Ill. Laws, PA 356
Specifies that a child sex offender may be present on school property if he or she is a parent or guardian of a student on the school grounds or has permission to be present.

IN   *1999 Ind. Acts, PL 214*
Provides additional conditions for probation or parole of sex offenders. Specifies conditions for sentencing as a repeat sexual offender.

IA   *1999 Iowa Acts, Chap. 61*
Defines "appropriate secure facility." Repeals time limit on filing a petition alleging that a person is a sexually violent predator. Grants full investigative powers to attorney general or prosecuting attorney prior to filing petition. Provides for the preservation of certain child abuse reports and authorizes the attorney general access to all child abuse records during an investigation. Allows alleged sexually violent predator to waive right to probable cause hearing. Permits continuance of hearing and outlines procedures. Increases time period during which trial must be held to determine if person is sexually violent predator. Establishes supervised release program for sexually violent predators and outlines departmental responsibilities. See also *Definitions/Offenses/Penalties* section.

1999 Iowa Acts, Chap. 112
Sec. 13   Permits a juvenile court officer to conduct risk assessments of juvenile sex offenders and to disclose the information to government agencies that are conducting confidential background investigations. Provides for lifetime registration for certain sex offenders and outlines procedures for the dissemination of information to the public regarding sex offenders.

KS   *1999 Kan. Sess. Laws, Chap. 164*
Sec. 38   Creates and defines new crime called "unlawful voluntary sexual relations" involving a minor under age 16 and a person between the ages of 16 and 19. Sets penalties.

LA   *1999 La. Acts, Act 541*
Requires that a protective order or consent agreement concerning a child who has been sexually molested shall remain in effect until the child is 18 years old.

ME   *1999 Me. Public Laws, Chap. 90*
Authorizes a minor to consent to a forensic examination after an alleged sexual assault.

1999 Me. Public Laws, Chap. 349
Makes it a crime to solicit a child, by means of a computer, to commit a prohibited act.

1999 Me. Public Laws, Chap. 438
Eliminates the statute of limitations for criminal prosecution of sexual abuse of a minor under age 16.

MN   *1999 Minn. Laws, Chap. 245*
Art. 8, Sec. 45   Modifies definition of "egregious harm" to include conduct towards a child that constitutes criminal sexual conduct.

Art. 8, Sec. 66   Modifies definitions of neglect, physical abuse, facility, mental injury and threatened injury.

NJ   *1999 N.J. Laws, Chap. 126*
Sec. 1   Expands the definition of "endangering the welfare of a child" to include the reproduction of a prohibited sexual act via the Internet or computer. Increases the classification of the crime to first degree if person charged is parent or has legal custody or care of the child. Specifies that lack of knowledge that a child is under age 16 or belief that the child is over age 16 cannot be used as a defense.

NM   *1999 N.M. Laws, Chap. 106*
Redefines sex offense to include solicitation to commit criminal sexual contact of a minor and kidnapping and false imprisonment of a victim under age 18 who is not a child of the offender.

PA   *1998 Pa. Laws, Act 126*
Defines sexual violence and rape to include use of child's likeness for photographing, videotaping, depicting on computer or filming.

SD   *1999 S.D. Sess. Laws, Chap. 119*
Increases the penalty for second convictions for criminal pedophilia.

TN   *1999 Tenn. Pub. Acts, Chap. 189*
Redefines "indecent exposure."

      1999 Tenn. Pub. Acts, Chap. 522
Requires all records and information in child sexual abuse cases to be confidential.

TX   *1999 Tex. Gen. Laws, Chap. 150*
Establishes a sex offender compliance unit within the Texas Department of Public Safety. See also *Organization/Oversight* section.

      1999 Tex. Gen. Laws, Chap. 1557
Establishes a risk assessment review committee to determine a sex offender's level of risk to the community. Outlines a screening tool to assesses the risk level of the offender to the community. See also *Organization/Oversight* section.

VA   *1999 Va. Acts, Chap. 659*
Increases the penalty for first offense possession of child pornography. Makes it a crime to use a communication system for accomplishment of sex crimes with children. Expands required sex offender registration to those making and possessing child pornography.

      1999 Va. Acts, Chap. 936
Establishes a Class 1 misdemeanor for sending sexually explicit electronic files or messages that are harmful to juveniles. See also *Definitions/Offenses/Penalties* section.

WA   *1999 Wash. Laws, Chap. 389*
Sec. 2   Establishes a statewide training program for those responsible for investigating child sexual abuse.

Sec. 3   Establishes a state-appointed work group to develop state guidelines for the development of child sexual abuse investigations.

Sec. 4   Requires each county to develop a written protocol for handling criminal child sexual abuse investigations.

Sec. 5   Adds specialized training in child sexual abuse investigations to the minimum training standards for caseworkers.

Sec. 6   Creates three pilot projects involving child sexual abuse investigations, each of which will use different methods and techniques to conduct and preserve interviews. Requires evaluations to be conducted on the effectiveness of each program.

WY   *1999 Wyo. Sess. Laws, Chap. 180*
        Defines crimes, fines and sentences related to sexual exploitation of children.

Sex Offender Registries

IL   *1999 Ill. Laws, PA 48*
        Sec. 5   Expands the lists of people required to register as sex offenders. Newly defines sexual predators.
        Requires those convicted of first degree murder of a child, sexually violent people and sexual predators to
        register for the rest of their lives. Outlines sex offender information disclosure.

        1999 Ill. Laws, PA 98
        Expands the list of sex offenders required to register to include people adjudicated sexually violent and
        those convicted of several misdemeanor sex crimes and non-forcible sex crimes with juveniles, if commit-
        ted after June 1999. Requires those convicted of first degree murder of a child, sexually violent people
        and sexual predators to register for the rest of their lives. Allows local and state police to disclose a sex
        offender's photo and employment, post them on the Internet and provide information on such offenders to
        anyone whose safety is jeopardized.

IL   *1999 Ill. Laws, PA 221*
        Increases penalties for registered sex offenders who provide false information. Requires registration infor-
        mation to be available within 72 hours after a request.

        1999 Ill. Laws, PA 224
        Requires sex offender information to include a photograph. Requires state police to make sex offender
        information available on the Internet. Allows state police to require biographical information from a
        person seeking information on a sex offender. Allows state police to limit access to the information.
        Allows law enforcement agencies to publish photos of registered sex offenders whose victims are age 13
        or younger in newspapers, magazines, on the Internet or on television.

        1999 Ill. Laws, PA 394
        Requires registered sex offenders to submit names and addresses of their places of work. Allows law
        enforcement agencies to notify people in offender's county of employment and to release registrant's
        photo and employment information to those likely to encounter the offender.

IN   *1999 Ind. Acts, PL 214*
        Requires that the sex and violent offender registry be placed on the Internet.

IA   *1999 Iowa Acts, Chap. 112*
        Sec. 19   Permits a juvenile court officer to conduct risk assessment for juvenile sex offenders and to
        disclose the information to government agencies that are conducting confidential background investiga-
        tions. Requires the Department of Public Safety to disclose the assessment of risk that offenders required
        to register pose of reoffending with the juvenile courts. Requires the juvenile court to share information
        with other departments to develop procedures for the assessment of risk for the juveniles who qualify for
        the sex offender registry.

KS   *1999 Kan. Sess. Laws, Chap. 164*
        Secs. 3, 29, 34 Expands the requirement for those who must submit blood and saliva specimens to include
        any convicted adult or juvenile who is required to register. Modifies the definition of sex offender in the
        Kansas Offender Registration Act to exclude a person who engages in consensual sexual acts. Requires
        lifetime offender registration for those convicted of an aggravated offense or for a second or subsequent
        offense.

MI   *1999 Mich. Pub. Acts, Act 86*
        Revises juvenile code to maintain consistency with the Sex Offenders Registration Act, including condi-
        tions under which fingerprints of the juvenile should be recorded.

NM   *1999 N.M. Laws, Chap. 106*
Specifies sex offender registration procedures for state residents and those who work or attend school in the state. Requires public access to registered sex offender information.

ND   *1999 N.D. Sess. Laws, Chap. 131*
Expands lists of crimes for which a conviction requires registration as a sex offender. Authorizes the court to make exceptions to registration requirements under certain conditions. Requires the court to consider certain factors when deciding whether a mental abnormality or predatory conduct exists to determine whether an individual must register. Expands list of circumstances under which an individual is required to remain registered as an offender. Expands list of individuals immune from liability for releasing information contained on registry under certain conditions to include state officers and school districts. Expands list of offenders required to register to include juveniles convicted of certain crimes. Details procedures for listing juveniles on registry and authorizes law enforcement agency to release information concerning juveniles to certain people.

TX   *1999 Tex. Gen. Laws, Chap. 56*
Outlines conditions of mandatory community supervision for violent offenders. Authorizes the establishment of "child safety zones" by a parole panel.

1999 Tex. Gen. Laws, Chap. 444
Clarifies sex offenders' civil commitments and registration requirements.
Outlines provisions of law when an offender is not in compliance.

1999 Tex., Gen. Laws, Chap. 1193
Defines new sex offender registration requirements.

1999 Tex. Gen. Laws, Chap. 1401
Creates requirements and procedures for people subject to sex offender registration to obtain driver's license and personal identification certificates.

1999 Tex. Gen. Laws, Chap. 1415
Clarifies registration requirements and expectations regarding conduct while under supervised release.

1999 Tex. Gen. Laws, Chap. 1557
Requires that information about certain offenders be published in the newspaper where the offender resides.

VA   *1999 Va. Acts, Chap. 659*
Increases the penalty for first offense possession of child pornography. Makes it a crime to use a communication system for accomplishment of sex crimes with children. Expands required sex offender registration to those making and possessing child pornography.

CHILD CARE AND EARLY CHILDHOOD EDUCATION

Administration

AR   *1999 Ark. Acts, Act 324*
Requires the Early Childhood Education Commission to provide an annual report to the legislature. Specifies that the commission examine recommendations of groups producing scientifically proven and cost effective results of child care and early childhood services. Requires the commission to recommend a state administrative structure.

    1999 Ark. Acts, Act 1222
Reduces membership on Early Childhood Commission and redefines the commission's policy goals. Creates the Division of Child Care and Early Childhood Education with approval by the commission. Creates, authorizes and defines membership for the Child Care Appeal Review Panel.

FL   *1999 Fla. Laws, Chap. 357*
Sec. 1   Establishes the Florida Partnership for School Readiness in the governor's office to coordinate programmatic, administrative and fiscal policies and to set standards for school readiness programs. Sets membership and appointment authority. Requires the partnership to adopt a statewide system for measuring school readiness, coordinate with specific commissions, institutions and the commissioner of education to assess available instruction and training of early childhood professionals, and approve local school readiness plans. Requires the establishment of county or multicounty school readiness coalitions and requires them to make plans to address all eligible children. Sets membership and terms. Requires the partnership to form local school readiness coalitions under certain circumstances.

IN   *1999 Ind. Acts, PL 121*
Sec. 6   Adds two members to the Interagency Coordinating Council for Children with Disabilities, including a Head Start agency representative and a state child care agency representative.

    1999 Ind. Acts, PL 211
Sec. 3   Establishes the Board for the Coordination of Child Care Regulation. Specifies membership, terms and duties. Requires that board make recommendations to legislature.

IA   *1999 Iowa Acts, Chap. 192*
Sec. 19   Adds a state public health employee to the state Child Care Advisory Council.

LA   *1999 La. Acts, HCR 259*
Creates a task force to study child care regulations and services in child care centers and homes, including other states' activities. Sets membership and duties. Requires a report to the Legislature, including recommendations.

ME   *1999 Me. Public Laws, Chap. 66*
Establishes the Business Advisory Commission on Quality Child Care Financing. Requires the commission to examine available financing and economic development incentives to encourage the development of quality child care and early education. Sets commission membership. Requires reports to the Legislature.

    1999 Me. Public Laws, Chap. 79
Renames the Task Force to Study Strategies to Support Parents as Children's First Teachers to the Task Force on Early Care and Education. Expands the membership to two additional legislators. Requires two reports to the Legislature.

    1999 Me. Public Laws, Chap. 529
Includes quality child care as part of the state's overall statewide goals to prevent child abuse and expands the definition of prevention programs to include the promotion of high-quality child care.

MN   *1999 Minn. Laws, Chap. 205*
        Art. 5, Sec. 19 ·Adds school-age providers to the membership of the statewide Advisory Task Force on Child Care Grants and other related issues.

NH   *1999 N.H. Laws, Chap. 135*
        Establishes an early childhood education commission to study, identify and prioritize early experiences, including parental involvement and teaching. Sets commission membership, appointment powers and duties. Requires a report to the legislature. States the importance of brain development in the first three years.

        1999 N.H. Laws, Chap. 184
        Makes certain changes to the membership and duties of the Advisory Council on Child Care.

SC   *1999 S.C. Acts, Act 99*
        Secs. 2-3, 5-7   Establishes the state First Steps to School Readiness office and requires it to provide information on successful strategies; review, support and provide technical assistance to county partnerships; submit an annual report about data collection; implement a standard fiscal accountability system; and coordinate the program with all related state programs. Establishes membership for county partnerships. Establishes county partnership requirements and duties, including an annual report that includes an evaluation and estimate of cost savings. Establishes a board of trustees to evaluate the partnerships. Requires legislatively-appointed and board-appointed committee members to oversee the evaluator's work. Requires the board to develop a comprehensive long-range improvement initiative, including recommendations for coordination and results-oriented measures and objectives. Requires specific state agencies to support the initiative.

TX   *1999 Tex. Gen. Laws, Chap. 33*
        Requires the governor to designate certain board members to handle issues related to children under age 3 with developmental delays. Expands the public's power to speak to the board about issues. Requires board members to complete a training program. Sets board member restrictions, a complaint process and responsibilities. Requires early identification of children under age 3 with developmental delay and interagency work on such children who are vulnerable to abuse or neglect. Requires parental involvement and an automated system. Requires an assessment of service effectiveness. Establishes a provider selection process. Requires the Interagency Council on Early Childhood Intervention to seek funding that maximizes federal, private and local sources. Requires a report to the Legislature.

UT   *1999 Utah Laws, Chap. 77*
        Adds members to the Child Care Licensing Advisory Committee. Lists membership requirements and requires annual membership changes.

WY   *1999 Wyo. Sess. Laws, Chap. 118*
        Limits Child Care Certification Board membership and makes other membership changes. Sets board decisionmaking process.

Background Checks and Screening

CO   *1999 Colo. Sess. Laws, Chap. 293*
        Adds certain criminal convictions to the list of background check findings that are grounds for denying licenses to family child care homes. Requires all child care applicants, owners and employees to obtain a criminal background record check. Exempts certain providers, but requires them to sign a statement affirming no convictions. Criminalizes a false statement by applicants and requires a notice be put on the application.

        Sec. 10   Authorizes a pilot study in three counties on background checks and requires a report to the legislature. Appropriates funds.

FL   *1999 Fla. Laws, Chap. 207*
Sec. 2 Prohibits misrepresentations regarding child care licensing to a parent or guardian, state licensing officials or law enforcement agency. Specifies issues that cannot be misrepresented. Provides penalties for misrepresentations made by child care personnel to parents or guardians if a child suffers harm.

GA   *1999 Ga. Laws, Act 320*
Requires certain child care centers to maintain satisfactory state and national fingerprint records to conduct sufficient background checks for prospective employees. Exempts from fingerprint checks those residing in a family child care home who are not present when a child is there.

      1999 Ga. Laws, Act 331
Ratifies the National Crime Prevention and Privacy Compact Act of 1998 by requiring the state Crime Information Center to establish and maintain a variety of criminal records and to disseminate this information in certain situations as it relates to prospective child care employees. Protects these records from distribution in other situations.

IA   *1999 Iowa Acts, Chap. 192*
Requires the state to notify parents, guardians and custodians of a child who is the victim of certain child abuse in a child care facility. Requires notification about the type of abuse, but prohibits identification of the victim, perpetrator or circumstances of the abuse.

MO   *1999 Mo. Laws, Chap. 210*
Establishes the Family Care Safety Registry for child care providers and requires the registry to be publicly accessible with a toll-free number in 2001. Requires any provider or worker in a licensed or license-exempt child care home or center or receiving state or federal funds to submit to a background check. Provides a penalty. Excludes certain child care providers. Requires the registry to contain certain background information. Requires license-exempt child care facilities, such as religiously operated centers, to conduct background checks on employees. Limits the state fee for conducting a background check. Allows for an appeal process. Requires an annual report to the legislature.

NH   *1999 N.H. Laws, Chap. 326*
Requires that individuals who have regular contact with children in a child care program submit background information to the state. Further defines compliance process for convictions for crimes that could pose a threat to a child.

NY   *1998 N.Y. Laws, Chap. 3*
Sets background check procedures for prospective child care employees.

      1998 N.Y. Laws, Chap. 600
Creates the crime of misrepresentation by a child care provider and defines reckless assault of a child.

UT   *1999 Utah Laws, Chap. 77*
Requires a family child care provider caring for more than five but fewer than eight children to obtain a state certificate to screen for child abuse or neglect.

VA   *1999 Va. Acts, Chap. 727*
Sec. 63.1-198.5 Requires child abuse and neglect record information checks and background checks for paid or volunteer staff of a child care center that provides services to state-funded families. Requires a center to provide copies of record checks. Requires applicants to provide a sworn statement of past proven abuse or neglect complaints, convictions or pending charges. Makes penalties for a false statement. Prohibits employing subjects of a proven complaint or conviction. Requires that information indicating abuse or neglect convictions or proven complaints be given to individuals refused employment. Specifies confidentiality rules.

Financing/Employer-Supported Programs

CA   *1998 Cal. Stats., Chap. 323*
        Secs. 25, 26 Extends the employer tax credits for child care construction startup costs, information and referral services costs, and contributions to a qualified care plan.

CO   *1999 Colo. Sess. Laws, Chap. 106*
        Extends the voluntary income tax checkoff contribution program for 10 years. Changes members' terms on the Child Care Improvement Oversight Committee. Transfers administration of the program from the Colorado Children's Campaign to the Colorado Office of Resource and Referral Agencies Inc. Increases the maximum percentage of voluntary contributions that can be spent on administration.

        1999 Colo. Sess. Laws, Chap. 293
        Sec. 7 Allows a state fine for a "negative licensing action" and creates a cash fund for improving child care quality from the fines collected.

FL   *1999 Fla. Laws, Chap. 304*
        Provides an ad valorem tax exemption for licensed child care facilities in an enterprise zone and for licensed Gold Seal Quality child care facilities by considering them educational institutions. Exempts from sales tax purchases of educational materials and toys by child care facilities that qualify as Gold Seal Quality care programs and provides health insurance.

        1999 Fla. Laws, Chap. 357
        Secs. 1, 6, 13 Establishes initiation grants for local school readiness plans, including more funds for plans approved earlier. Offers incentive bonuses to local coalitions with plans that clearly show quality enhancement without reducing the number of children served. Authorizes multiple funding sources for school readiness programs, including state, federal, lottery or local funds and specific subsidized child care and early education funds. Requires the state Partnership for School Readiness to recommend to the Legislature a plan for combining program funds and transportation. Caps administrative costs at 5 percent. Requires private sector membership on local coalitions. Requires recommendations on methods to increase public-private partnerships in school readiness plans. Appropriates $330,000 to implement the act.

GA   *1999 Ga. Laws, Act 19*
        Increases the income tax credit to 50 percent against tax liability for the cost of operating an employer-provided or employer-sponsored child care. Creates an income tax credit of 75 percent of the cost of operating an on-site child care center. Allows an employer who constructs an on-site children's care center to receive a 10 percent credit per year of the construction costs for 10 years.

ME   *1999 Me. Public Laws, Chap. 66*
        Establishes the Business Advisory Commission on Quality Child Care Financing. Requires the commission to examine available financing and economic development incentives to encourage the development of quality child care and early education. Sets the commission membership. Requires reports to the Legislature.

        1999 Me. Public Laws, Chap. 272
        Adds quality child care to the types of businesses for state financing that contribute to Maine's business, family and environmental development. Specifies which costs will be financed, including construction, training and accreditation.

        1999 Me. Public Laws, Chap. 296
        Requires the state to award annual grants for educational programs for children under age 6 who have developmental delays. Establishes a funding formula and contract procedure requirements. Requires the state to review regional budgets for compliance with program requirements. Defines developmental delays for children from birth to age 3 and from age 3 to age 6.

1999 Me. Public Laws, Chap. 401
Sec. NNN   Allows an income tax credit for child care expenses of up to $500 and doubles the amount of the credit for parents who use "quality child care." Defines quality child care as child care provided that meets minimum licensing standards and is accredited or uses quality standards or indicators. Allows a corporate tax credit of 30 percent of costs or $30,000 for investing in child care services. Allows an individual tax credit of $1,000 for at least $10,000 in child care expenditures over 10 years.

Sec. OOO-5   Creates the Quality Child Care Education Scholarship Fund. Appropriates $150,000 for scholarships for child care workers who enroll in early childhood education or child development courses at an accredited college or university. Requires the state to set eligibility, loan amounts and scholarship terms.

1999 Me. Public Laws, Chap. 515
Requires the state to adopt rules allowing after-school care for students ages 12 to 15. Appropriates $525,000 for these services. Appropriates $962,850 for school-aged child care subsidies. Appropriates funds for incentives for child care providers to offer care during odd hours and in underserved geographic areas.

MD   *1999 Md. Laws, Chaps. 583, 584*
Creates an additional nonrefundable state tax credit for child care and dependent expenses up to 25 percent of the federal credit claimed for that year with incomes less then $30,000. Requires a report to the legislature on the effectiveness of the tax credit program.

MN   *1999 Minn. Laws, Chap. 205*
Art. 1, Secs. 62, 64   Directs the state to assist employers to establish pre-tax child care accounts. Requires a report to the Legislature. Requires the state to encourage businesses and other organizations to donate materials to help children under age 4 develop skills for reading and school success.

Art. 1, Sec. 71   Makes state appropriations for child care development grants.

NV   *1999 Nev. Stats., Chap. 584*
Sec. 7   Appropriates $300,000 for continued support of the child care training program operated by the City of Las Vegas.

SC   *1999 S.C. Acts, Act 99*
Secs. 2-4   Requires state First Steps School Readiness office grants to be awarded in two levels, one for development and planning and one for implementation. Establishes grant criteria and process, including considering the percentage of students eligible for free and reduced price lunch program when allocating grants. Prohibits supplantation of other funds. Requires a 15 percent local match and encourages private contributions. Allows termination of grants or targeted assistance where no progress has been made. Allows tax return contributions to the school readiness fund. Establishes a separate fund for both state appropriations and nongovernmental funds for the initiative.

TX   *1999 Tex. Gen. Laws, Chap. 33*
Sec. 8   Requires the Interagency Council on Early Childhood Intervention to seek funding for services for children under age 3 with developmental delays that maximizes federal, private and local sources.

1999 Tex. Gen. Laws, Chap. 394
Sec. 13   Establishes an employer tax credit of up to $50,000 or 50 percent of costs for operating, construct-ing, renovating or purchasing child care from a child care center or registered family child care home. Requires a biennial report to the Legislature on the implementation and fiscal effect of this credit.

1999 Tex. Gen. Laws, Chap. 1433
Requires that the state spend federal child care funds or other available funds for a scholarship program that pays $1,000 to eligible child care employees for expenses incurred in obtaining certain child devel-opment or child care credentials or degrees. Allows for a state-paid bonus or wage supplementation for certain scholarship recipients. Caps the total biennial amount at $2 million.

UT   *1999 Utah Laws, Chap. 272*
Establishes an individual income tax credit of $100 for an at-home parent with a child under age 1 if the parent earns less than $3,000 per year in wages or business income and the gross income of all taxpayers filing the return is less than $50,000. Makes an appropriation from the General Fund to replace the Uniform School Fund revenues.

Low-Income/Welfare Reform

CA   *1998 Cal. Stats., Chap. 329*
Makes eligibility requirements uniform for Stage I and Stage II child care under CalWORKs by excluding SSI benefits and state supplemental benefits from the income definition. Requires that former CalWORKs recipients who cannot make the transition to Stage II because of no funded slot be eligible for up to 24 months after they leave cash aid, or until they are ineligible. Allows former CalWORKs recipients to receive child care in Stage I and Stage II for up to 24 months after they leave cash aid or until they are ineligible.

CO   *1999 Colo. Sess. Laws, Chap. 323*
Requires the state Department of Human Services, with input from the state Department of Education, to seek six additional pilot agencies through an RFP to provide community consolidated child care services. States that the purposes of the pilot projects is to increase quality, meet families' child care needs, and integrate early care with education programs. Requires the state to select six pilot agencies to mentor the new pilot projects. Allows the state to add pilot projects if appropriate. Requires applying agencies to report specific program information. Requires an annual review and an independent evaluation. Appropriates $470,000 from federal child care funds to implement the act.

FL   *1999 Fla. Laws, Chap. 241*
Allows families enrolled in the state's welfare-to-work program (WAGES) who are paid to be counted toward meeting staff-to-child ratios.

      1999 Fla. Laws, Chap. 304
Expands subsidized child care eligibility to 200 percent of the federal poverty level (FPL) for children of working families enrolled in the Child Care Executive Partnership Program. Allows licensed Gold Seal certified child care providers to be reimbursed at the market rate for children who are eligible for subsidized child care.

      1999 Fla. Laws, Chap. 357
Sec. 1   Establishes school readiness programs' eligibility priority for children from birth to kindergarten age who are at risk or economically disadvantaged up to 150 percent of the FPL. Maintains eligibility with a sliding fee scale. Applies a waiting list and a single point of entry to this program. Authorizes specific subsidized child care and early education funds for local school readiness programs.

IL   *1999 Ill. Laws, PA 331*
Sec. 11-20.1   Requires department to notify recipients of the availability of 12 months of child care and medical assistance after cash assistance is ended due to earnings.

IA   *1999 Iowa Acts, Chap. 192*
Secs. 35-36   Establishes state child care assistance eligibility to include a participant who is employed, a person whose earned income is considered in determining eligibility, and a person participating in activities approved under Job Opportunity and Basic Skills (JOBS). Eliminates the child care deduction for determining family investment program eligibility and assistance amounts. Allows those receiving transitional child care benefits to continue to receive them until their eligibility expires or they fail to meet program requirements.

      1999 Iowa Acts, Chap. 203
Secs. 2, 4   Authorizes the state to transfer part of the 1998 Temporary Assistance for Needy Families (TANF) appropriation to community-based programs for children from birth to age 5. Requires that the funds be used by communities to enhance quality child care in support of parent employment and have a

primary emphasis on low-income families. Requires funds to be provided to communities in a flexible way. Specifies strategies to be used, including developing child care capacity, sick child care, night shift child care and linkages with early education systems. Appropriates approximately $16.8 million in TANF funds for state child care assistance.

ME   *1999 Me. Public Laws, Chap. 383*
Allows transitional child care services for families eligible for TANF that have at least one adult working and that request termination of benefits.

1999 Me. Public Laws, Chap. 515
Requires the state to maximize federal early childhood funds as a result of increased state expenditures. Makes appropriations for additional child care subsidies, including school-aged child care subsidies.

MD   *1999 Md. Laws, Chap. 541*
Authorizes the state Department of Education as the lead agency for implementing and administering the redesigned rate-setting structure for nonresidential child care programs. Specifies appeal process for new rates.

MN   *1999 Minn. Laws, Chap. 205*
Secs. 13, 16   Requires counties to make a preliminary eligibility determination based on family size, income and authorized activity for all child care assistance applications. Requires counties to review and update the child care assistance waiting list at least every six months.

Sec. 26   Establishes a child support collection account for public assistance reimbursement and requires that funds in the account be used for child care programs.

Art. 1, Secs. 1, 6, 8-10, 14, 24, 31, 33, 48 and 63   Adds child care assistance programs to the list of exceptions for the data privacy act. Allows interdepartmental disclosure of data used to administer programs. Excludes child care assistance from income in the child care assistance program. Specifies that a provider of a child cannot be a member of the family receiving child care assistance. Expands transitional child care assistance to include job search. Makes eligibility and assistance changes to the at-home infant child care program. Reduces the work requirement from 20 hours to 10 hours per week for full-time students eligible for child care. Removes the prohibition against the state reducing parent copayments with the addition of family members. Directs the state to develop and distribute a child care assistance application form with a notice of eligibility requirements and penalties for wrongfully obtaining assistance. Requires the state to enforce program integrity and fraud prevention for child care assistance programs. Changes child care copayments for families below 75 percent of the state medium income (SMI).

Art. 1, Secs. 10, 12, 19   Adds job search and at-home infant care subsidy to the eligible uses of the child care fund. Allows distribution of additional funds based on certain criteria. Authorizes the state to supervise and distribute money to counties that administer child care programs and modifies the county allocation distribution formula. Requires training and support services to be provided to counties.

MN   *1999 Minn. Laws, Chap. 205*
Art. 1, Sec. 24   Removes requirement that a family must be a two-parent family to receive the at-home infant child care subsidy. Expands the definition of parent to include birth or adoptive parent or stepparent for the purposes of this program. Requires the determination of the amount of the at-home infant child care subsidy to include family size. Specifies that receipt of at-home infant care assistance does not establish an employer-employee relationship between any member of the family and the county or state.

Art. 1, Sec. 25   Removes exemption from child care assistance time limit for high school students participating in a postsecondary program while pursuing a high school diploma. Eliminates automatic eligibility for child care assistance for financially eligible students who have received assistance for one academic year.

Art. 1, Secs. 61, 66   Requires the state to develop a plan for integrating child care and early childhood education programs and services. Requires the plan to focus on cost-effective services and centrality of programs, including accessibility to services, nontraditional hour care, infant care, and sick care and special needs child care. Requires the state to report to the Legislature on the plan. Requires the state to study ways to consolidate child care, transitional child care and basic sliding fee programs into one child care assistance program for welfare recipients. Requires a report to the Legislature.

Art. 1, Secs. 65, 71, 72   Requires additional state funding to early childhood family education aid programs to school districts with children under age 5. Makes state appropriations for school readiness programs, early childhood family education aid, Head Start, school-age care, low-income child care assistance, child care for TANF recipients and child care development grants. Transfers TANF funds to the basic sliding fee program and child care services development grants.

NM   *1999 N.M. Laws, Chap. 12*
Makes a TANF block grant appropriation for training participants to become licensed child care providers. Appropriates state welfare funds for early childhood and family support and education training programs to include before- and after-school programs for children ages 5 to 8 and classes to develop job skills and leadership skills for parents. Requires programs to be offered in areas that lack certified child care. Requires measurable performance standards, identification of target clients, and tracking and reporting.

NY   *1998 N.Y. Laws, Chap. 397*
Requires the state to study child care use patterns and increasing needs for child care services of low-or moderate-income families, with particular emphasis on such needs for minority group members. Requires a report to the Legislature, including recommendations to improve child care availability for families with the most acute need.

SC   *1999 S.C. Acts, Act 99*
Sec. 2   Establishes the school readiness grant criteria and process, including considering the percentage of students eligible for free and reduced price lunch program when allocating grants.

TX   *1999 Tex. Gen. Laws, Chap. 719*
Requires the state to submit proposed actions on the Child and Adult Care Food Program to the state's advisory committee for comment, unless federal law requires immediate action. Requires the state to notify organizations of changes in the program. Authorizes the advisory committee to conduct public hearings, refer issues for discussion and recommend modifications.

        1999 Tex. Gen. Laws, Chap. 469
Sec. 1   Requires the Texas Workforce Commission to work with local work force development boards to review the child care funding formula. Specifies that the review consider funding areas with the greatest need for child care services based on number of children in poverty, poverty-based programs and families receiving public assistance. Requires a legislative report.

VT   *1999 Vt. Acts, Act 62*
Sec. 140   Appropriates $2 million to implement a rate increase for licensed and registered child care providers. Appropriates $500,000 to adjust the sliding fee scale for individuals with income below 82 1/2 percent of SMI. Appropriates funding to continue to provide quality incentive bonuses at 15 percent above the rate for programs that become accredited and to providers that receive a degree or are employed in a licensed or registered child care program. Appropriates funds for a child care mentoring program.

Preschool Services

CO   *1999 Colo. Sess. Laws, Chap. 323*
Requires the state Department of Human Services, with input from the state Department of Education, to seek six additional pilot agencies through an RFP to provide community consolidated child care services. States that the purposes of the pilot projects is to increase quality, meet families' child care needs, and integrate early care with education programs. Requires the state to select six pilot agencies to mentor the

new pilot projects. Allows the state to add pilot projects if appropriate. Requires applying agencies to report specific program information. Requires an annual review and an independent evaluation. Appropriates $470,000 from federal child care funds to implement the act.

CT   *1999 Conn. Acts, Act 230*
Allows 5 percent of the state's school readiness program spaces to be reserved for 5-year-olds if they have participated for at least a year. Increases the appropriations percentage for priority school districts in the school readiness grant program. Reduces the appropriations amount dedicated to the competitive grant program. Increases the amount of funds a town may use for coordination, program evaluation and administration if the town provides a minimum amount of local funds for those purposes. Requires [such] information to be provided to the state for a program evaluation. Authorizes the state to use 10 percent of a town's eligible funding to earmark supplemental grants to other towns if a town does not submit an approved priority district's plan. Requires information on health insurance, medical provider and history for each child in a school readiness program. Requires grants to pay for staff development and education, quality assurance personnel and technical assistance. Requires the state to develop assessment measures to evaluate programs.

FL   *1999 Fla. Laws, Chap. 304*
Establishes an Early Head Start Collaboration Grants Program to assist local agencies in securing Head Start programs.

      1999 Fla. Laws, Chap. 357
Sec. 1   Requires local school readiness plans to include a developmentally appropriate curriculum, appropriate ratios, a healthy and safe environment, enhancement of child development, and a resource and referral network. Requires local coalitions to increase parents' training and involvement in their child's preschool and provide family literacy programs.

Secs. 1, 8   Establishes the Florida Partnership for School Readiness in the governor's office to coordinate programmatic, administrative and fiscal policies, and standards for school readiness programs. Sets membership and appointment authority. Requires the partnership to adopt a statewide system for measuring school readiness, including specific uniform screening data and expectations, a control group evaluation system, and outcome measures. Requires an assessment of available training for early childhood education professionals. Requires local school readiness plans and sets state approval and funding authority for these plans.

IA   *1999 Iowa Acts, Chap. 192*
Sec. 1   Exempts from the definition of child care an instructional program for children at least age 4 who are attending prekindergarten administered by a nonpublic school system.

ME   *1999 Me. Public Laws, Chap. 515*
Requires the state to adopt rules that allow for full-day, year-round Head Start programs.

MN   *1999 Minn. Laws, Chap. 205*
Art. 1, Sec. 71   Makes state appropriations for school readiness programs, early childhood family education aid and Head Start.

SC   *1999 S.C. Acts, Act 99*
Secs. 2-4   Establishes the state First Steps to School Readiness office through county partnerships, public and private funds and family support services. Establishes program goals, including parent support, high-quality preschool programs, and community mobilization efforts. Requires grants to be awarded in two levels, one for development and planning and one for implementation. Establishes grant criteria and process. Lists focus areas for activities and services, including school readiness, family support, child health, quality child care, transportation and affordability. Prohibits supplantation of other funding. Allows termination of grants or targeted assistance where no progress has been made. Allows tax return contributions to the school readiness fund. Establishes a separate fund for both state appropriations and nongovernmental funds for the initiative.

Regulation and Licensing

CA   *1998 Cal. Stats., Chap. 329*
Requires that state-funded child care provider training to CalWORKs recipients include information about becoming a licensed provider. Requires that certain license-exempt providers who are compensated under Stage I of the CalWORKs child care program be registered as trustline providers.

CO   *1999 Colo. Sess. Laws, Chap. 293*
Defines "negative licensing action" as denying, suspending or revoking a license. Requires the state to notify parents when a family child care home or child care center receives one. Allows a state fine and creates a cash fund for improving child care quality from the fines collected. Requires the state to rule on the on-site public availability of child care inspection reports and display of the license in a prominent place during operational hours. Requires the state to send a written notice to a facility that is subject to an inspection for which there are no serious violations.

Sec. 7   Prohibits alcohol use by those providing care to a child, with exceptions. Allows for a fine or license denial, suspension or revocation.

FL   *1999 Fla. Laws, Chap. 206*
Allows substitute care providers to be licensed as both foster care and day child care providers and to receive both subsidized child care and foster care payments for the same child if care is provided 24 hours a day.

1999 Fla. Laws, Chap. 241
Allows families enrolled in the state's welfare-to-work program (WAGES) who are paid to be counted toward meeting staff-to-child ratios.

1999 Fla. Laws, Chap. 304
Creates a large family child care home classification. Establishes requirements for observational and developmental assessment of young children. Increases training requirements for child care personnel, including family child care home operators. Authorizes specialized child care facilities to care for mildly ill children. Requires a child care director's credential by 2003.

1999 Fla. Laws, Chap. 357
Sec. 1   Requires the Florida Partnership for School Readiness to adopt a statewide system for measuring school readiness, including requiring specific screening data and expectations. Requires local school readiness plans to include a developmentally appropriate curriculum, appropriate ratios, a healthy and safe environment, enhancement of child development, and a resource and referral network.

HI   *1999 Hawaii Sess. Laws, Act 242*
Includes certain types of residential community units to be eligible for providing family child care. Requires townhouse projects to allow family child care homes that meet certain conditions. Allows immunity from liability for certain associations. Allows associations to place liability and insurance conditions for homes that provide child care.

IL   *1999 Ill. Laws, PA 268*
Sec. 5   Establishes that committing offenses against children in or near a child care facility is an aggravating factor in sentencing.

IA   *1999 Iowa Acts, Chap. 189*
Defines a children's center as a privately-funded facility that serves seven or more children at once, is not under the custody or authority of a government agency, and offers certain services, including child care and family support services. Requires the state to establish and review certification and licensing standards for the protection of children. Prohibits the state from establishing program standards for the centers.

1999 Iowa Acts, Chap. 192
Sec. 1   Exempts from the definition of child care an instructional program for children at least age 4 who are attending prekindergarten administered by a nonpublic school system, a youth program, a before-and-after-school program, a church-based program providing care to children while the parents are attending a church activity, and a program that operates one day per week that meets certain conditions.

Secs. 2, 4, 11   Requires the state to implement a family and group child care home pilot project in interested counties and authorizes expansions. Prohibits a child care center from providing services if denied a license pending an evidentiary hearing outcome. Allows the state to reduce licenses to one-year provisional licenses and places restrictions on those licenses. Requires a Level III registered child care home provider in the pilot project to have an assistant if caring for more than eight children for more than two hours.

KS   *1999 Kan. Sess. Laws, Chap. 19*
Makes each day in violation of child care facility licensing regulations a separate violation, punishable by up to $500 per violation.

LA   *1999 La. Acts, Act 558*
Sec. 1   Reduces the fee collected by the state fire marshal for child care home inspections. Specifies that fees be used to employ inspection personnel and prohibits other fees from being collected for inspections. Eliminates the state's' responsibility for assisting state fire marshal with inspecting child care homes. Requires homes to be inspected for fire safety regardless of the certifying agency.

1999 La. Acts, Act 1237
Exempts tax-exempt religious organizations from consideration as child care centers if they are open for less than 24 hours in a continuous seven-day week. Defines related or relative of child caregiver as natural or adopted child or grandchild or child in legal custody of caregiver. Specifies that the residence of a caregiver relative is not considered a child care center. Reduces the minimum weekly hours of care at a child care center from 20 to 12.5.

ME   *1999 Me. Public Laws, Chap. 276*
Requires an annual lead hazard screening of a child care center or preschool with exceptions and prohibits a child care center or preschool from being licensed, certified, approved or state-funded unless it has been screened. Allows family child care homes to be inspected for lead when a lead-poisoned child has been identified and allows the department to provide technical assistance.   Authorizes penalties.

1999 Me. Public Laws, Chap. 363
Defines day care center and excludes certain settings from the definition. Specifies penalties for child care licensure violations. Provides a mechanism to close child care facilities immediately when conditions exist that threaten children. Allows the state to issue temporary licenses when licensed providers move to new locations. Requires that revenue from penalties go to a special social services account.

MD   *1999 Md. Laws, Chap. 68*
Requires family child care providers to hold a certain basic first aid training and CPR certification and requires child care centers to have at least one staff person for every 20 children in care who holds a certain basic first aid training and CPR certification.

1999 Md. Laws, Chap. 352
Prevents homeowners' associations from prohibiting the use of a residence as a family child care home until the lot owners, other than the developer, have 90 percent of the votes in the homeowners' association. Repeals the ability of a homeowners' association to regulate the number of family child care homes.

1999 Md. Laws, Chap. 410
Permits unannounced state inspections of family child care homes in a year without an initial or renewal inspection. Requires an inspection prior to registration and at least biennially thereafter.

MI   *1998 Mich. Pub. Acts, Act 440*
Requires that child care facilities have an appropriately CPR-certified person on duty at all times.

MN   *1999 Minn. Laws, Chap. 205*
Art. 1, Sec. 34   Removes language defining "accredited" as being accredited only by the National Association for the Education of Young Children when determining a bonus to centers and family child care homes.

Art. 5, Sec. 2   Defines nonlicensed child care provider as excluded from state licensing requirements.

MO   *1999 Mo. Laws, Chap. 210*
Authorizes action against child care facilities when there is a threat to children. Requires the state to revoke the registration of a registered child care provider paid with public funds for due cause. Requires registered providers be at least age 18. Requires registered providers to meet certain health and safety standards.

MT   *1999 Mont. Laws, Chap. 135*
Allows the state to issue a three-year license to a provider who has no licensing criteria deficiencies.

NH   *1999 N.H. Laws, Chap. 185*
Creates the Credentialing of Personnel in Early Care and Education Programs. Requires the state to issue a credential to any child care and early childhood education professional who has satisfied the state's education and training licensing requirements. Requires the state to set rules and a fee.

        1999 N.H. Laws, Chap. 326
Exempts school-age programs located in schools from providing documentation of approval pertaining to fire, health and zoning.

OH   *1998 Ohio Laws, SB 212*
Adds administrators and employees of child day camps and residential camps to list of people required to report suspected abuse or neglect.

OK   *1999 Okla. Sess. Laws, Chap. 233*
Modifies and adds definitions and expands list of exempted entities.

TX   *1999 Tex. Gen. Laws, Chap. 1129*
Specifies staff-to-child ratios, group sizes and square footage requirements for child care facilities as minimum standards for which the state must conduct a comprehensive cost-benefit analysis and economic impact study that includes families and licensed providers.

UT   *1999 Utah Laws, Chap. 77*
Clarifies when a provider's children count for licensing purposes. Disallows a certified family child care provider from taking care of more than two children under age 2. Requires a family child care provider caring for more than five but fewer than eight children to obtain a state certificate to screen for child abuse or neglect.

VA   *1999 Va. Acts, Chap. 454*
Expands the list of accrediting organizations that, upon accreditation, enable certain private prekindergarten programs to be exempt from licensure.

School-Age Child Care/Child Care in Public Schools

CA   *1998 Cal. Stats., Chaps. 318-320*
Establishes the After-School Learning and Safe Neighborhoods Partnerships Program to create incentives for after-school enrichment programs for children from kindergarten through ninth grade. States the purpose of the programs are a safe environment, educational enrichment, tutoring, homework assistance and recreational activities. Requires programs to operate at school sites during certain numbers of days and

until a certain hour, and allows local programs to operate during summer and vacation. Makes all students in the school eligible. Requires competitive awards and minimum percentages of students who are eligible for free or reduced meals. Provides renewable incentive grants of up to $5 per day per child for schools. Provides minimum amounts for grants to schools and specifies percentages for elementary, middle and high schools. Requires a 20:1 child-to-staff ratio. Requires a 50 percent match from local school districts. Requires an interagency collaborative planning process.

IA   199 Iowa Acts, Chap. *192*
        Sec. 1   Exempts from the definition of child care a youth program, a before- and after-school care program, a church-based program providing care to children while the parents are attending a church activity, and a program that operates one day per week that meets certain conditions.

ME   *1999 Me. Public Laws, Chap. 515*
        Requires the state to adopt rules allowing after-school care for students ages 12 to 15. Appropriates $525,000 for these services. Appropriates $962,850 for school-aged child care subsidies.

MN   *1999 Minn. Laws, Chap. 205*
        Art. 1, Sec. 44   Authorizes certain school districts to allow certain groups to use school facilities for school-age child care programs. Requires that school-age child care programs have access to school facilities if the facilities are not in use. Allows school districts to establish rules regarding school-age programs. Encourages school districts to coordinate school-age care programs with other education programs, instruction and services provided by the district, government or nonprofit agencies.

        Art. 1, Sec. 71   Makes state appropriations for school-age care.

        Art. 5, Secs. 6, 12-17   Makes school-age care programs and legal nonlicensed providers eligible to receive grants.

        Art. 5, Sec. 19   Adds school-age providers to the membership of the statewide Advisory Task Force on Child Care Grants and other issues.

NH   *1999 N.H. Laws, Chap. 326*
        Exempts school-age programs located in schools from providing documentation of approval pertaining to fire, health and zoning.

NM   *1999 N.M. Laws, Chap. 12*
        Appropriates state welfare funds for early childhood and family support and education training programs to include before- and after-school programs for children ages 5 to 8 and classes to develop job skills and leadership skills for parents.

OH   *1998 Ohio Laws, SB 212*
        Adds administrators and employees of child day camps and residential camps to the list of people required to report suspected abuse or neglect.

Support for Providers/Training/Resource and Referral

CA   *1998 Cal. Stats., Chap. 329*
        Requires that state-funded child care provider training to CalWORKs recipients include information about becoming a licensed provider. Requires that certain license-exempt providers who are compensated under Stage I of the CalWORKs child care program be registered as trustline providers.

CT   *1999 Conn. Acts, Act 230*
        Requires school readiness program grants to pay for staff development and education, quality assurance personnel and technical assistance.

DE   *Vol. 70 Del. Laws, Chap. 173*
      Sec. 3   Requires that all public and private early childhood education providers contracting with the Department of Education ensure that every employee receive a minimum of one hour of training every year in the detection and reporting of child abuse.

FL   *1999 Fla. Laws, Chap. 304*
      Exempts from sales tax purchases of educational materials and toys by child care facilities that qualify as Gold Seal Quality Care programs and provide health insurance. Requires the state to study how to make affordable health insurance available to child care providers. Requires a child care director's credential by 2003.

      Increases training requirements for child care personnel, including family child care home operators.

      1999 Fla. Laws, Chap. 357
      Secs. 1, 8   Requires the Partnership for School Readiness to coordinate with specific commissions, institutions and the commissioner of education to assess available instruction and training for early childhood professionals. Requires the assessment to include articulation of training, career and academic programs and career paths. Requires local school readiness plans to include a resource and referral network.

HI   *1999 Hawaii Sess. Laws, Act 242*
      Includes certain types of residential community units to be eligible for providing family child care. Requires townhouse projects to allow family child care homes that meet certain conditions. Allows immunity from liability for certain associations. Allows associations to place liability and insurance conditions for homes that provide child care.

      1999 Iowa Acts, Chap. 192
      Requires an interdepartmental leadership council for child care training and development. Requires participation by community colleges, higher education, child care resource and referral services among others. Requires a proposal to improve support for child care providers, including core competencies, professional development levels, a professional experience registry, a unified training and technical assistance approach, an articulation process for academic credit, and a financing plan.

IA   *1999 Iowa Acts, Chap. 203*
      Sec. 49   Requires the state to identify and list child care providers who are nationally accredited as Gold Seal quality providers. Encourages resource and referral services to use the designation. Requires an annual recognition week for such providers in April. Authorizes a one-time cash award to certain Gold Seal providers. Specifies amounts.

ME   *1999 Me. Public Laws, Chap. 401*
      Sec. OOO   Establishes the Early Care and Education Revolving Loan Program to provide financial assistance to early care and education businesses. Allows loan assistance of up to $100,000 and specifies financing terms and loan amounts for certain loans. Specifies eligibility and interest rates for loans. Requires semiannual reports to the state and allows for audits.

      Sec. OOO-5   Creates the Quality Child Care Education Scholarship Fund. Appropriates $150,000 for scholarships for child care workers who enroll in an early childhood education or child development courses at an accredited college or university. Requires the state to set eligibility, loan amounts and scholarship terms.

      1999 Me. Public Laws, Chap. 515
      Appropriates funds for increased wages, training and facilities improvements for child care programs. Appropriates funds for incentives for child care providers to offer care during odd hours and in underserved geographic areas. Appropriates funds to child care resource development centers.

1999 Me. Public Laws, Chap. 529
Includes quality child care as part of the state's overall statewide goal to prevent child abuse and expands the definition of prevention programs to include the promotion of high-quality child care. Requires applicants to the Maine Children's Trust be made public with applicants' permission.

MD   *1999 Md. Laws, Chap. 352*
Prevents homeowners associations from prohibiting the use of a residence as a family child care home until the lot owners, other than the developer, have 90 percent of the votes in the homeowners association. Repeals the ability of a homeowners association to regulate the number of family child care homes.

MN   *1999 Minn. Laws, Chap. 205*
Art. 1, Sec. 37   Increases to 24 months the amount of time a child care provider must provide child care services for a loan to be forgiven.

Art. 5, Secs. 3, 7   Requires state rules for funding organizations to operate child care resource and referral programs that include application forms, timelines, and standards for renewal. Clarifies requirements and duties of a child care resource and referral program.

Art. 5, Secs. 6, 12-17   Shifts authority and responsibilities from regional advisory committees to the state for distributing funds for child care center services grants and family child care technical assistance grants. Requires the regional committees to make funding recommendations to child care resource and referral programs. Authorizes that 10 percent of the funds be set aside for statewide training, development, collaboration and research initiatives. Authorizes resource and referral programs to apply for this funding and allows up to 90 percent of the grant funds go to child care resource and referral programs. Requires a 25 percent local match for a child care center services grant and no match for a family child care technical assistance grant. Adds certification; emergency assistance for child care programs; new programs for the creation, expansion or improvement of programs that serve ethnic immigrant and refugee communities; and recruitment initiatives that expand and build capacity and improve the quality of care provided by legal nonlicensed child care providers as being eligible to receive a grant. Makes school-age care programs and legal nonlicensed providers eligible to receive grants for centers.

NM   *1999 N.M. Laws, Chap. 12*
Makes a TANF block grant appropriation for training welfare recipients to become licensed child care providers.

NV   *1999 Nev. Stats., Chap. 584*
Sec. 7   Appropriates $300,000 for continued support of the child care training program operated by the City of Las Vegas.

TX   *1999 Tex. Gen. Laws, Chap. 833*
Allows state repayment of student loans of child care workers who work more than 30 hours per week. Requires that the worker must hold an early childhood degree and agree to work in child care in the state for two years. Limits loan repayment amounts. Prioritizes eligibility if there are insufficient funds. Provides for a trust fund and state allocations to it. Provides for state collection of the loan if conditions are unmet.

1999 Tex. Gen. Laws, Chap. 1433
Requires the development of a scholarship program that provides $1,000 to eligible child care employees to pay expenses incurred in obtaining certain child development or child care credentials or degrees. Specifies that eligible child care employees must intend to obtain a certain educational qualification and agree to work in child care for at least 18 additional months. Allows for a state-paid bonus or wage supplementation for a scholarship recipient who cares for a child under age 6 after the 18-month period. Specifies that the state use federal child care funds or other available funds and caps the total biennial amount at $2 million.

VT   *1999 Vt. Acts, Act 62*
Sec. 140   Appropriates funding to continue to provide quality incentive bonuses at 15 percent above the rate for programs that become accredited and to providers that receive a degree or are employed in a licensed or registered child care program. Appropriates funds for a child care mentoring program.

1999 Vt. Acts, H 181
Requires that state-registered family child care homes with 12 or fewer children be permitted to use a single-family residential property. Establishes a committee to study the impact of zoning ordinances on family child care homes. Sets membership appointment authority.

CHILD SUPPORT

Administrative Liens and Subpoenas

FL   *1999 Fla. Laws, Chap. 375*
Sec. 12   Authorizes the agency to impose a fine for failure to comply with administrative subpoenas for information necessary for action in child support orders.

Sec. 15   Allows an obligor to consent in writing to a notice of intent to levy.

MN   *1999 Minn. Laws, Chap. 196*
Sec. 7   Grants the child support agency administrative authority to subpoena information needed to establish, modify, or enforce a child support, and request sanctions for failure to respond to a subpoena; establishes procedures for service of subpoenas. Also grants the agency administrative authority to secure assets by seizing payments from other agencies, attaching or seizing assets in financial institutions or retirement funds, and imposing liens.

1999 Minn. Laws, Chap. 245
Secs. 13, 20   Allows individuals owing child support who have a lien against property due to arrearage claims to provide the court with proof that all balances are paid in order to remove the lien, and requires court to be notified if a lien on property is released by the local assistance office due to partial payment of balance owed.

MS   *1999 Miss. Laws, Chap. 512*
Sec. 16   Stipulates that an unpaid support payment becomes a judgment against the obligor after 30 days and that the judgment is a lien against property.

MT   *1999 Mont. Laws, Chap. 579*
Secs. 3, 6, 8   Allows child support agency in cases of child support arrearages to conduct hearings on claims that property is exempt from administrative liens, specifies procedures for such hearings, and permits the agency to issue and process liens for support through administrative action. Also requires warrants for child support liens to include information regarding exemptions, and specifies procedures for the obligor to request such a hearing.

PA   *1998 Pa. Laws, Act 127*
Sec. 4   Outlines conditions where overdue support becomes a lien against property, and procedures to determine the priority and amount of a lien against property; and establishes procedures to execute liens against property for overdue support. Also allows agency to charge a fee to issue a lien certification and directs the agency to send information regarding liens to credit bureaus. Protects the agency from liability in case of errors related to issuance of liens except in cases of willful misconduct.

TX   *1999 Tex. Gen. Laws, Chap. 556*
Sec. 20   Clarifies that a child support lien attaches to all nonexempt property and lists the property that is subject to a lien.

Sec. 51   Directs the IV-D agency to file a lien when an obligor has a delinquency of at least $5,000 and the obligor owns property or resides within the state.

Agency Administration and Financing

AR   *1999 Ark. Acts, Act 1514*
Eliminates State Commission on Child Support. Reduces quarterly administrative fees for payments directed through court or state child support clearinghouse, and incorporates these fees into original child support order. Defines and distinguishes "overdue support" versus "past-due support."

CA   1998 Cal. Stats., Chap. 329
            Sec. 18   Requires county automated systems to be in compliance with distribution requirements by Oct.
            1, 1998.   Requires department and Health and Welfare Data Agency to work with U.S. Department of
            Health and Human Services to determine compliance.   Specifies systems not in compliance will not
            receive general fund money for meeting requirements.

            Requires counties to cooperate with department on annual child support automation plan by Dec. 1, 1998,
            and each December after. Withholds state and federal funds for automation until county agrees to annual
            plan.

            Sec. 19   Requires the department to establish a steering committee to provide advice on development and
            implementation of a long-term solution for a statewide automation system.   Specifies the committee will
            develop standards, goals, priorities, objectives and an evaluation model to guide the department in a
            study and report.   Allows the department to provide funds based on availability to replace up to 100
            percent of a county's administrative funding reduction for federal penalties due to noncompliance with
            automation. Specifies funding sources for the automated system. Requires counties to pay for the nonfederal
            share of ongoing operational and maintenance costs of respective consortia.   Reduces each county's funds
            for automation administrative support due to penalties if the system does not received federal approval by
            Sept. 30, 2001, and further reduces funds for any county that delays federal approval after the deadline.

            Authorizes department, Health and Welfare Agency Data Center and county district attorneys to establish
            a statewide automated child support enforcement system to comply with federal law and increase child
            support collections.   Permits creation of interim automated child support system to comply with federal
            law. Specifies automated system shall consist of no more than four linked counties, an State Disbursement
            Unit, a statewide case registry and all other necessary databases and interfaces.   Also requires counties to
            select one of seven automated systems by Oct. 1, 1998.

            Requires counties that are not selected to be part of the automated system to submit an amendment to the
            county's automation cooperation play to the department within 90 days.   Specifies the amendment must
            include a plan of conversion to one of the selected systems.   Withholds state and federal funds for child
            support automation efforts for the period of noncompliance for counties that fail to submit an amended
            plan. Withholds state and federal funds for child support automation efforts for the period of noncompli-
            ance for counties that fail to agree to the amended plan.

            1998 Cal. Stats., Chap. 404
            Implements the Legislative Analyst Office's child support enforcement incentive plan, whereby counties
            can qualify for state funds based upon meeting certain support enforcement criteria.   Sets criteria and
            formula for incentives.

CA   1998 Cal. Stats., Chap. 899
            Requires state contracts exceeding $100,000 to contain language regarding the state policy on impor-
            tance of child and family support obligations and a statement of compliance with all earnings assignment
            orders.

CO   1999 Colo. Sess. Laws, Chap. 274
            Sec. 1   Changes the October 1, 1999, sunset of family support registries in the district courts to Jan. 1,
            2001.

            Sec. 7   Repeals current federal incentive payment distribution to counties.

            Sec. 8   Requires that 100 percent of any federal incentives received be passed to the counties and that the
            state create rules for distributing payments based on performance measures, and prohibits counties from
            reducing county funding of child support due to receipt of incentive payments, and requires that payments
            be spent consistent with federal law.

FL   *1999 Fla. Laws, Chap. 375*
Sec. 13   Requires the court to temporarily order that child support payments be redirected if the child is residing with a relative caretaker, or was residing with a relative caretaker and now is residing with the original payee.

Sec. 14   Redefines "automated administrative enforcement" according to federal law.

GA   *1999 Ga. Laws, Act 337*
Sec. 1   Clarifies that a motion to enforce alimony or child support through a contempt order does not constitute a new action or require payment of a new filing fee.

IN   *1999 Ind. Acts, Act 1590*
Sec. 5   Requires child support agency to establish a program to regulate contracts with private organizations for child support enforcement services.

Sec. 6   Specifies that child support incentive payments received by counties will not take the place of regular county expenditures for the child support program

IA   *1999 Iowa Acts, Chap. 127*
Sec. 1   Specifies that subsidized guardianship payments be treated the same as foster care payments for the purposes of child support recovery.

Sec. 2   Requires income withholding orders filed by the child support recovery unit to include the name and address of the appropriate child support recovery unit rather than any other signatures.

Sec. 3   Allows the child support recovery unit to pay a fee to financial institutions for costs related to the quarterly data match, and allows the unit to pay an additional fee to financial institutions for automation programming required to conduct the quarterly data matches.

1999 Iowa Acts, Chap. 203
Sec. 13   Appropriates funds for a public awareness campaign to emphasize the importance of parental involvement and payment of child support.

LA   *1999 La. Acts, Act 762*
Sec. 1   Allows an obligor to obtain an order directing child support payments be made to the agency rather than an individual.

1999 La. Acts, Act 1089
Sec. 1   Redefines "absent parent" and defines "noncustodial parent" the same as "absent parent," clarifies that the child support agency provides services to, and that an order to pay child or spousal support may be obtained by, any individual, including the noncustodial parent, regardless of whether the individual has received public assistance or there is a delinquency.

MD   *1999 Md. Laws, Chap. 486*
Sec. 1   Requires any private contractor for child support services to offer employment to any former state employees working for an existing contractor who are affected by the transfer of the contract, and directs the Department of Human Resources to establish state jurisdictions to provide child support services in competition with the privatized demonstration contractor, and clarifies employment provisions related to the demonstration jurisdictions.

MN   *1999 Minn. Laws, Chap. 196*
Sec. 7   Grants the child support agency administrative authority to recognize and enforce support orders from other states; order parties to submit to genetic testing for establishment of paternity; subpoena information needed to establish, modify or enforce a child support and request sanctions for failure to respond to a subpoena and establishes procedures for genetic testing and service of subpoenas. Also grants the agency administrative authority to direct obligor or other payor to send payments to the SDU; order income withholding; and secure assets by seizing payments from other agencies, attaching or seizing

assets in financial institutions or retirement funds, and imposing liens. The agency also may increase the amount of monthly support payments to collect arrearages; subpoena an employer or payer for information regarding compensation and benefits; and request sanctions for failure to respond.

Sec. 2 Eliminates statutory references to the previous administrative process for actions related to child support, and replaces references to administrative law judges with child support magistrates. Also repeals the previous administrative process for child support.

1999 Minn. Laws, Chap. 205
Sec. 26 Establishes a child support collection account for collections assigned to the state for reimbursement of public assistance, and directs that funds in the account be used for child care programs.

1999 Minn. Laws, Chap. 245
Sec. 9 Removes definition of central child support collections agency as a third party for purposes of creditor collection efforts against child support obligors or obligees.

Sec. 10 Requires department to establish a revolving account to cover funds issued in error due to insufficient funds or other reasons. Requires administrative cost appropriations and all recoupments against payments from the account to be deposited in the revolving account and appropriated to the department. Allows unspent balances in the account to remain until they are spent.

Sec. 22 Allows the department to continue planning a child support assurance demonstration project by administering federal money granted for this purpose.

MS   *1999 Miss. Laws, Chap. 512*
Sec. 1 Grants child support agency authority to establish administrative procedures for genetic testing, modification of child support orders, income withholding, and issuing liens and subpoenas, and to use administrative procedures in interstate child support cases.

Sec. 4 Specifies that a parent is delinquent in child support payments and out of compliance with an order for support if a payment is 30 days overdue.

MO   *1999 Mo. Laws, Chap. 452*
Sec. 452.340 Directs that, when the noncustodial parent receives a parenting time abatement, the amount will be recorded in the automated child support system.

Sec. 452.350 Permits employers to charge a $6 fee per month for income withholding, gives employers the option of sending payments to the SDU rather than the circuit court clerk, and specifies how withheld income should be divided among multiple families.

Sec. 454.432 Requires that overpayments be recorded in the automated child support system in IV-D and non-IV-D cases.

Sec. 454.533 Establishes a trust fund for deposit of child support payments, requires any interest earned in the fund to be paid to the state general revenue fund, and specifies that any principal in the fund is not state funds.

Sec. 454.551 Permits the state to collect a fee of up to $25 for insufficient funds checks sent to the SDU.

1999 Mo. Laws, Chap. 556
Sec. A Extends the statute of limitations to three years for prosecution of false affidavits and false declarations made to public officials relating to child support arrearages.

MT   *1999 Mont. Laws, Chap. 579*
Secs. 2, 13 Defines "support debt," "support obligation" and "support order" to include fines, fees, penalties and interest that the department can collect related to child support or spousal maintenance and support.

Sec. 5 Prohibits agency from collecting a handling fee from the obligee, and prohibits district courts from ordering the agency to collect and charge fees except as authorized in statute.

Sec. 10 Outlines procedures for notification to obligor and obligee of administrative review of child support orders, specifies information that parties must provide to the agency as part of the child support order, and requires the agency to keep the information confidential.

Secs. 11,12 Clarifies definition of permissible "alternative arrangement" between the obligee and obligor for child support payments.

NE   *1999 Neb. Laws, LB 407*
Sec. 1 Establishes a Child Support Commission to make recommendations regarding the child support guidelines adopted by the Supreme Court, and specifies the members that should serve on the commission, including two legislators. Also outlines areas for the commission to consider, and requires the commission to submit an annual report to the Supreme Court and to the executive board of the Legislative Council.

1999 Neb. Laws, LB 637
Sec. 5 Directs courts to utilize statewide automated system for establishment, modification, or enforcement of a support order, and withholds child support funding from counties where the district courts do not comply.

NV   *1999 Nev. Stats., Chap. 185*
Sec. 5 Directs that all payments be made to the child support agency or its designated representative for appropriate disbursement.

NC   *1999 N.C. Sess. Laws, Chap. 293*
Sec. 3 Directs that child support payments shall be made on a monthly basis, and clarifies that this requirement does not affect garnishment of wages based on an obligor's pay period.

ND   *1999 N.D. Sess. Laws, Chap. 141*
Increases the number of court and public officials who may certify child support case registry information; requires state to use high-volume automated administrative enforcement in intrastate as well as interstate cases; mandates the Social Security number of any applicant for any license or permit to be recorded; and shifts support payment deposits from state disbursement unit fund to state treasury.

1999 N.D. Sess. Laws, Chap. 284
Establishes interest on unpaid child support as part of the child support obligation and creates priority by which partial payments of child support are applied.

OK   *1999 Okla. Sess. Laws, Chap. 422*
Sec. 4 Directs established or modified court orders to be forwarded to the central case registry.

TX   *1999 Tex. Gen. Laws, Chap. 40*
Defines district attorney, community supervision department and local registry responsibilities regarding enforcement and distribution of child support orders and payments.

1999 Tex. Gen. Laws, Chap. 228
Requires Office of Attorney General (OAG) to share all information relating to support collections with the Department of Protective and Regulatory Services (DPRS). Requires DPRS to create a division dedicated to finding parents and to use contractors to increase collection of child support. Requires OAG to set membership for a work group to facilitate the sharing of child support information.

1999 Tex. Gen. Laws, Chap. 556
Secs. 2, 50 Moves responsibilities for child support program from attorney general's office to IV-D agency.

Sec. 18   Allows child support enforcement measures to be used for collection of fees and costs related to child support orders.

Sec. 48   Authorizes a county domestic relations office with a cooperative agreement with the IV-D agency to collect an initial child support service fee.

Sec. 50   Removes laws requiring attorney general to establish a work group to create a unified child support system, and other provisions related to the federal Welfare Reform Act of 1996 that have been accomplished or are no longer relevant.

Sec. 51   Requests that the IV-D agency include in its biennial report to the legislature information regarding use and effectiveness of enforcement tools, and the impact of the use of private contractors for some IV-D functions.

Secs. 51, 82   Establishes an interagency work group, specifies agency membership of the work group, lists the specific goals for the work group, and gives deadlines for completion of the work. Establishes a county advisory work group to assist the IV-D agency in developing and changing child support programs that affect counties, specifies membership of the county work group, lists the specific goals for the county work group, and gives deadlines for completion of the work. Establishes an information resources steering committee, specifies members of the committee, directs the IV-D agency director to appoint other members, lists the goals of the committee, and gives deadlines for completion of the work.

Sec. 54   Requires the IV-D agency to establish an ombudsman program to process and track complaints against the IV-D agency, directs the agency to create a statewide process for receipt and resolution of complaints, and specifies information to be collected regarding complaints.

Sec. 55   Prohibits certain courts and court officials from charging certain fees for services in IV-D cases.

Sec. 76   Allows the IV-D agency to obtain information regarding a criminal history from the FBI for a potential employee or other person potentially providing services to the agency.

Sec. 79   Directs the attorney general to redesign and improve the child support enforcement system, establishes that the attorney general's oversight of the child support program will be subject to legislative review, sets parameters for portions of program subject to legislative review, requires the attorney general to submit a report to the Legislature by Oct. 15, 2000, regarding the improvements in the child support system, and directs the Sunset Advisory Commission of the Legislature to report findings to the Legislature in 2001.

Sec. 80   Directs the attorney general to investigate alternate sources of revenue for operation of the child support program, including a cost-benefit analysis, specifies what the cost-benefit analysis should include and requires the attorney general to submit a report to the Legislature by Oct. 15, 2000, with the findings.

1999 Tex. Gen. Laws, Chap. 859
Authorizes a domestic relations office to provide an informal forum for delinquent obligors to negotiate an agreed repayment schedule. Authorizes same office to review information from national directory of new hires and state case registry records to help in collection and distribution of support payments.

WV   *1999 W. Va. Acts, Chap. 10 - 2nd Special Session*
Sec. 48A-1A-21   Clarifies that filing an action concerning establishment or enforcement of child support constitutes an application to receive services from the child support agency, and allows an individual the option to decline such services.

WY   *1999 Wyo. Sess. Laws, Act 66*
Grants power to child support agency to appear in judicial proceedings concerning establishment, enforcement and modification of child support orders. Clarifies who is eligible for child support agency services.

Child Support Enforcement Procedures

CA *1998 Cal. Stats., Chap. 249*
Mandates Judicial Council to evaluate success of the recently implemented child support commissioner system.

IL *1999 Ill. Laws, PA 397*
Sec. 5 Requires that interest be charged on unpaid support obligations after 30 days.

IN *1999 Ind. Acts, Act 1590*
Sec. 2, 4 Defines private organization with which a prosecuting attorney may contract to provide child support enforcement services and allows prosecuting attorneys to contract with a private organization to provide child support enforcement services.

IA *1999 Iowa Acts, Chap. 203*
Sec. 13 Appropriates funds for a public awareness campaign to emphasize the importance of parental involvement and payment of child support.

LA *1999 La. Acts, Act 57*
Sec. 1 Specifies that disobeying custody or spousal support orders can be contempt of court, and allows court to order probation for up to two years for disobeying child support, spousal support, or custody or visitation orders.

1999 La. Acts, Act 559
Mandates suspension of driver's licenses for failure to pay child support, contempt for failure to pay or criminal neglect of family proceeding. Gives court discretion for period of suspension.

1999 La. Acts, HCR 341
Urges department to create a brochure for custodial parents to explain options for collecting unpaid child support.

1999 La. Acts, SR 59
Urges department to use available measures to collect child support from self-employed people.

MD *1999 Md. Laws, Chap. 358*
Sec. 1 Authorizes background checks of child support arrearages for applicants for foster home approval, and requires regulations to take into account any child support arrearages in considering foster home applications.

MA *1998 Mass. Acts, Act 483*
Increases penalties and fines for aiding someone in concealing an asset to avoid a support order to 2 and one-half years in prison and/or $5,000, respectively.

MN *1999 Minn. Laws, Chap. 196*
Sec. 7 Grants the child support agency administrative authority to request sanctions for failure to respond to a subpoena, and increase the amount of monthly support payments to collect arrearages.

1999 Minn. Laws, Chap. 245
Sec. 14 Allows court to suspend interest on a child support debt if obligor cannot pay due to physical or mental disability or receipt of supplemental security income, other disability benefits or need-based public assistance.

NV *1999 Nev. Stats., Chap. 638*
Sec. 1 Allows a defendant charged with failure to pay child or spousal support to claim as a defense inability to pay the support, and specifies conditions that may not be considered an inability to pay support, including voluntary unemployment, excessive spending and indebtedness.

Sec. 3   Designates penalties for persons convicted of failure to pay support, and specifies that failure to pay support is a felony if the person's arrearages are $10,000 or more, or this is the person's second conviction of failure to pay support and arrearages are $5,000 or more.

NH   *1999 N.H. Laws, Chap. 327*
Sec. 1   Reclassifies non support as a felony if the obligor has not paid in over a year or the arrearage is over $10,000, or the obligor has previously been convicted on non support.

NC   *1999 N.C. Sess. Laws, Chap. 293*
Sec. 2   Directs the court to enter appropriate sanctions if an obligor is found in civil or criminal contempt for the third or subsequent time for failure to comply with a child support order.   Also requires a court-ordered payment plan for arrearages to provide for repayment within a reasonable amount of time, and directs the obligor to make an initial payment of at least 5 percent of the delinquent amount or $500, whichever is less.

ND   *1999 N.D. Sess. Laws, Chap. 146*
Permits a court to enforce a visitation order by using any method available for enforcing a child support order that is also appropriate to enforcing a visitation order.

1999 N.D. Sess. Laws, Chap. 281
Shifts burden of proof to the obligor to prove inability to pay support.

1999 N.D. Sess. Laws, Chap. 284
Establishes interest on unpaid child support as part of the child support obligation and creates priority by which partial payments of child support are applied.

OK   *1999 Okla. Sess. Laws, Chap. 301*
Requires noncustodial parents to pay child support even if the custodial parent interferes with or does not permit visitation with the child, prohibits the custodial parent from interfering with a visitation order, and permits prosecution of individuals who violate a child support or visitation order for civil contempt.

TX   *1999 Tex. Gen. Laws, Chap. 1348*
Sets a Class 4 collection priority for collection of delinquent support against the estate of a deceased delinquent obligor.

1999 Tex. Gen. Laws, Chap. 228
Requires Office of Attorney General (OAG) to share all information relating to support collections with the Department of Protective and Regulatory Services (DPRS). Requires DPRS to create a division dedicated to finding parents and to use contractors to increase collection of child support.

1999 Tex. Gen. Laws, Chap. 1072
Mandates OAG to refer underemployed obligors in arrears to appropriate employment services providers and requires Texas Workforce Commission to provide services to such individuals. Requires effectiveness study, by January 31, 2001, of such referrals to employee assistance programs. Authorizes, defines duties, and funds child support court monitors. Authorizes state disbursement unit to transmit payments electronically to appropriate recipients.

1999 Tex. Gen. Laws, Chap. 556
Sec. 51   Requests that the IV-D agency include in its biennial report to the legislature information regarding use and effectiveness of enforcement tools, and the impact of the use of private contractors for some IV-D functions.

UT   *1999 Utah Laws, Chap. 89*
Makes criminal nonsupport a third-degree felony and clarifies that receiving support from another source in not a defense for nonsupport.

WV   *1999 W. Va. Acts, Chap. 10 - 2nd Special Session*
        Sec. 61-5-29   Limits the use of inability to pay to an affirmative defense, which shifts the burden of proof
        to the state to prove the obligor's ability to pay.

Court Practices and Procedures

AL   *1999 Ala. Acts, Act 443*
        Sec. 1   Redefines "claim" to include nonpayment of child support pursuant to a court order.

CA   *1998 Cal. Stats., Chap. 249*
        Mandates judicial council to evaluate success of the recently implemented child support commissioner
        system.

FL   *1999 Fla. Laws, Chap. 375*
        Sec. 18   Clarifies that a county court judge or clerk of the court may not refuse a marriage license to
        noncitizens who are unable to provide a Social Security number, alien registration number or other iden-
        tification number on their application.

GA   *1999 Ga. Laws, Act 337*
        Sec. 1   Clarifies that a motion to enforce alimony or child support through a contempt order does not
        constitute a new action or require payment of a new filing fee.

LA   *1999 La. Acts, Act 210*
        Sec. 1   Outlines certain procedures for registering support orders with another court and changing jurisdic-
        tion to another court.

        1999 La. Acts, Act 447
        Prohibits attorneys representing the department to also represent any party involved in custody or visita-
        tion disputes where the department is providing support services. Permits either party to raise any issue
        relating to custody of child and clarifies that custody or visitation matters need not be specifically in-
        cluded in original documents for parties to raise or courts to decide issue.

        1999 La. Acts, Act 559
        Mandates suspension of driver's licenses for failure to pay child support, contempt for failure to pay or
        criminal neglect of family proceeding. Gives court discretion for period of suspension.

        1999 La. Acts, Act 563
        Permits obligors and employers to be notified in writing of income withholding orders rather than by
        personal service.

MN   *1999 Minn. Laws, Chap. 196*
        Sec. 2   Requires the Supreme Court to establish an expedited child support hearing process designed to
        handle support and paternity matters in compliance with federal law and to adopt rules to implement the
        expedited process, requires all IV-D cases to be handled by the expedited process, and prohibits non-IV-D
        cases from using the expedited process. Also allows a party in a IV-D case to go to a district court if other
        issues related to domestic abuse, custody or visitation, or property are involved, and allows counties to
        decide if the process will include contempt or paternity actions. Specifies goals for the expedited process.

        Instructs the state court administrator to provide for the administration of the expedited process in each
        judicial district, and allows the Office of Administrative Hearings to contract with the Supreme Court for
        administrative law judges to serve as child support magistrates for a specified period of time.

        Sec. 3   Allows proceedings in the expedited process to be reported using electronic recording equipment
        under specified circumstances.

Sec. 4   Requires the court, upon motion of a party, to conduct a hearing to review compliance with visitation and child support orders, and directs the court administrator to provide simplified pro se forms for requesting a review.

Sec. 6   Grants that the child support agency is a party in IV-D cases involving an assignment of support, and specifies the rights of the agency in other IV-D cases.

Sec. 7   Defines the role of non-attorney employees and oversight responsibilities of the county attorney in IV-D cases, specifies information to be included in financial worksheet prepared by non-attorney employees, and directs that the information be filed with the court or child support magistrate at least 5 days before a hearing. Also allows a non-attorney employee to prepare appropriate documents in uncontested matters under the direction of the county attorney.

Sec. 8   Requests the Supreme Court to develop forms for use in execution of support judgments.

Sec. 9   Encourages judicial districts to utilize the existing expertise of child support administrative law judges in appointing child support magistrates.

Sec. 10   Directs the Supreme Court to evaluate expedited administrative process, and grants the court limited access to confidential information for purposes of the evaluation. Requests the court to submit the evaluation and recommendations to the Legislature by Dec. 15, 2000.

1999 Minn. Laws, Chap. 245
Sec. 12   Requires court administrator to enter child support orders upon court decision. Requires orders to be docketed upon filing of the affidavit.

Secs. 16, 18   Requires renewed child support judgements to be equal to the unpaid balance plus the accrued unpaid interest, and allows renewal of judgements until paid. Also allows the court to enter and docket additional judgments for unpaid child support balances, and specifies each judgment must be treated separately for reasons of enforcement and receipt.

MS   *1999 Miss. Laws, Chap. 512*
Sec. 12   Allows parties to agree to a modification of support, directs that such agreements acknowledged and filed before clerks of the court be treated the same as modifications entered by the court, and outlines methods by which agency must notify parties of intent to modify support orders.

Sec. 13   Outlines procedures for agency to notify obligor of a hearing to establish support, allows parties to agree to a payment plan for child support arrearages and directs such agreements acknowledged and filed before clerks of the court, to be treated the same as a judgment for overdue support entered by the court.

Sec. 15   Requires an order for support to specify the amount to be paid and how often payment is to be made, directs payments to be made to the department if the child or parent receives public assistance, and limits retroactivity of support orders to one year prior to commencement of an action. Also grants court continuing jurisdiction in cases enforced by the agency, and establishes requirements for notification of subsequent enforcement actions.

MT   *1999 Mont. Laws, Chap. 579*
Sec. 9   Clarifies procedures for service of summons on the child support agency.

NV   *1999 Nev. Stats., Chap. 169*
Sec. 3   Expands the class of persons to whom district attorneys must provide certain services for the support of children.

Sec. 4   Clarifies that the court must appoint the welfare division as guardian ad litem for the child in paternity actions if the interests of the child are not adequately represented by the appointment of the district attorney.

NC   *1999 N.C. Sess. Laws, Chap. 293*
Sec. 2   Directs the court to enter appropriate sanctions if an obligor is found in civil or criminal contempt for the third or subsequent time for failure to comply with a child support order. Also requires a court-ordered payment plan for arrearages to provide for repayment within a reasonable amount of time, and directs the obligor to make an initial payment of at least 5 percent of the delinquent amount or $500, whichever is less.

ND   *1999 N.D. Sess. Laws, Chap. 140*
Clarifies that due and unpaid support obligations and payments and judgments are not subject to statutes of limitation.

        1999 N.D. Sess. Laws, Chap. 142
Expands role of clerk of court regarding income withholding and notice for failure to pay. Removes notice requirement from state disbursement unit.

TX   *1999 Tex. Gen. Laws, Chap. 1348*
Sets a priority for collection of delinquent support against the estate of a deceased delinquent obligor.

        1999 Tex. Gen. Laws, Chap. 1072
Mandates attorney general's office to refer underemployed obligors in arrears to appropriate employment services providers and requires Texas Workforce Commission to provide services to such individuals. Requires effectiveness study, by Jan. 31, 2001, of such referrals to employee assistance programs. Authorizes, defines duties, and funds child support court monitors. Authorizes state disbursement unit to transmit payments electronically to appropriate recipients.

        1999 Tex. Gen. Laws, Chap. 556
Sec. 3   Prohibits a party from requesting a jury trial for a suit to determine parentage.

Sec. 8   Allows court to order that a party other than a parent may receive, hold or disburse child support payments in IV-D cases where neither parent has physical custody of the child.

Sec. 11   Specifies receipt and disbursement procedures if jurisdiction is changed to another court.

Sec. 14   Permits a court to modify a custody order so a person with actual physical custody of a child can receive child support payments on behalf of the child if the person with legal custody has voluntarily relinquished care, control and possession of the child for at least six months.

Secs. 15, 19   Specifies that a court retains jurisdiction over a child support case until all current support and arrearages are paid.

Sec. 16   Requires an order to appear before a judge on a child support matter to be forwarded to the Texas Crime Information Center and the National Crime Information Center.

Sec. 17   Mandates information that must be contained in enforcement orders for civil contempt.

Sec. 28   Gives employer and obligor the option of notifying the court or the IV-D agency when employment is terminated.

Secs. 41, 42, 43, 47   Outline duties and authority of child support masters.

Sec. 52   Prohibits clerk of the court from terminating an assignment of support and redirecting payments to the obligee.

Sec. 54   Allows IV-D agency to hire private process servers, and specifies procedures for service process.

Sec. 65   Sets procedures for a court hearing if parties do not agree to all issues in a child support case at a negotiation conference.

VA   *1999 Va. Acts, Chap. 690*
Permits courts to require custodial parents to present documentation to verify employment-related child care costs.

WV   *1999 W. Va. Acts, Chap. 10 - 2nd Special Session*
Sec. 48A-4-20   Specifies standards for a circuit court review of the family law master recommendation in a case.

Sec. 48A-4-9   Requires that a scheduled final hearing on a support order cannot be continued without agreement of the parties or a review of the temporary parenting plan and support order. Also directs the family law master, if a party claims inability to pay fees and costs, to determine whether either party is able to pay, and, if so, to assess payment as part of a recommended order.

Secs. 51-2A-1 through 51-2A-11   Creates new family law division of county circuit courts, specifies procedures for appointment and election, qualifications, responsibilities, and allocation of family law masters in the state. Also outlines procedures for removal, suspension or discipline of family law masters, and sets rules for compensation. Specifies rules of practice and procedure, matters to be heard, and contempt powers for family law masters.

Sec. 51-3-14   Removes outdated language regarding the court security fund, and directs that, beginning in 2000, certain fees and costs received for the court security fund be transmitted to the family court fund.

Sec. Sec. 61-5-29   Limits the use of inability to pay to an affirmative defense, which shifts the burden of proof to the state to prove the obligor's ability to pay.

WY   *1999 Wyo. Sess. Laws, Act 66*
Grants power to child support agency to appear in judicial proceedings concerning establishment, enforcement, and modification of child support orders.

Guidelines and Modifications

AR   *1999 Ark. Acts, Act 1075*
Establishes procedure by which child support obligation is adjusted when the obligation for one child expires.

CT   *1999 Conn. Acts, Act 193*
Sec. 3   Limits income that may be counted for child support purposes to the first 45 hours per week.

FL   *1999 Fla. Laws, Chap. 359*
Sec. 1   Requires court to adjust child support awards based on amount of time spent with each parent and other factors. Removes specific provision that court may reduce awards up to 50 percent for 28 consecutive days with the noncustodial parent.

GA   *1999 Ga. Laws, Act 426*
Sec. 1   Clarifies time frames and requirements for three-year reviews and modifications of child support orders

IA   *1999 Iowa Acts, Chap. 203*
Sec. 5   Directs department to adopt rules and procedures for pilot programs for services to custodial and noncustodial parents. Directs Department of Human Services to develop procedures to expedite the establishment and adjustment of support obligations that may deviate from guidelines, with the consent of both parents; changes in income withholding orders, based on individual circumstances; satisfaction of portion of support owed the state, contingent upon cooperation and compliance of noncustodial parent with project requirements; and adjustment of visitation/shared custody arrangements to enhance the ability of parents to meet parental obligations.

LA   *1999 La. Acts, Act 153*
Extends current review of child support guidelines and requests accompanying findings and recommendations to be submitted to the House Civil Law and Procedure Committee 60 days prior to the convening of the 2000 regular session. Directs that public meetings be held regarding support guidelines.

1999 La. Acts, Act 156
Authorizes court to award support beyond maximum schedule guidelines when parties' combined adjusted monthly gross income exceeds a certain level.

1999 La. Acts, HCR 245
Urges judicial council to conduct required review of the child support guidelines and recommend any improvements.

ME   *1999 Me. Public Laws, Chap. 327*
Sec. 1   Requires that an obligor receive credit for any disability payments made to a child due to the obligor's disability, and specifies, that when support is calculated, the obligation shall not be reduced by dependent benefits paid to the child, and that credit received cannot exceed the amount of the current obligation.

MN   *1999 Minn. Laws, Chap. 245*
Sec. 5   Allows judge to include payment for mother's lost wages due to pregnancy in child support order.

Secs. 16, 18   Requires renewed child support judgements to be equal to the unpaid balance plus the accrued unpaid interest, and allows renewal of judgements until paid. Also allows the court to enter and docket additional judgments for unpaid child support balances, and specifies each judgment must be treated separately for reasons of enforcement and receipt.

Sec. 23   Requires department to study the feasibility of a fair, consistent statewide policy for forgiving child support arrearages. Requires legislative report.

MS   *1999 Miss. Laws, Chap. 512*
Sec. 12   Allows parties to agree to a modification of support, directs such agreements acknowledged and filed before clerks of the court to be treated the same as modifications entered by the court, and outlines methods by which agency must notify parties of intent to modify support orders.

Sec. 15   Requires an order for support to specify the amount to be paid and how often payment is to be made, directs payments to be made to the department if the child or parent receives public assistance, and limits retroactivity of support orders to one year prior to commencement of an action. Also grants court continuing jurisdiction in cases enforced by the agency, and establishes requirements for notification of subsequent enforcement actions.

MO   *1999 Mo. Laws, Chap. 452*
Sec. 452.340   Directs that when the noncustodial parent receives a parenting time abatement, the amount will be recorded in the automated child support system. Specifies that a parent's obligation to pay child support ends no later than the child's second birthday unless the parental support order extends the support past the child's 22nd birthday because the child is physically or mentally incapacitated and incapable of self-support. Also establishes simplified procedures for terminating an order of child support that do not require a court appearance by either party.

MT   *1999 Mont. Laws, Chap. 579*
Sec. 7   Grants the agency the authority to set a support amount based on the child support guidelines when a party fails to appear for a hearing to determine support and the agency has financial information about the party.

NE   *1999 Neb. Laws, LB 407*
Sec. 1   Establishes a child support commission to review and make recommendations regarding the child support guidelines adopted by the Supreme Court, and specifies the members that should serve on the

commission, including two legislators. Also outlines areas for the commission to consider, and requires the commission to submit an annual report to the Supreme Court and to the executive board of the legislative council.

NC   *1999 N.C. Sess. Laws, Chap. 293*
Sec. 16   Establishes procedures for verification of an obligor's income for purposes of establishing or modifying a child support order.

ND   *1999 N.D. Sess. Laws, Chap. 143*
Clarifies when a judgment or order may require child support after majority. Extends effect of order into summer school session if a child did not graduate high school at the end of the preceding school year.

1999 N.D. Sess. Laws, Chap. 144
Includes consideration of extended periods of time a minor child spends with the obligor parent in determining support decisions.

1999 N.D. Sess. Laws, Chap. 145
Exempts an employee benefit, over which the employee doesn't have significant control, from gross income determination.

OK   *1999 Okla. Sess. Laws, Chap. 422*
Sec. 2   Creates a formula to calculate child support in cases of split custody. Allows the court to order an informal review and adjustment process once per year, involving an exchange of information between the parents, and specifies procedures for the informal review.

Instructs the court to consider income from secondary employment when computing gross income, and creates a self-support reserve for the obligor by taking into account a federal earned income tax credit. Also instructs the court to base child support obligations on both parents' income once a base obligation is determined using the obligor's income, and clarifies the base obligation calculation in cases of sole custody.

Adds provisions to the child support guidelines to account for shared parenting time, and defines shared parenting time as more than 92 overnights per year that the child spends with each parent, and specifies a formula to calculate a shared parenting time adjustment.

Orders child care expenses to be added to child support obligations, and adds extraordinary medical, visitation, and transportation expenses to deviations courts may consider when determining child support.

Specifies that changes to the guideline schedule does not by itself create a material change of circumstance warranting modification of support orders, and that subsequent children born or adopted does not by itself create a material change of circumstance warranting modification of support orders, and prohibits retroactive modification of child support.

Requires final support orders to include a statement of past due support and interest, allows the court to order an informal review and adjustment process once per year, involving an exchange of information between the parents, and specifies procedures for the informal review, and requires the court to include in a support order provisions for any anticipated changes that will affect the order.

Sec. 3   Creates a mandatory minimum payment for very low income obligors, increases the guideline award schedule for most other income levels, and extends the schedule to monthly incomes up to $15,000. Also directs the court to order additional support beyond what is specified if more than six children are involved.

Sec. 5   Allows creation of periodic forgiveness programs for obligors who owe large amounts of past due support.

TX   *1999 Tex. Gen. Laws, Chap. 43*
Establishes release from prison as a circumstance that warrants modification of child support order if obligor's support was reduced or suspended during prison time.

1999 Tex. Gen. Laws, Chap. 506
Permits extension of support beyond age 18 for child enrolled in a joint high school/junior college program.

1999 Tex. Gen. Laws, Chap. 556
Secs. 12, 13   Extends child support guidelines to situations of multiple families.

Sec. 6   Mandates a legislative review of the child support guidelines prior to each legislative session and deletes requirement for an advisory committee appointed by the Supreme Court for guideline review. Also requests the IV-D agency to submit a biennial report to the legislature concerning the guidelines, and specifies certain data the report must contain.

Sec. 9   Specifies that support orders will terminate if the obligor and obligee become married or remarried, unless a nonparent or agency has custody of the child.

Sec. 64   Identifies procedures for review of child support orders once a voluntary acknowledgment of paternity has been filed, and specifies certain information to be contained in the notice of review.

1999 Tex. Gen. Laws, Chap. 891
Directs that any benefits received by a child from an obligor parent's disability payments should be subtracted from obligor's required support payment.

1999 Tex. Gen. Laws, Chap. 943
Clarifies principal amount upon which interest will accrue when support is delinquent.

VA   *1999 Va. Acts, Chap. 836*
Eliminates the use of 110 days as a trigger for a shared parenting deviation. Increases the multiplier from 1.25 to 1.4 for a more gradual decrease in support for those days spent with support obligor. Defines "day" for custody purposes.

WV   *1999 W. Va. Acts, Chap. 10 - 2nd Special Session*
Sec. 48-2-15   Specifies that support orders include a statement requiring parents to report any changes in gross income larger than 15 percent to the child support agency and the other party, and directs the court to consider costs and care associated with a minor or adult child's physical or mental disability when determining alimony, child support, or maintenance payments.

Sec. 48A-1-3   Prohibits courts from awarding prejudgment interest in a child support or alimony action except in specific circumstances.

Sec. 48A-1A-19   Amends definition of gross income and clarifies definition of overtime compensation for purposes of calculating child support.

Sec. 48A-1B-3   Makes technical amendments to the child support guideline schedule and in the provisions for incomes above the guideline schedule, resulting in an increase in some child support amounts and a decrease in others.

Sec. 48A-1B-6   Raises the adjusted monthly gross income level that requires an additional calculation to determine ability to pay to $1,550.

Sec. 48A-1B-11   Allows a modification of a child support order for a substantial change of circumstance, and clarifies that a potential change of more than 15 percent in the support amount is a substantial change of circumstance. Also creates an expedited process for modification of a support order in certain circumstances.

Sec. 48A-1B-14   Adds needs of another child or children to whom obligor owes a duty of support, extent to which the obligor's income depends on nonrecurring or non-guaranteed income, and considerations for low-income families, as allowable reasons for deviations from the child support guidelines.

Sec. 48A-1B-16   Grants court discretion to order that a portion of the support be placed in a trust for the child if the amount of ordered child support is over $2,000 per month.

Sec. 48A-2-17   Requires the child support agency, upon receipt of notice from an employer, to send a notice to an obligor who is no longer employed, informing the obligor of the availability of a modification and other services of the agency.

Health or Medical Support

MN   *1999 Minn. Laws, Chap. 245*
        Sec. 5   Allows judge to include payment for mother's lost wages due to pregnancy in child support order.

MT   *1999 Mont. Laws, Chap. 545*
        Secs. 3, 5   Allows a speedy dissolution of marriage when the parties have children if the parties have a parenting plan and the children have orders for child and medical support, and requires court to seal parenting plans at the request of either party.

        1999 Mont. Laws, Chap. 579
        Sec. 14   Removes provisions requiring parents to reimburse Medicaid expenses in certain circumstances.

NV   *1999 Nev. Stats., Chap. 185*
        Sec. 8   Requires the enforcing authority to send by first class mail any notices requiring an employer or organization to enroll a child in a health plan pursuant to a medical support order.

OK   *1999 Okla. Sess. Laws, Chap. 422*
        Sec. 2   Directs that medical and dental insurance be split between both parents based on their income and added to the child support obligation, and adds extraordinary medical, visitation, and transportation expenses to deviations courts may consider when determining child support.

TX   *1999 Tex. Gen. Laws, Chap. 556*
        Sec. 23   Specifies conditions under which an order for income withholding may be issued, and information that must be contained in such an order, including whether the obligor is providing health insurance for the child through the obligor's employer.

Income Withholding

CT   *1999 Conn. Acts, Act 193*
        Secs. 6, 13   Requires all child support payments collected by income withholding to be sent to the SDU rather than the obligee, and directs the SDU to distribute all payments within two business days of receipt. Clarifies that, when orders for withholding exceed the maximum amount that can be withheld from a person's paycheck, the SDU will determine allocation.

GA   *1999 Ga. Laws, Act 450*
        Secs. 1, 2   Clarifies income withholding procedures.

        Sec. 3   Requires that all child support orders with income deduction orders be made through the family support registry.

IL   *1999 Ill. Laws, PA 212*
        Secs. 20, 25, 30, 40   Requires that all support payments for support orders entered or modified after Oct. 1, 1999, be made to the SDU in cases where child support services are being provided by the agency and in any cases with income withholding, and establishes procedures for the agency to notify obligors and employers to make payments to the SDU.

1999 Ill. Laws, PA 212

Sec. 35   Details the data requirements for income withholding notices, and directs payers to make payments to the SDU. Directs payments through income withholding to be sent to the SDU instead of to the obligee or public office. Removes provision directing Department of Public Aid to redirect income withholding to obligee when it no longer is authorized to receive payments. Directs the SDU to keep accurate records of income withholding payments and establishes that records of payments from the SDU can be submitted as legal evidence.

IA   *1999 Iowa Acts, Chap. 203*

Sec. 5   Directs department to adopt rules and procedures for pilot programs for services to custodial and noncustodial parents. Directs department to develop procedures to expedite changes in income withholding orders, based on individual circumstances.

MN   *1999 Minn. Laws, Chap. 196*

Sec. 7   Grants the child support agency administrative authority to order income withholding. The agency also may subpoena an employer or payor for information regarding compensation and benefits, and request sanctions for failure to respond.

MS   *1999 Miss. Laws, Chap. 512*

Sec. 17   Grants agency the authority to implement administrative income withholding orders, and specifies procedures for notification and administration of withholding orders.

Sec. 18   Directs that payments from income withholding be paid to the agency for orders enforced by the agency, and allows the court to designate an entity or person to receive payments for orders not enforced by the agency.

MO   *1999 Mo. Laws, Chap. 452*

Sec. 452.350   Permits employers to charge a $6 fee per month for income withholding, and gives employers the option of sending payments to the SDU rather than the circuit court clerk, and specifies how withheld income should be divided among multiple families.

NV   *1999 Nev. Stats., Chap. 185*

Secs. 1, 2   Specifies that initial income withholding notices to employers be sent by first class mail and if withholding does not commence, a second notice be sent by certified mail, and allows employers to be penalized for not complying with an income withholding order after they have received the second notice sent by certified mail.

Sec. 5   Directs that all payments be made to the child support agency or its designated representative for appropriate disbursement.

1999 N.C. Sess. Laws, Chap. 293

Sec. 3   Directs that child support payments shall be made on a monthly basis, and clarifies that this requirement does not affect garnishment of wages based on an obligor's pay period.

Sec. 16   Establishes procedures for verification of an obligor's income for purposes of establishing or modifying a child support order.

Sec. 18   Clarifies that a request for withholding be filed in the office of the court that entered the order for support.

Secs. 19, 20   Directs a payor who receives notice of income withholding to send payments to the SDU instead of the clerk of the court.

NC   *1999 N.C. Sess. Laws, Chap. 293*

Secs. 5, 6   Allows income withholding orders from other states in cases where the obligor is receiving unemployment from state, to be sent directly to the North Carolina Employment Security Commission, without registering the support order in a North Carolina court, and prohibits the Employment Security Commission from withholding more than 25 percent of unemployment benefits.

ND   *1999 N.D. Sess. Laws, Chap. 142*
       Expands role of clerk of court regarding income withholding and notice for failure to pay.

       1999 N.D. Sess. Laws, Chap. 141
       Permits first-class mail as sufficient notice for income withholding authorization.

TX   *1999 Tex. Gen. Laws, Chap. 556*
       Sec. 22   Grants authority to IV-D agency to order income withholding for arrearages when no current support is owed, and to extend the payment period if the payment schedule would cause unreasonable hardship.

       Sec. 23   Specifies conditions under which an order for income withholding may be issued, and information that must be contained in such an order, including whether the obligor is providing health insurance for the child through the obligor's employer.

       Sec. 24   Allows an order or judicial writ of withholding to be delivered to the employer by electronic transmission.

       Sec. 25   Directs IV-D agency to prescribe forms for income withholding and specifies that such forms may be used to request voluntary withholding.

       Sec. 26   Requires employer to transmit amount withheld no later than two business days after the pay date for payments made by electronic means, lists data that must be included with transmitted payments, and specifies where employers must remit income withholding payments.

       Sec. 27   Lists circumstances in which an employer may be fined for willfully violating an income withholding order.

       Sec. 28   Gives employer and obligor the option of notifying the court or the IV-D agency when employment is terminated.

       Sec. 29   Directs an employer who sends a payment to an incorrect agency or person to send payment to correct agency or person no later than two business days after receiving the returned payment.

       Sec. 31   Specifies that only the IV-D agency may issue an administrative income withholding order, and lists conditions when the agency may do so.

       Sec. 32   Clarifies procedures for agency to notify parties of an administrative withholding order.

       Secs. 34, 35   Notes exceptions for required information the agency must send to the obligor for notice of income withholding orders, and exceptions of when the obligor may request a review disputing the identity of the obligor or existence or amount of arrearages.

       Sec. 54   Requests IV-D agency to establish a toll-free telephone line for employers for questions regarding income withholding.

       1999 Tex. Gen. Laws, Chap. 1580
       Creates employer responsibility to obligor for any amount of support withheld but not distributed, including interest.

VA   *1999 Va. Acts, Chap. 56*
       Charges employers with embezzlement for withholding wages and then failing to distribute court-ordered support.

1999 Va. Acts, Chap. 577
Simplifies wage withholding procedures when the United States is the employer.

Information Sharing and Confidentiality Safeguards

CA   *1998 Cal. Stats., Chap. 511*
Sets process for seeking an *ex parte* order prohibiting disclosure of identifying information of a party or child in an interstate child support case when the court finds that disclosure would place party or child at unreasonable risk.

        1998 Cal. Stats., Chap. 1056
Permits disclosure of files maintained by a public entity pursuant to a child support enforcement program to a county welfare department for specified purposes.

CO   *1999 Colo. Sess. Laws, Chap. 274*
Sec. 2   Specifies that child support orders include parties' residential and mailing addresses; and eliminates requirement that orders include parties' telephone numbers, driver's license numbers and employer information.

        Sec. 10   Requires that children's Social Security number and parents' dates of birth be collected in the state case registry.

FL   *1999 Fla. Laws, Chap. 375*
Sec. 1   Requires parties to provide full names, dates of birth, and Social Security numbers of minor children in dissolution of marriage pleadings.

        Sec. 2   Requires full name, date of birth, and Social Security number of each minor child that is the subject of a child support order to be included in the order, and specifies that Social Security numbers will be a separate attachment in the file.

        Sec. 11   Eliminates the statutory requirement that the Department of Revenue and Department of Insurance enter into a cooperative agreement to share insurance information.

        Sec. 16   Requires the child support agency to enter into an agreement with the Federal Parent Locator Service for data matches, adds certain information to data required to be kept by financial institutions for obligors with arrearages, and allows financial institutions to provide the required data to the agency for all individual accounts held by the institution with the stipulation that the information only be used for administration of the child support program.

        Sec. 17   Requires the agency to release information from the parent locator service to any agency providing child support enforcement to non IV-D clients.

        Sec. 18   Clarifies that a county court judge or clerk of the court may not refuse a marriage license to noncitizens who are unable to provide a Social Security number, alien registration number, or other identification number on their application.

IL   *1999 Ill. Laws, PA 212*
Secs. 20, 25, 30, 40 Directs that information be forwarded to the state case registry for orders for support entered or modified by the circuit court, orders where services are being provided by the agency, and administrative orders, and requires parties to report changes in information to a clerk of the court within five business days of the change.

        1999 Ill. Laws, PA 212
Sec. 35   Requires income withholding notices to include the date of entry of the order for support, the Social Security numbers of the parties, and the signature of the obligee or name and telephone number of a representative of a public office, and to direct payer to make payments to the SDU.

Directs payments due to income withholding orders to be sent to the SDU instead of the obligee or public office. Requests the obligee to notify the SDU of a change of address within seven days, requests the obligor to notify the obligee, public office and clerk of the circuit court of a change of payor within seven days, and removes provision directing department of public aid to redirect income withholding to obligee when it is no longer authorized to receive payments.

IN   *1999 Ind. Acts, Act 1590*
Sec. 3   Allows the parent locator service to be used to locate parents who owe child support.

Sec. 8   Requires that Social Security numbers be included on marriage forms unless the applicant objects; requires the form to state that the applicant is not required by law to provide a Social Security number on a marriage application; specifies that Social Security numbers only be used for child support program activities; and specifies that anyone who willfully violates confidentiality regarding Social Security numbers commits an infraction.

Secs. 10, 11   Requires parties to a child support order to inform the clerk of the court of the Social Security numbers of any child affected by the order, and requires that Social Security numbers be kept confidential and used only for the purposes of the child support program.

LA   *1999 La. Acts, Act 213*
Sec. 1   Implements procedures to safeguard confidential information contained in the state case registry, including in cases of domestic violence, and adds the child support agency to entities that have access to the protective order registry.

1999 La. Acts, Act 519
Allows department to publish names of delinquent child support obligors under certain criteria.

1999 La. Acts, Act 563
Permits obligors and employers to be notified in writing of income withholding orders rather than by personal service. Requires names and Social Security numbers to be included within obligor information forwarded to the recipient or the department, whichever is appropriate, within seven days of order entry.

1999 La. Acts, Act 1003
Specifies which information concerning an obligor may be released to an obligee's attorney retained to assist in the recoupment of delinquent child support.

MD   *1999 Md. Laws, Chap. 358*
Sec. 1   Authorizes background checks of child support arrearages for applicants for foster home approval, and requires regulations to take into account any child support arrearages in considering foster home applications.

MN   Sec. 7   Allows the child support agency to share certain information in order to perform its duties.

1999 Minn. Laws, Chap. 196
Sec. 10   Directs the Supreme Court to evaluate the expedited process, and grants the court limited access to confidential information for purposes of the evaluation. Requests the court to submit the evaluation and recommendations to the Legislature by Dec. 15, 2000.

1999 Minn. Laws, Chap. 245
Sec. 1   Allows data in welfare system to be released to evaluate child support program performance and to identify and prevent fraud.

Sec. 2   Requires court child support orders to include names and Social Security numbers of the parties.

Sec. 3   Allows child support enforcement agencies to request confidential information from all state agencies, departments, boards or bureaus that is necessary to establish paternity and child support orders and distribute support collections. Requires information be withheld from credit companies. Removes responsibility of child support agencies for providing responses to requests for information about individuals owing child support requested by employers, utility companies, insurance companies, financial institutions, credit companies and labor associations.

MS   *1999 Miss. Laws, Chap. 512*
Sec. 1   Adds residential and mailing addresses, telephone numbers, driver's license numbers, employer information, and records of restraining or protective orders indicating domestic violence to case data to be recorded in the central case registry.

Sec. 14   Establishes confidentiality safeguards in child support cases where there is domestic violence, and specifies that any unauthorized disclosure of information made in good faith shall not be considered a violation of confidentiality safeguards.

Sec. 15   Requires parties to a paternity or child support proceeding to give notice of change of address within five days.

MT   *1999 Mont. Laws, Chap. 27*
Sec. 1   Eliminates sunset provisions on requirements for new hire reporting and financial institution data match, and on requirements to collect Social Security numbers for occupational and professional license applications, marriage license applications, records of divorce decrees and support orders, and commercial driver's license applications.

Sec. 2   Requires collection of Social Security numbers on death certificates when the state's federal exemption expires.

1999 Mont. Laws, Chap. 29
Sec. 3   Prohibits use of the Social Security number on driver's licenses as the distinguishing number without the authorization of the licensee.

Secs. 4, 5   Requires an applicant for a hunting, fishing, trapping or wildlife conservation license to provide a Social Security number, and directs that the number is to be kept confidential except for purposes of the child support program. Also directs that the Social Security number of an applicant for a wildlife conservation license be deleted from any electronic database five years after the application is made for the most recent license.

1999 Mont. Laws, Chap. 579
Sec. 10   Specifies information that parties must provide to the agency as part of the child support order, and requires the agency to keep the information confidential.

NV   *1999 Nev. Stats., Chap. 526*
Requires courts in divorce, paternity establishment and child support actions to provide Social Security numbers to the child support agency or other enforcing entity as required, and to safeguard the confidentiality of Social Security numbers collected in the court orders.

OK   *1999 Okla. Sess. Laws, Chap. 422*
Sec. 2   Requires the Social Security numbers of all parties to be included in paternity or child support orders.

PA   *1998 Pa. Laws, Act 127*
Sec. 2   Clarifies that government agencies may only require Social Security numbers on license applications if an individual has a Social Security number, and directs government agencies to protect the confidentiality of Social Security numbers collected on license applications. Allows courts to punish contempt for violation of a visitation or custody order by denying, in addition to not renewing or suspending operating licenses.

Sec. 3   Directs employers to provide information regarding employment, compensation and benefits of an employee or contractor to the child support agency, a county domestic relations section or the child support agency of another state upon request, and imposes a civil penalty for failure to comply with such a request.

Sec. 4   Directs the agency to send information regarding liens to credit bureaus.

TX   *1999 Tex. Gen. Laws, Chap. 859*
Authorizes a domestic relations office to provide an informal forum for delinquent obligors to negotiate an agreed repayment schedule. Authorizes same office to review information from national directory of new hires and state case registry records to help in collection and distribution of support payments.

1999 Tex. Gen. Laws, Chap. 228
Requires Office of Attorney General (OAG) to share all information relating to support collections with the Department of Protective and Regulatory Services (DPRS).

1999 Tex. Gen. Laws, Chap. 556
Sec. 16   Requires orders to appear before a judge to be forwarded to the Texas Crime Information Center and the National Crime Information Center.

Sec. 37   Directs the bureau of vital statistics to release information contained in forms to IV-D agency or any other authorized person, and directs the bureau and the IV-D agency to adopt a memorandum of understanding regarding collection and transfer of information for paternity acknowledgment.

Sec. 39   Requests bureau of vital statistics to share information regarding registry, birth records, and acknowledgments of paternity on receipt of a request for such information.

Sec. 53   Allows IV-D agency to release information for purposes not prohibited by federal law.

Sec. 56   Clarifies that the parent locator service can be used to obtain information for support and paternity establishment as well as enforcement purposes, and specifies who may receive information from the parent locator service.

Sec. 58   Authorizes IV-D agency to enter into a consortium with other states and contract with a vendor for services related to data matches with financial institutions.

Sec. 62   Directs the state case registry to provide information as directed and restricted by federal law.

Sec. 69   Directs Social Security numbers of the mother and father on certain forms to be made available to federal agencies.

Sec. 73   Directs Social Security numbers to be recorded on death certificates.

Sec. 76   Allows the IV-D agency to obtain information regarding a criminal history from the FBI for a potential employee or other person providing services to the agency.

Secs. 77, 78   Clarifies that the Department of Transportation may require an applicant for a driver's license to provide a Social Security number only for purposes relating to child support enforcement.

Interstate Enforcement

CA   *1998 Cal. Stats., Chap. 511*
Sets process for seeking an ex parte order prohibiting disclosure of identifying information of a party or child in an interstate child support case when the court finds that disclosure would place party or child at unreasonable risk.

CT   *1999 Conn. Acts, Act 193*
Sec. 4   Directs the IV-D agency to use high-volume automated administrative enforcement for interstate cases at the request of another state, specifies how the agency may request similar assistance from other

states, and clarifies that assistance provided to another state does not mean that the case is transferred to Connecticut's IV-D agency. Also directs the agency to keep records regarding assistance offered in interstate cases.

Sec. 9   Clarifies jurisdiction issues related to interstate child support cases.

IN   *1999 Ind. Acts, Act 1590*
Secs. 12-33 Makes technical changes in compliance with Uniform Interstate Family Support Act (UIFSA).

LA   *1999 La. Acts, Act 210*
Sec. 1 Outlines certain procedures for registering support orders with another court and changing jurisdiction to another court.

1999 La. Acts, Act 561
Sec. 1   Repeals current procedures for interstate enforcement of support by income assignment.

1999 La. Acts, Act 1003
Specifies which information concerning an obligor may be released to an obligee's attorney retained to assist in the recoupment of delinquent child support.

MN   *1999 Minn. Laws, Chap. 196*
Sec. 7 Grants the child support agency administrative authority to recognize and enforce support orders from other states.

MS   *1999 Miss. Laws, Chap. 512*
Sec. 1 Grants child support agency authority to use administrative procedures in interstate child support cases.

Sec. 19   Directs agency to use automated administrative enforcement measures for interstate cases.

MT   *1999 Mont. Laws, Chap. 579*
Sec. 1   Modifies child support jurisdiction laws to conform to federal full faith and credit requirements.

NV   *1999 Nev. Stats., Chap. 74*
Sec. 1 Makes technical changes to UIFSA statute, which governs interstate child support orders.

NC   *1999 N.C. Sess. Laws, Chap. 293*
Secs. 5, 6   Allows income withholding orders from other states in cases where the obligor is receiving unemployment from North Carolina, to be sent directly to the North Carolina Employment Security Commission, without registering the support order in a North Carolina court, and prohibits the Employment Security Commission from withholding more than 25 percent of unemployment benefits.

Sec. 7 Orders the agency to use automated systems and seize assets in response to requests for assistance and information from other states, and to transmit requests to other states for information and assistance from their automated systems.

TX   *1999 Tex. Gen. Laws, Chap. 556*
Sec. 58 Authorizes IV-D agency to enter into a consortium with other states and contract with a vendor for services related to data matches with financial institutions.

License Restrictions

AL   *1999 Ala. Acts, Act 440*
Sec. 1 Redefines "license" as it relates to child support to include sporting licenses, and requires agencies administering licenses to drive, or recreational and sporting licenses, to collect Social Security numbers on license applications.

AR   *1999 Ark. Acts, Act 1514*
Reduces to 60 days the notice of suspension of a driver's license when a noncustodial parent fails to execute a support installment agreement with agency, and requires Department of Finance and Administration to maintain registry of vital information for all residents issued noncommercial driver's licenses starting Oct. 1, 2000.

FL   *1999 Fla. Laws, Chap. 375*
Sec. 4   Specifies that child support payments are delinquent after 15 days, and permits the obligor's driver's license or motor vehicle registration to be suspended.

GA   *1999 Ga. Laws, Act 275*
Sec. 1   Adds salespersons and investment advisor representatives to list of professions that can have licenses denied, suspended, denied renewal of, or revoked for failure to pay child support.

LA   *1999 La. Acts, Act 559*
Mandates suspension of driver's licenses for failure to pay child support, contempt for failure to pay or criminal neglect of family proceeding. Gives court discretion for period of suspension.

MN   *1999 Minn. Laws, Chap. 245*
Sec. 8   Permits the court to suspend or revoke a recreational license for support arrearages equal to or greater than six months or for noncompliance with a subpoena or warrant in a child support proceeding. Allows individual owing support to provide proof of compliance to the court. Requires court to notify licensing agency of release on suspension or revocation within 15 days of receiving proof of compliance.

MS   *1999 Miss. Laws, Chap. 512*
Sec. 5   Allows licensed attorneys representing an obligee to submit a record of child support arrearages to the agency for purposes of enforcing license penalties.

Sec. 6   Requires that, in license suspension procedures, the agency must furnish records of arrearages within 48 hours of a request for such records, and allows license suspensions for individuals who fail to comply with a subpoena or warrant relating to paternity or child support proceedings.

Sec. 7   Removes laws allowing agency to enter interagency agreements with licensing entities and allowing entities to receive federal reimbursement for license restriction activities.

MT   *1999 Mont. Laws, Chap. 27*
Sec. 1   Eliminates sunset provisions on requirements to collect Social Security numbers for occupational and professional license applications, marriage license applications, records of divorce decrees and support orders, and commercial drivers' license applications.

1999 Mont. Laws, Chap. 29
Sec. 3   Prohibits use of the Social Security number on driver's licenses as the distinguishing number without the authorization of the licensee.

Secs. 4, 5   Requires an applicant for a hunting, fishing, trapping, or wildlife conservation license to provide a Social Security number, and directs that the number is to be kept confidential except for purposes of the child support program. Also directs that the Social Security number of an applicant for a wildlife conservation license be deleted from any electronic database five years after the application is made for the most recent license.

NV   *1999 Nev. Stats., Chap. 74*
Sec. 3 Exempts Division of Wildlife from requiring a statement concerning compliance with child support obligations when issuing recreational licenses and permits.

1999 Nev. Stats., Chap. 217
Repeals provision requiring an applicant for the issuance or renewal of a driver's license to sign a statement regarding whether the applicant is in compliance with a child support order.

ND   *1999 N.D. Sess. Laws, Chap. 141*
Mandates the Social Security number of any applicant for any license or permit to be recorded.

PA   *1998 Pa. Laws, Act 127*
Sec. 2   Removes provision allowing court to revoke operating licenses for violation of visitation or custody orders.

Sec. 5   Extends immunity provisions relating to license suspensions to certain people responsible for issuing fish, game, and sporting licenses.

Sec. 7   Grants the agency authority to take administrative action to prohibit the issuance or renewal of licenses or require suspension of a license of an obligor.

TX   *1999 Tex. Gen. Laws, Chap. 556*
Sec. 61   Establishes certain defenses for individuals subject to a license suspension for child support delinquencies.

Secs. 77, 78   Clarifies that the Department of Transportation may require an applicant for a driver's license to provide a Social Security number only for purposes relating to child support enforcement.

New Hire Reporting

MT   *1999 Mont. Laws, Chap. 27*
Sec. 1   Eliminates sunset provisions on requirements for new hire reporting.

Paternity Establishment

AR   *1999 Ark. Acts, Act 1054*
Requires a notarized affidavit from the putative father for inclusion in the putative father registry.

CA   *1998 Cal. Stats., Chap. 390*
Allows juvenile courts to issue restraining orders, custody and visitation orders, and paternity orders in delinquency cases.

CO   *1999 Colo. Sess. Laws, Chap. 274*
Sec. 5   Requires a new birth certificate to be issued if the court determines that a parent and child relationship exists.

IN   *1999 Ind. Acts, Act 1352*
Sec. 1   Establishes required guidelines for proof of paternity for inheritance purposes.

IA   *1999 Iowa Acts, Chap. 203*
Sec. 5   Directs department to adopt rules and procedures for pilot programs for services to custodial and noncustodial parents. Directs department to develop procedures to expedite.

LA   *1999 La. Acts, Act 524*
Permits uncontested paternity to be established by affidavit.

1999 La. Acts, Act 790
Sec. 1   Expands the time frame during which a putative father may disavow paternity from 180 days to 1 year.

1999 La. Acts, Act 834
Sec. 1   Clarifies provisions for determining the surname of an out-of-wedlock child.

1999 La. Acts, Act 918
Sets procedure for testing and potentially excluding presumed fathers, then testing an alleged father for paternity.

1999 La. Acts, Act 922
Permits a court in a suit alleging paternity by a man other than the presumed father to order the presumed father or fathers to submit to paternity testing before ordering an alleged father to submit to paternity testing. Also directs courts to resolve paternity issues in chambers if the presumed father or fathers are unknown to the parties or unavailable to submit to testing.

1999 La. Acts, Act 1021
Suspends, until August 15, 2000, the period in which a minor born between March 1-September 1, 1982, may establish parentage for survivor benefits.

1999 La. Acts, Act 1127
Clarifies and details new affidavit requirements in determining chain of custody for DNA samples in paternity cases.

MN   *1999 Minn. Laws, Chap. 196*
Sec. 7   Grants the child support agency administrative authority to order parties to submit to genetic testing for establishment of paternity; establishes procedures for genetic testing.

MS   *1999 Miss. Laws, Chap. 512*
Sec. 1   Grants child support agency authority to establish administrative procedures for genetic testing.

Secs. 2, 3   Outlines procedures for administrative orders for genetic testing, establishes the presumption that a refusal to submit to testing is an admission of paternity, and requires agency to pay fees for initial genetic testing if ordered by the agency.

Sec. 6   Allows license suspensions for individuals who fail to comply with a subpoena or warrant relating to paternity or child support proceedings.

Secs. 9, 10, 11   Allows a voluntary paternity acknowledgment to be rescinded within the earlier of 60 days or the date of judicial proceedings related to the child, and specifies conditions for a court challenge of such acknowledgment after that time.

NV   *1999 Nev. Stats., Chap. 169*
Sec. 4   Clarifies that the court must appoint the welfare division as guardian ad litem for the child in paternity actions if the interests of the child are not adequately represented by the appointment of the district attorney.

NC   *1999 N.C. Sess. Laws, Chap. 293*
Sec. 1   Clarifies that a written acknowledgment of paternity is the same as a legal judgment of paternity for purposes of establishing child support.

ND   *1999 N.D. Sess. Laws, Chap. 141*
Sets process for voluntary paternity establishment. Expands courts' authority to modify custody and visitation in orders for future support.

OK   *1999 Okla. Sess. Laws, Chap. 396*
Sec. 21   Requires dismissal of any pending court or administrative collection proceedings and release from court or department-ordered support payments if challenger of paternity is determined not to be the father by an administrative or judicial proceeding.

Requires state registrar of vital statistics to remove the name of any person listed as the father from the birth certificate upon notice that the party has been determined not to be the father. Specifies the records will be corrected and the birth certificate changed to reflect the father's name upon paternity establishment.

Allows statement acknowledging paternity to be withdrawn by the mother or acknowledging father within 60 days after the statement is filed or by the date of the administrative or judicial proceeding relating to the child that involves both parties, including child support order proceeding, whichever date is earlier.

Limits reasons for a court challenge of a signed, voluntary paternity acknowledgment to claims of fraud, duress or material mistake of fact. Permits challenges to be submitted within 60 days of signing of paternity agreement. Specifies that legal responsibilities of any party, including child support payments, shall not be suspended during the paternity challenge, except for good cause.

Sec. 22   Specifies that a signed, voluntary acknowledgment of paternity is considered a legal finding of paternity.

1999 Okla. Sess. Laws, Chap. 422
Sec. 2   Requires the Social Security numbers of all parties to be included in paternity or child support orders.

TX   *1999 Tex. Gen. Laws, Chap. 556*
Sec. 2   Requires notice to IV-D agency if a petition requests rescission of voluntary acknowledgment of paternity.

Sec. 3   Prohibits a party from requesting a jury trial for a suit to determine parentage.

Sec. 7   Removes presumption that a man is the biological father of a child in certain situations.

Secs. 36, 37, 38 Establishes procedures and guidelines for voluntary acknowledgment of paternity, prohibits bureau of vital statistics from charging a filing fee for voluntary paternity acknowledgment, allows a minor to sign an acknowledgment or denial of paternity, and directs that a signed acknowledgment of paternity is a legal finding of paternity.

Establishes guidelines and procedures for rescinding or contesting a voluntary acknowledgment of paternity, sets a time limit of 60 days or the date of a hearing relating to paternity for rescinding an acknowledgment of paternity, and narrows permissible grounds for attacking paternity judgments.

Specifies that any statements admitting paternity signed before September 1, 1999 are valid and binding, directs bureau of vital statistics to create forms for acknowledgment and denial of paternity and lists information to be included on the forms, including notice of legal rights and responsibilities imposed or terminated as a result of the paternity acknowledgment or denial.

Secs. 37, 39   Directs the bureau of vital statistics and the IV-D agency to adopt a memorandum of understanding regarding collection and transfer of information for paternity acknowledgment, and mandates bureau of vital statistics to share information regarding registry, birth records, and acknowledgments of paternity on receipt of a request for such information.

Sec. 64   Identifies procedures for review of child support orders once a voluntary acknowledgment of paternity has been filed, and specifies certain information to be contained in the notice of review.

Sec. 71   Allows a supplementary birth certificate to be filed for a person whose parentage is determined by an acknowledgment of paternity.

Sec. 72   Directs person responsible for filing a birth certificate when parents are unmarried to communicate certain information regarding paternity establishment to the parents, and outlines procedures for recording an acknowledgment of paternity.

Public Assistance and Child Support

FL   *1999 Fla. Laws, Chap. 375*
        Sec. 11   Clarifies that payment of public assistance money to or on behalf of a dependent child creates an obligation in an amount determined by application of the child support guidelines, and that such amounts collected be deposited into the general revenue fund.

IL   *1999 Ill. Laws, Act 212*
        Sec. 20   Clarifies when child support payments should be made to the SDU in cases involving public assistance.

MN   *1999 Minn. Laws, Chap. 205*
        Sec. 26   Establishes a child support collection account for collections assigned to the state for reimbursement of public assistance, and directs that funds in the account be used for child care programs.

        1999 Minn. Laws, Chap. 245
        Sec. 1   Allows data in welfare system to be released to evaluate child support program performance and to identify and prevent fraud.

        Sec. 4   Directs welfare agency to retain portion of child support payments to the extent necessary to reimburse state for public assistance payments.

        Sec. 14   Allows court to suspend interest on a child support debt if obligor cannot pay due to physical or mental disability or receipt of supplemental security income, other disability benefits or need-based public assistance.

        Sec. 23   Requires department to study the possibility of passing full or partial child support payment to custodial parent. Requires legislative report.

MO   *1999 Mo. Laws, Chap. 454*
        Sec. 454.415   Specifies the child support payment distribution procedures for the SDU in TANF cases.

MT   *1999 Mont. Laws, Chap. 29*
        Sec. 1   Includes unpaid support that accrued before an applicant received public assistance as support that is assigned to the state for reimbursement purposes.

NV   *1999 Nev. Stats., Chap. 169*
        Sec. 1   Directs the court, before issuing or modifying a child support order, to determine if any of the parties are receiving or have ever received public assistance, and prohibits the court from waiving arrearages in cases where a party received public assistance without providing notice and an opportunity for a hearing to the division of welfare.

PA   *1998 Pa. Laws, Act 127*
        Sec. 6   Specifies distribution procedures for arrearages accrued during the time a family is receiving cash assistance, and directs that all child support arrears collected prior to Oct. 1, 1998, be distributed according to agency procedures.

TX   *1999 Tex. Gen. Laws, Chap. 556*
        Sec. 52   Prohibits clerk of the court from terminating an assignment of support and redirecting payments to the obligee.

        Sec. 54   Directs the IV-D agency to adopt rules governing noncompliance by a recipient of public assistance and to send notice of noncompliance to the department, and allows the IV-D agency or court to require a noncustodial parent to work, have a plan to pay overdue support, or participate in work activities to pay overdue support.

Sec. 75   Directs IV-D agency not to impose sanctions on a showing of good cause for noncompliance with requests for information in a case of a person receiving public assistance.

WY   *1999 Wyo. Sess. Laws, Act 66*
         Sec. 1   Expands obligations for recipients of welfare employment services program to include cooperation with establishment and modification of child support orders.

State Disbursement Unit

CA   *1998 Cal. Stats., Chap. 329*
         Sec. 19   Specifies automated system shall consist of no more than four linked counties, an State Disbursement Unit (SDU), a statewide case registry, and all other necessary databases and interfaces.

CO   *1999 Colo. Sess. Laws, Chap. 274*
         Sec. 9   Adds maintenance payments to those collected and disbursed by the family support registry, and requires party making maintenance payments to pay a processing fee.

CT   *1999 Conn. Acts, Act 193*
         Secs. 6, 13   Requires all child support payments collected by income withholding to be sent to the SDU rather than the obligee, and directs the SDU to distribute all payments within two business days of receipt. Clarifies that when orders for withholding exceed the maximum amount that can be withheld from a person's paycheck, the SDU will determine allocation.

FL   *1999 Fla. Laws, Chap. 375*
         Sec. 3   Directs that all child support payments from initial orders issued on or after Jan. 1, 1994, that have income withholding be paid to the SDU.

         Sec. 6   Requires the state disbursement unit to collect a fee for non-agency child support payments processed by the SDU, and share 40 percent of the fee with the depository where the case is located; prohibits the SDU, in cases where the fee is not collected, from taking it from the support payment.

         Sec. 7   Establishes the SDU and requires that all support payments be processed by the SDU beginning on October 1, 1999, or earlier if the unit is operational.

         Sec. 9   Penalizes local depositories that fail to comply with the cooperative agreement between the Department of Revenue and the Florida Association of Court Clerks, and removes previous statute regarding failure to comply and appropriate penalties.

         Sec. 10   Requires the child support agency to establish rules for procedures for a recipient of SDU services to contest the amount collected, date collected, amount distributed, distribution timing or calculation of arrears, and allows agency to establish procedural rules for recovery of overpayments.

GA   *1999 Ga. Laws, Act 450*
         Sec. 3   Establishes Family Support Registry, defines duties and procedures for collection and processing of payments through the Family Support Registry, and requires that all child support orders with income deduction orders be made through the Family Support Registry.

IL   *1999 Ill. Laws, PA 212*
         Sec. 20   Directs the Department of Revenue to send collected delinquent payments to the SDU.

         Establishes the SDU beginning Oct. 1, 1999; directs the agency to contract with another governmental unit or private entity to operate the SDU; and allows the agency to operate the SDU for no more than 12 months if no contract is in effect. Also directs payments to be collected and disbursed by the SDU for all cases receiving services from the agency and all orders entered after Jan. 1, 1994, with income withholding, and establishes collection and disbursement procedures for the SDU.

Specifies that all payments collected by the SDU that are assigned to the state be held in a separate trust fund outside the state treasury, and removes provision allowing disbursements from the trust fund to cases receiving child support services from the agency.

Clarifies when child support payments should be made to the SDU in cases involving public assistance.

Secs. 20, 25, 30, 40 Requires all support payments for support orders entered or modified after Oct. 1, 1999, to be made to the SDU in cases where child support services are being provided by the agency and in any cases with income withholding, and establishes procedures for the agency to notify obligors and employers to make payments to the SDU.

Sec. 22 Establishes that the county where the principal office of the SDU is located is the venue for proceedings against parties that submit insufficient funds checks or checks that are returned for nonpayment for any reason.

Sec. 35 Requires income withholding notices to direct payor to make payments to the SDU. Also requires a copy of the withholding notice to be filed with the clerk of the circuit court. Directs that income withholding payments be sent to the SDU instead of the obligee or public office. Removes provision directing Department of Public Aid to redirect income withholding to obligee when it is no longer authorized to receive payments. Directs the SDU to keep accurate records of income withholding payments and establishes that records of payments from the SDU can be submitted as legal evidence.

IL   *1999 Ill. Laws, PA 212*
Secs. 5, 10, 15, 45 Directs various state agencies to send child support payments deducted from warrants and other payments to the SDU.

IA   *1999 Iowa Acts, Chap. 127*
Sec. 2 Requires income withholding orders filed by the child support recovery unit to include the name and address of the appropriate child support recovery unit rather than any other signatures.

Sec. 3 Allows the child support recovery unit to pay a fee to financial institutions for costs related to the quarterly data match, and allows the unit to pay an additional fee to financial institutions for automation programming required to conduct the quarterly data matches.

LA   *1999 La. Acts, Act 562*
Sec. 1 Removes law allowing certain courts to collect and disburse child support payments, and requires all collection and disbursement to be done by the SDU.

MN   *1999 Minn. Laws, Chap. 196*
Sec. 7 Grants the agency administrative authority to direct obligor or other payor to send payments to the SDU.

MO   *1999 Mo. Laws, Chap. 452*
Specifies that child support payments must be directed to the SDU, including all orders issued after Oct. 1, 1999, and sets notice requirements, distribution procedures and subpoena compliance procedures for the SDU. Gives employers the option of sending payments to the SDU rather than the circuit court clerk, and specifies how withheld income should be divided among multiple families.

1999 Mo. Laws, Chap. 454
Sec. 454.415 Specifies the child support payment distribution procedures for the SDU in TANF cases.

Secs. 454.430, 454.495 Designates the SDU as a trustee for the agency or person to whom child support is to be paid without the need for an additional court hearing.

Sec. 454.530 Requires the agency to establish an SDU and authorizes the agency to contract with a private company for operation of the SDU. Also requires an annual audit if the SDU is privatized.

Mandates that the SDU disburse received funds within two days and requires the SDU to create an electronic funds transfer system.

Sec. 454.551   Permits the state to collect a fee of up to $25 for insufficient funds checks sent to the SDU.

Sec. 454.565   Mandates an annual audit of the SDU, beginning in 2000.

NE   *1999 Neb. Laws, LB 637*
Secs. 2, 4, 7   Creates SDU to be operated by designee of the child support division, subject to legislative confirmation, directs child support division to reimburse counties for unrecovered costs for processing and disbursement of child support order payments until SDU is operative, requires that payments be disbursed within two days of receipt, and instructs child support division to promulgate rules and regulations for SDU.

Sec. 3   Establishes study to determine best method for collection and disbursement of child support payments in compliance with federal law, designates executive board of Legislative Council to oversee study, and clarifies that study shall not delay implementation of wage withholding procedures.

Sec. 6   Creates Title IV-D Support Payment Cash Fund for collection and disbursement of child support payments.

NV   *1999 Nev. Stats., Chap. 155*
Sec. 2   Establishes the SDU, specifies that interest and income earned by the fund will be credited to the fund, and that the amount of a check sent to the fund that is not honored for payment will be charged against the fund, and directs that money in the fund be used to comply with provisions of federal law.

Sec. 3   Directs that all money collected in fees, costs, interest payments, attorney's fees, incentive payments or other payments not collected for support of children be deposited in the state general fund and not the SDU.

1999 Nev. Stats., Chap. 185
Sec. 5   Directs that all payments be made to the child support agency or its designated representative for appropriate disbursement.

NC   *1999 N.C. Sess. Laws, Chap. 293*
Sec. 4   Requires that child support payments in IV-D cases be made to the SDU, and allows child support payments in non-IV-D cases to be made to the SDU.

Sec. 11, 23   Allows court to order child support payments to be made to the SDU.

Sec. 12, 21   Requires the SDU to transmit payments received through any means to the appropriate recipient.

Secs. 13, 14   Directs the SDU, in non-IV-D cases, to notify clerks of the court of child support payments received.

Sec. 17   Directs entities receiving notices of garnishment to send payments to the SDU rather than to the clerk of the court.

Secs. 19, 20   Directs a payer who receives a notice of income withholding to send payments to the SDU instead of to the clerk of the court.

Sec. 22   Designates that the SDU is responsible for collection and disbursement of support payments for all cases.

ND	*1999 N.D. Sess. Laws, Chap. 141*
Shifts support payment deposits from SDU fund to state treasury.

1999 N.D. Sess. Laws, Chap. 142
Expands role of clerk of court regarding income withholding and notice for failure to pay. Removes notice requirement from SDU.

TX	*1999 Tex. Gen. Laws, Chap. 1072*
Authorizes SDU to transmit payments electronically to appropriate recipients.

1999 Tex. Gen. Laws, Chap. 556
Sec. 9   Adds SDU, in addition to local registry or IV-D agency, as an entity to which support payments must be sent in IV-D cases.

Sec. 10   Allows payments by electronic funds transfer to be made to the SDU, and prohibits an obligor from making payments by electronic funds transfer directly to the account of the obligee if the payment is required to be made to the SDU. Also allows SDU to comply with a subpoena or order to produce a child support payment record.

Sec. 11   Specifies receipt and disbursement procedures if jurisdiction over order is changed to another court.

Sec. 26   Requires employer to transmit amount withheld no later than two business days after the pay date for payments made by electronic means, lists data that must be included with transmitted payments, and specifies where employers must remit income withholding payments.

Sec. 68   Directs the SDU to make available to local registries certain information regarding child support cases. Also establishes additional guidelines for the work group overseeing establishment and operation of the state case registry and SDU and directs the IV-D agency to develop additional procedures for operation of the state case registry and SDU.

Directs the SDU to distribute payments within two business days of receipt. Specifies certain procedures for recording payments by the SDU and local registries.

WY	*1999 Wyo. Sess. Laws, Act 51*
Sec. 1   Establishes administrative payment process for SDU.

CHILD WELFARE

Administration/Research

AR   *1999 Ark. Acts, Act 401*
Sec. 1   Provides that child health and safety are the paramount concerns, in accordance with ASFA.

1999 Ark. Acts, Act 1318
Requires a study of the agency rules and regulations relating to children in need of care, particularly children in protective custody. Requires a report to the legislature by Jan. 10, 2000.

CA   *1998 Cal. Stats., Chap. 311*
Sec. 71   Authorizes any county to enter into performance agreements with private, nonprofit agencies to encourage innovation in the delivery of children's services, to develop services not available in the community and to promote change in the child welfare system.

1998 Cal. Stats., Chap. 785
Requires the state to contract for an evaluation of the adequacy of current child welfare services budgeting methodology. Requires a report to the Legislature by Jan. 30, 2000. Requires state to convene an advisory group to assist the contractor.

FL   *1999 Fla. Laws, Chap. 206*
Clarifies duties of the Child Welfare System Estimating Conference. Authorizes pilot programs for the provision of targeted case management services for children in the child welfare system. States legislative findings and lists goals for children in foster care.

HI   *1999 Hawaii Sess. Laws, Act 116*
Permits the director of human services, rather than the governor, to appoint members to the Blueprint Pilot Project, to expand the size of the child protective services reform coordinating committee to include two line staff of the child protective services unit, and to extend the project through June 30, 2002.

ME   *1999 Me. Public Laws, Chap. 87*
Establishes the Commission to Study Children in Need of Services to study truancy, runaways, emancipation and related issues. Specifies membership. Requires a report to the Legislature.

1999 Me. Public Laws, Chap. 392
Recognizes the authority of Maine Indian tribes under the federal Indian Child Welfare Act. Clarifies that children in the custody of Indian tribes are eligible for all foster care programs administered by the state. Excepts Indian foster family homes from the state licensing requirement.

MI   *1998 Mich. Pub. Acts, Act 517*
Extends the authority currently held by the Child Welfare Agency to newly-created county juvenile justice agencies.

NV   *1999 Nev. Stats., Chap. 435*
Secs. 12-15   Creates rural and local advisory boards to expedite proceedings for placement of children. Specifies membership and duties.

1999 Nev. Stats., LR 53
Requires an interim study and a report to the Legislature on the integration of state and local child welfare systems in Nevada.

NY   *1999 N.Y. Laws, Chap. 7*
Secs. 9, 56   Amends statement of legislative intent to include reference to paramount importance of child health and safety, in accordance with ASFA. Requires a study and a report to the governor and the Legislature on the extent to which victims of domestic violence have their children removed.

ND   *1999 N.D. Sess. Laws, Chap. 282*
        Secs. 16-19, 26 Adds to general responsibilities of Department of Human Services under Titles IV-B and IV-E of Social Security Act. Requires the Legislative Council to consider studying the impact of ASFA.

OH   *1998 Ohio Laws, HB 484*
        Requires the Department of Alcohol and Drug Addiction Services and the Department of Human Services to develop a joint state plan to improve accessibility and timeliness of addiction services for parents of at risk children. Adds reasonable efforts to prevent or eliminate the need to remove a child from home to the responsibilities of a public children services agency.

OK   *1999 Okla. Sess. Laws, Chap. 396*
        Secs. 1-5 Creates a Child Welfare System Review Committee. Outlines membership, duties and purpose.

TN   *1999 Tenn. Pub. Acts, Chap. 508*
        Directs the state to implement the recommendations of the Child Welfare League of America regarding staffing, training, foster care, adoption services, resolution of interagency issues related to TennCare, and review of the role of children's services agencies. Expresses legislative intent that the state enhance foster care services. Requires a report to the legislature. Specifies required contents of annual reports.

UT   *1999 Utah Laws, Chap. 104*
        Expands membership and modifies other aspects of the Families, Agencies and Communities Together State Council.

WV   *1999 W. Va. Acts, Act 5 - 1st Special Session*
        Repeals the 1997 Child Placement Alternatives Act. Requires Department of Health and Human Services and Division of Juvenile Services to present a coordinated plan of child welfare and juvenile justice services to a designated legislative task force. Requires Division of Juvenile Services to develop and annually update its comprehensive plan to establish a unified system for social and rehabilitative programming and treatment of juveniles. Requires several cabinet-level members and other officials to develop and agree to criteria for construction, renovation, acquisition or repair of juvenile facilities. Authorizes Juvenile Services director to modify a juvenile's dispositional order. Clarifies purpose for state plan for predispositional juvenile detention centers. Sets Division of Juvenile Services responsibilities, which previously were performed by Department of Health and Human Services. Sets priority for hiring at juvenile detention and correction facilities. Prioritizes medical treatment choices for juveniles under state care. Adds Division of Juvenile Services to agencies required to keep juvenile records confidential except in specified circumstances.

Adoption

AL   *1999 Ala. Acts, Act 435*
        Provides that consent or relinquishment of a minor for adoption may be implied by the failure by the father to offer prebirth support.

AZ   *1999 Ariz. Sess. Laws, Chap. 347*
        Requires that people seeking certification as preadoptive parents submit fingerprints. Provides that the certification requirements do not apply to licensed foster parents seeking to adopt. Modifies consent requirements. Specifies deadlines for adoption hearings related to children in foster care. Allows for waiver of probationary period in certain circumstances.

AR   *1999 Ark. Acts, Act 518*
        Sec. 2,3 Repeals minimum time that petitioner must have custody for court to find that adoption is in the best interest of the child.

        Specifies conditions under which state may grant a child eligibility for an adoption subsidy without first searching for a family willing to adopt without a subsidy.

1999 Ark. Acts, Act 1229
Sec. 1   Requires certified statement from putative father registry to be obtained upon filing of a petition for adoption and prior to the entry of an adoption decree in certain cases. Requires confidential information about child and adoptive parents to be removed from notice given to putative father.

CA   *1998 Cal. Stats., Chap. 329*
Secs. 28-29   Establishes a program for special training and services to facilitate the adoption of children who are HIV positive or born to a substance abusing mother, based on the TIES for Adoption program in Los Angeles.

         1998 Cal. Stats., Chap. 572
Broadens juvenile court authority to terminate parental rights and expedite adoption process if child is likely to be adopted.

         1998 Cal. Stats., Chap. 1056
Prohibits state or an adoption agency from denying an adoptive placement because the prospective adoptive family lives outside the jurisdiction, in accordance with ASFA. Directs the state to establish a statewide adoption exchange. Requires the reinvestment of any adoption incentive payments under ASFA to provide post-adoption services. Requires that a nonresident who relinquishes a child to the state for adoption first receive counseling in his or her state of residence. Requires that private adoption agencies employ a supervisor with at least five years of experience. Authorizes county adoption agencies to contract with out-of-state adoption agencies.

CO   *1999 Colo. Sess. Laws, Chap. 259*
Requires an adoption investigation to include a check of the central child abuse registry. Requires the department to develop a vendor list of qualified home study providers. Allows providers to promote the adoption of available children through education and public information campaign. Requires the state to establish standards for home studies in which the criteria shall include assessing the abilities of prospective adoptive families to meet the needs of a child with special needs. Establishes fees for investigations and home studies. Authorizes waiver of fee if it poses a barrier to the adoption of a child. Requires the adoption investigation to include access to the central child abuse registry to obtain information on the prospective adoptive parent(s).

Requires the department to establish a statewide adoptive family resource registry. Allows the state to accept and expend donations to establish the registry. Defines "public adoption" as an adoption involving a child who is in the legal custody and guardianship of the county department of social services that has the right to consent to adoption for that child. Requires the department to evaluate the adoptive placement process of children in custody and report to the Legislature.

         1999 Colo. Sess. Laws, Chap. 270
Authorizes expedited methods of adoption of children in custodial adoptions and kinship adoptions when the birth parents have abandoned the child. Excepts custodial and kinship adoptions from certain background investigation requirements. Requires that any convictions of certain felonies be acknowledged in stepparent, custodial and kinship adoptions.

         1999 Colo. Sess. Laws, Chap. 283
Authorizes confidential intermediaries to inspect adoption records. For adoptions before Sept. 1, 1999, allows access to adoption information to certain persons only through intermediaries. For later adoptions, opens adoption records to certain individuals, unless birth parent requested confidentiality. Provides for consent to release of identifying information. Limits access to records and contact with an adoptee where family has adopted two or more siblings.

CT   *1999 Conn. Acts, Act 166*
Requires good faith efforts to place a child for adoption if the permanency plan is adoption. Requires establishment of a central registry of all children for whom the permanency plan is adoption and a system to monitor progress in implementing permanency plans.

Encourages state to contract with child-placing agencies to arrange for adoption of children. Authorizes waiver of child care subsidy income standards for families that adopt children out of foster care. Adds such families to the priority list for child care subsidies.

Prohibits delay of placement for adoption on the basis of race, color or national origin. Expresses preference for placement of siblings together.

Requires that reports in adoption proceedings contain information on physical, mental and genetic history of child and history of abuse suffered by child. Provides that records relating to child are available to adoptive parents.

Allows state to provide post-adoption counseling and referral services. Establishes an advisory committee on adoption promotion. Requires certain adoption workers to complete cultural sensitivity training. Requires state to designate a minority recruitment specialist for foster and adoptive families. Specifies duties.

1999 Conn. Acts, Act 252
Directs establishment of an adoption resource exchange and preparation of an information handbook for individuals interested in adopting a special needs child. Enacts into law the Interstate Compact on Adoption and Medical Assistance. Provides for waiver of income standards so that child care subsidies may be provided to families that adopt special needs children.

ID   *1999 Idaho Sess. Laws, Chap. 314*
Requires notice of termination of parental rights and adoption hearings to man considered to be child's father.

IN   *1999 Ind. Acts, PL 200*
Secs. 3, 6-23, 32-33   Establishes time frames for paternity actions if an adoption of the child is pending. Requires a petition for adoption to state whether the petitioner has been convicted of certain crimes. Makes other procedural changes to adoption statute regarding notice to and rights of putative fathers. Prohibits a court from granting an adoption if the petitioner has been convicted of a specified felony. Provides that appropriations to the program for adoption of hard to place children does not revert to general fund at the end of the year. Places restrictions on payments by an adoptive family to a birth mother to cover expenses of pregnancy and childbirth. Creates the offense of adoption deception.

IA   *1999 Iowa Acts, Chap. 138*
Secs. 1, 4, 6   Specifies individuals authorized to perform pre-adoption background investigations and author report. Outlines procedures for completion and submission of report. Eliminates requirement that document certifying parental rights have been terminated in another country be approved by the immigration and naturalization service. Requires the state to accept, instead, any official document from country of origin demonstrating a legal release or approval for adoption. Specifies individuals authorized to offer pre-adoption counseling to birth parents considering adoption.

IA   *1999 Iowa Acts, Chap. 203*
Sec. 46   Requires the Department of Human Services to submit recommendations to the General Assembly regarding the addition of respite care to the special services provided to families that adopt special needs children, and the continuation of special services to a foster child for a reasonable time following issuance of an adoption decree.

LA   *1999 La. Acts, Act 695*
Adds two requirements to a father's consent to termination of parental rights and/or adoption.

1999 La. Acts, Act 884
Adds "any other genetic or familial condition or health problem" question to statement of family history form and lists medical record limitations on adoptions occurring prior to Sept. 11, 1981.

1999 La. Acts, Act 1062
Expands provisions for intrafamily adoptions and requires abuse/neglect and criminal records checks in such situations. Gives priority to intrafamily adoptions when there is a conflict. Sets time period to challenge adoption for fraud. Sets allowable fees and expenses for private adoptions. Specifies that payment or receipt of anything of value for the procurement of a child is prohibited, except reasonable expenses. Prohibits a minor's parent from waiving mental health counseling after adoption. Details required efforts to notify alleged or adjudicated father prior to adoption. Revises provisions relating to court review of adoption and record checks of prospective adoptive parents.

1999 La. Acts, Act 1243
Clarifies jurisdiction and domiciliary requirements in adoption proceedings.

1999 La. Acts, Act 1268
Enacts a new title of the Children's Code to provide for adoption of foreign orphans.

1999 La. Acts, H Con. Res. 282
Requests the House and Senate committees on health and welfare to function as a joint committee to study the methods by which children are identified and placed when adoption is indicated.

ME   *1999 Me. Public Laws, Chap. 265*
Permits designation of a preadoptive parent's home as a foster home for the purpose of placing a child prior to adoption.

MD   *1999 Md. Laws, Chap. 320*
Authorizes the state to join the Interstate Compact on Adoption and Medical Assistance.

1999 Md. Laws, Chap. 503
Requires all private employers and certain state and local government units that provide paid leave to employees following the birth of a child to provide the same paid leave to employees following the adoption of a child.

MI   *1998 Mich. Pub. Acts, Act 495*
Requires an adoption facilitator to provide a prospective adoptive parent with certain nonidentifying information about the prospective adoptee. Requires the facilitator to hold a conference with the prospective adoptive parent to review and discuss information.

MN   *1999 Minn. Laws, Chap. 245*
Art. 8, Sec. 1, 41 Requires the state registrar to provide a copy of an adopted person's birth certificate to an Indian tribe for purposes of determining eligibility for membership.

Art. 8, Sec. 34 Allows an adoptive parent to appeal a commissioner's denial of adoption assistance.

Art. 8, Sec. 35 Authorizes the commissioner to enter into contracts with licensed child placing agencies in other states.

Art. 8, Sec. 36 Clarifies the requirements for reimbursement of nonrecurring adoption expenses.

Art. 8, Secs. 37, 39 Allows a child to be eligible for post-adoption service grants until age 22, if he or she remains dependent on the adoptive parents and is enrolled in a secondary education program.

MO   *1999 Mo. Laws, Chap. 135*
Sec. A Requires that special needs adoption tax credit be taken half upon placement of the child and half when adoption is final. Sets new limits on credit. Authorizes the transfer and sale of credit.

1999 Mo. Laws, Chap. 453
Sec. A Prohibits court from waiving criminal background check when pre-adoption investigation is waived in certain adoption proceedings.

MT   *1999 Mont. Laws, Chap. 21*
Secs. 1-5   Replaces the phrase "hard to place" with "special needs" for determining eligibility for adoption subsidies and defines "special needs." Eliminates examples of what constitutes reasonable efforts to place a child without a subsidy. Allows licensed child placement agencies to approve families for subsidized adoptions. Requires subsidy for child with mental or physical handicap to continue until child reaches age 21. Clarifies services and items allowable under subsidy agreements.

1999 Mont. Laws, Chap. 257
Secs. 4,15, 16,18-19, 20   Clarifies that relinquishment and consent to adopt must specify that relinquishment ends all parental rights and obligations.

Allows the court to waive the requirement of a preplacement evaluation in cases of stepparent adoptions.

Requires stepparent wishing to adopt to obtain termination of parental rights for noncustodial parent prior to adoption. Repeals the requirement that child's parent who is not stepparent's spouse consent to the adoption.

Requires adoption decree to include objection of either parent to the child obtaining information from original birth certificate after age 18 and requires notice of such information to be given to Vital Statistics Bureau.

NV   *1999 Nev. Stats., Chap. 74*
Prohibits a stay of adoption proceedings for the enforcement of child support.

1999 Nev. Stats., Chap. 435
Secs. 1-2   Requires child-placing agencies to give preference to the placement of a child for adoption together with his siblings. Requires courts considering adoption petitions by foster parents to strongly consider the emotional bond between child and foster parent.

NH   *1999 N.H. Laws, Chap. 18*
Removes the prohibition against homosexuals acting as adoptive or foster parents.

1999 N.H. Laws, Chap. 40
Establishes a committee to study the feasibility of open adoption. Requires a report to the legislature on or before November 1, 1999.

NY   *1998 N.Y. Laws, Chap. 531*
Requires that adoption petitions be filed and heard in the same county that termination of parental rights petition is pending or termination was ordered.

1999 N.Y. Laws, Chap. 7
Secs. 25, 27   Requires that adoption incentive payments under ASFA be used for preventive services and post-adoption services. Requires the provision of medical assistance to handicapped adoptive children.

NC   *1999 N.C. Sess. Laws, Chap. 190*
Sec. 5   Authorizes the state to join the Interstate Compact on Adoption and Medical Assistance.

ND   *1999 N.D. Sess. Laws, Chap. 148*
Authorizes the court to waive pre-adoption investigation in relative adoptions other than stepparent adoptions under certain conditions. Defines "relative."

1999 N.D. Sess. Laws, Chap. 282
Sec. 25   Authorizes the state to join the Interstate Compact on Adoption and Medical Assistance.

OH   *1998 Ohio Laws, HB 484*
Authorizes the state to enter into one or more interstate compacts for the provision of medical assistance and other social services to special needs adopted children. Requires agencies to consider giving preference to an adult relative over a non-relative caregiver when determining an adoptive placement.

OK   *1999 Okla. Sess. Laws, Chap. 396*
Secs. 18-19   Outlines procedures for completion of criminal records background checks. Requires national background check for all adults living in potential adoptive home who have not resided in state continuously for 10 years. Details procedures for updating existing home studies. Outlines procedures for the completion of a home study for international adoptions. Requires people who complete home studies to receive certain training.

SC   *1999 S.C. Acts, Act 82*
Clarifies and limits ability to appeal final adoption orders.

UT   *1999 Utah Laws, Chap. 251*
Requires a report to the Legislature by Oct. 1, 1999, on the funding of services to families who have adopted foster children.

      1999 Utah Laws, Chap. 178
Extends from 30 days to 90 days the period during which a child must be placed with an adoptive parent for the parent to qualify for an adoption indemnity benefit under insurance policies that cover maternity benefits.

VA   *1999 Va. Acts, Chap. 1028*
Establishes that a birth father's consent to adoption is not necessary when the birth father was convicted of carnal knowledge of a child between the ages of 13 and 15 and the child to be adopted was conceived as a result of the violation. Bars the person convicted from having a legitimate interest in the custody and visitation of a child conceived as a result of the violation.

Financing/Training

CA   *1998 Cal. Stats., Chap. 1056*
Appropriates $330,000 to implement ASFA.

FL   *1999 Fla. Laws, Chap. 193*
Authorizes the department to annually certify local funds for the state match for eligible Title IV-E expenditures.

      1999 Fla. Laws, Chap. 206
Clarifies that the privatization of child welfare services does not require additional funding by local jurisdictions. Provides guidelines for the distribution of federal funds earned by the state and community-based agencies in excess of the amount appropriated by the legislature. Requires a report to the Legislature, including performance outcomes.

IA   *1999 Iowa Acts, Chap. 111*
Secs. 9-10   Establishes new timelines for the submission of regional plans for containing child welfare expenditures and decategorization agreements.

      1999 Iowa Acts, Chap. 203
Secs. 4, 15   Appropriates $23.5 million from the TANF block grant for child and family services. Appropriates $107.5 million from the general fund for such services. Sets an expenditure target for group foster care. Requires that, in the event that expenditure targets for group foster care are being exceeded, group placements be examined for possible termination. Continues the goal that not more than 15 percent of foster children may be in care for more than 24 months. Requires continuation of decategorization program. Authorizes expenditure of funds for subsidized guardianship program.

MN   *1999 Minn. Laws, Chap. 245*
        Art. 8, Secs. 6-8   Allows federal child welfare funds to be claimed by contracted staff of a local social service agency and an American Indian tribe.

NY   *1999 N.Y. Laws, Chap. 7*
        Sec. 57   Appropriates $3.5 million to implement ASFA, of which $2.2 million is to be used for fingerprinting.

ND   *1999 N.D. Sess. Laws, Chap. 34*
        Sec. 10   Requires counties to reimburse the state for a certain portion of foster care and subsidized adoption costs in excess of the amount provided by the federal government under Title IV-E.

UT   *1999 Utah Laws, Chap. 101*
        Defines on-the-job training requirements for state child welfare workers.

Legal Procedures/Policy/Records

AR   *1999 Ark. Acts, Act 401*
        Sec. 5   Requires that all hearings involving foster children be closed. Adopts notice provisions in ASFA.

CA   *1998 Cal. Stats., Chap. 706*
        Permits minors age 12 or older to appear in court without guardian or counsel to request or oppose a protective or restraining order. Permits persons under age 12 to appear with guardian in same situations.

ME   *1999 Me. Public Laws, Chap. 189*
        Allows a foster parent, preadoptive parent or relative caregiver to attend a review or hearing, unless excluded by the judge. Requires a report to the Legislature. Allows state child welfare agency to include foster parent in meetings with child. Requires a report to the Legislature.

MI   *1999 Mich. Pub. Acts, Act 530*
        Extends family court jurisdiction in abuse and neglect cases to include authority over nonparent adults in family service plans and termination of parental rights. Defines "nonparent" adult.

MT   *1999 Mont. Laws, Chap. 566*
        Sec. 8   Adopts notice provisions in ASFA.

NY   *1999 N.Y. Laws, Chap. 7*
        Secs. 5, 18, 30, 44   Requires that notice of permanency hearings be given to foster parents, preadoptive parents and relative caregivers, in accordance with ASFA.

ND   *1999 N.D. Sess. Laws, Chap. 282*
        Sec. 4   Provides that juvenile court has concurrent jurisdiction with district court for appointment of guardian.

OH   *1998 Ohio Laws, HB 484*
        Adopts notice provisions of ASFA.

SC   *1999 S.C. Acts, Act 104*
        Sec. 9   Extends civil immunity to conveners of family group conferences.

Out-of-Home Placement/Foster Care

AL   *1999 Ala. Acts, Act 437*
        Establishes a kinship foster care program. Authorizes payment of the full foster care rate to approved relatives. Requires the state to develop eligibility standards and to conduct background checks.

AZ   *1999 Ariz. Sess. Laws, Chap. 198*
Provides that a child in foster care has the right to maintain contact with friends, siblings and other relatives.

AR   *1999 Ark. Acts, Act 401*
Sec. 2   Defines "long-term foster care."

      1999 Ark. Acts, Act 1319
Sec. 1   Clarifies that non-psychiatric residential treatment facilities and other facilities licensed by the Child Welfare Board are not to be considered long-term care facilities. Specifies that child welfare agencies licensed by the board are exempted from licensure by Office of Long-Term Care and Health Services Agency and Commission.

      1999 Ark. Acts, Act 1363
Sec. 1   Establishes advance notice requirements for changing placements of children in foster care and outlines procedures. Creates exception when child's health or safety necessitates an immediate change.

CA   *1998 Cal. Stats., Chap. 311*
Requires counties to make available to child-placing agencies information about educational options for children in licensed children's institutions. Requires cooperation to ensure transfer of records when a foster child transfers to another educational setting.

Requires state to investigate any threat to health and safety of children placed out of state. Imposes additional safety requirements with respect to children placed out of state.

Requires group homes to operate with a provisional license for the first 12 months. Imposes additional requirements on members of group home boards of directors. Imposes additional disclosure requirements for licensure of community care facilities. Requires fingerprinting of applicants for licensure as a community care facility. Authorizes state to create substitute group home employee registries.

Requires the state to implement regulations regarding the duties of group home facility manager. Requires a certification program for administrators of group homes. Imposes other duties on group homes. Authorizes revocation or suspension of a license on the grounds of financial malfeasance.

Adds to training requirements imposed on state licensing personnel.

Specifies circumstances in which minors placed out of state may be removed and returned to court for review of the suitability of the placement.

Requires counties to provide mental health screening, assessment and treatment for certain children in group care.

States the intent of the Legislature that the foster care state plan be amended to ensure that all eligible children up to age 21 may be served by the Independent Living Program.

Requires the state to issue to all county placing agencies and the courts, current best practice guidelines for the assessment of a child receiving foster care and child welfare services. Requires the state to establish a pilot project to test the effectiveness of using best practice standards for such assessment.

Revises procedures for the establishment of a group home's rate classification level.

Provides for an increase in reimbursement rates to foster care providers. Requires an annual financial audit of foster family agencies and group homes.

Requires a task force to recommend changes to facilitate prosecution of illegal activities regarding funds paid to community care facilities.

Repeals procedures for determination of the level of care required by foster children. Requires that foster children placed out of state be visited at least once monthly by a county social worker.

Establishes the Office of the State Foster Care Ombudsman.

Requires the state to conduct a reexamination of the role of the foster care system.

1998 Cal. Stats., Chap. 329
Secs. 21, 22   States legislative intent that the Department of Social Services work with counties, federal officials, kinship caregivers and other interested parties to develop a Kinship Care Program separate from the existing foster care program. Prohibits payment of foster care funds on behalf of a child determined to be eligible solely on the basis of the decision in *Land vs. Anderson*.

1998 Cal. Stats., Chap. 1055
Establishes the Kinship Guardianship Assistance Payment (Kin-GAP) Program to provide financial assistance for dependent children placed in legal guardianship with a relative. Amends court procedures pertaining to establishment of a legal guardianship for a minor adjudicated to be dependent.

1998 Cal. Stats., Chap. 1056
Caps at $5,000 the amount of accumulated savings that may be retained by a ward of the state under the ward's Independent Living Program case plan. Requires the state to submit for public comment regulations regarding mother and infant programs in group homes.

CO   *1999 Colo. Sess. Laws, Chap. 272*
Creates Child Mental Health Treatment Act. Sets county and mental health agency procedures for when a mental health needs assessment is needed. Directs when a dependency or neglect action regarding children with mental health needs is warranted. Requires mental health agencies and Department of Human Services to report certain information regarding crossover between child mental health needs and neglect and dependency out-of-home placement. Permits parents to petition state for mental health services for minor child. Repeals act July 1, 2003.

1999 Colo. Sess. Laws, Chap. 293
Sec. 6   Requires the state to rule on the process of foster homes becoming recertified every three years. Requires foster home applicants seeking certification to provide a list of departments and agencies that previously certified the home. Directs the state to conduct a reference check of the applicant.

Sec. 7   Prohibits any person providing care to a child from using alcohol around children. Exempts foster care parents under certain conditions.

CT   *1999 Conn. Acts, Act 166*
Provides that any person licensed to accept placement of a child is deemed to be licensed as a foster family or prospective adoptive family.

DE   *Vol. 70 Del. Laws, Chap. 77*
Eliminates the need for home evaluations for dependent children who have been living with related adults who do not meet the legal definition of relative, where such individuals have been providing adequate care.

FL   *1999 Fla. Laws, Chap. 168*
Requires the department to specify behaviors or conditions under which the department must take a child into custody or petition the court for removal from the home. Specifies that these factors must include noncompliance with the case plan and prior abuse reports with findings that involve the child or caregiver.

1999 Fla. Laws, Chap. 193
Allows the department to place a child in a foster home that otherwise meets licensing requirements if the state and local records checks do not disqualify the home and the department is awaiting results from the federal criminal records check.

1999 Fla. Laws, Chap. 206
Specifies minimum levels of liability insurance that must be carried by certain community-based foster care and related service providers. Limits damages that may be recovered against such providers. Clarifies immunities from liability. Requires that foster care workers whose positions are being privatized shall be given hiring preference by providers. Allows foster care providers to also be licensed as family day care homes and receive both child care and foster care payments for the same child. Extends the deadline for privatization of foster care in District 5.

GA   *1999 Ga. Laws, Act 447*
Sec. 1 Authorizes the department to take temporary custody of a child for up to seven days without court order when parent cannot care for child due to emergency or illness. Outlines rights, duties and responsibilities of department. Grants immunity to department for its actions during period of temporary custody.

HI   *1999 Hawaii Sess. Laws, Act 271*
Requires the department to establish a procedure for the timely enrollment of foster children into a health insurance program.

Requires foster boarding home applicants to successfully complete foster parent training within the first year following placement of the first child in a new special licensed or relative foster home. Defines foster parent training.

IN   *1999 Ind. Acts, PL 211*
Secs. 1-2, 4-5 Defines "special needs foster family home" and "therapeutic foster family home." Specifies licensure requirements. Defines "special needs foster child" and "therapeutic foster child."

1999 Ind. Acts, PL 118
Allows a school corporation to enter into an agreement to pay transfer tuition to a nonprofit corporation that educates children placed in a child care facility under certain circumstances.

IA   *1999 Iowa Acts, Chap. 55*
Clarifies that compensation to foster parents from foster home insurance fund for property damage in licensed foster home is at replacement cost. Changes foster parent deductible from a per-occurrence liability to an annual liability. Eliminates provisions that fund is not liable for claims under certain circumstances. Changes limitations on fund coverage amounts from calendar year to state fiscal year.

1999 Iowa Acts, Chap. 111
Sec. 1 Requires that children with mental retardation or other developmental disability, voluntarily placed out-of-home and under court supervision, be placed in family foster homes contingent upon the receipt of a federal Medicaid waiver.

1999 Iowa Acts, Chap. 203
Sec. 15 Authorizes expenditure of funds for a subsidized guardianship program. Specifies eligibility criteria and payment maximums.

KS   *1999 Kan. Sess. Laws, Chap. 156*
Sec. 12 Allows continued placement of an adjudicated delinquent in a child welfare placement unless the offender was adjudicated for a felony or a second or subsequent misdemeanor.

LA   *1999 La. Acts, Act 770*
Clarifies the meaning of "least restrictive disposition."

1999 La. Acts, Act 990
Establishes a Grandparent Subsidy Program for grandparents and stepgrandparents who have legal custody or guardianship of their grandchildren or stepgrandchildren.

1999 La. Acts, Act 1062
Adds large family child care homes to the statutory definition of "child care facility." Redefines "foster family home." Defines "large family child care home." Adds certain juvenile facilities to the list of care providers exempt from the Child Care Facilities Licensing Act.

1999 La. Acts, Act 1173
Requires notification of local educational agencies of an application for licensure to provide residential treatment, group home care, shelter care and other forms of care.

1999 La. Acts, Act 1356
Prohibits a juvenile who committed a felony-grade or misdemeanor-grade delinquent act from being placed in a shelter care facility under any circumstances.

ME   *1999 Me. Public Laws, Chap. 216*
Provides a tuition waiver for those age 17 or 18 who have resided in foster care for at least one year.

1999 Me. Public Laws, Chap. 265
Permits designation of a preadoptive parent's home as a foster home for the purpose of placing a child prior to adoption.

1999 Me. Public Laws, Chap. 382
Requires the state to consider giving preference to an adult relative when making placement decisions.

1999 Me. Public Laws, Chap. 392
Recognizes the authority of Maine Indian tribes under the federal Indian Child Welfare Act. Clarifies that children in the custody of Indian tribes are eligible for all foster care programs administered by the state. Excepts Indian foster family homes from the state licensing requirement.

MD   *1999 Md. Laws, Chaps. 355, 356*
Renames the existing state Citizen Board of Review of Foster Care for Children to be the State Citizens' Review Board for Children.

1999 Md. Laws, Chap. 358
Authorizes the Social Services Administration to conduct background checks for child support arrearages on certain applicants for foster care home approval. Allows the administration to consider any child support arrearage in determining whether to approve or disapprove the applicant.

1999 Md. Laws, Chap. 541
Authorizes the state Department of Education as the lead agency for redesigning and implementing the rate setting structure for nonresidential child care programs. Specifies appeal process for new rates.

MA   *1998 Mass. Acts, Chap. 459*
Limits the liability of foster parents from claims made against them by a child in their care under certain circumstances.

MI   *1998 Mich. Pub. Acts, Act 478*
Specifies the responsibilities of the family division of the circuit court in committing a juvenile to either the Child Welfare Agency or to an appropriate county juvenile justice agency.

1998 Mich. Pub. Acts, Act 519
Requires the Family Independence Agency (FIA) to expedite licensing of child care facilities when those facilities are being developed to contract with a county juvenile agency. Requires FIA to review such application within 10 days and decide upon issuing a license within 60 days. Provides power of mandamus for applicants if FIA fails to act within said time period.

MN   *1999 Minn. Laws, Chap. 216*
Art. 6, Sec. 7   Requires human services commissioner to develop standards for foster care homes that provide therapeutic services.

Art. 6, Secs. 20-24   Requires state Supreme Court chief justice to convene a juvenile out-of-home placement task force. Sets membership and responsibilities and requires report to the Legislature.

Requires corrections and human services commissioners to find ways to collect comprehensive information on juvenile out-of-home placement spending and placements. Requires commissioners to convene a task force to adopt uniform definitions for measuring juvenile residential program completion rates and to study issues regarding culturally appropriate screening, assessment, case management and direct services. Requires Department of Human Services to identify and correct errors to ensure accuracy of its juvenile out-of-home placement database.

1999 Minn. Laws, Chap. 245
Art. 8, Sec. 2   Prohibits licensure of residential facilities that accept out-of-state children that do not have an agreement with the sending entity for the payment of medical expenses.

Art. 8, Sec. 9   Specifies provider qualifications and service requirements for residential treatment facilities for children with severe emotional disturbance. Establishes funding procedures and payment rates. Outlines the counties' and commissioners' responsibilities in the collection and report of program outcomes.

Art. 8, Sec. 19   Outlines the responsibilities of local social service agencies in the placement and review of children in foster homes.

Art. 8, Sec. 20   Clarifies that siblings should be placed together in out-of-home placements at the earliest possible time.

Art. 8, Sec. 21   Requires social services to provide information regarding permanent placement to parents who are considering voluntary placement.

Art. 8, Secs. 26-33   Expands the Relative Custody Assistance Program to include an important friend of the child and relatives who live outside of the state. Clarifies procedures for determining the amount of assistance a relative receives under the program.

Art. 8, Sec. 58   Clarifies procedures for the review of the foster care status of a child.

MO   *1999 Mo. Laws, Chap. 208*
Adds legislative findings to the "Grandparents as Foster Parents Program" statute. Lowers the age of eligible grandparents from 55 to 50. Authorizes the state to allow other relatives of a child to participate in the program if there are no grandparents willing to do so. Authorizes the provision of ancillary services. Provides that funding for cash assistance and other services shall be funded from state maintenance of effort funds. Allows non-eligible grandparents to apply for foster care reimbursement, to be funded with TANF. Specifies that such persons will be subject to time limits and work requirements.

MT   *1999 Mont. Laws, Chap. 127*
Requires the department to provide reimbursement for outpatient counseling to people who have experienced the death of a foster child in a youth care facility.

NE   *1999 Neb. Laws, LB 240*
Adds department to list of entities required to report all foster care placements to State Foster Care Review Board. Specifies information that must be included in report. Expands membership of board.

NV   *1999 Nev. Stats., Chap. 508*
Authorizes counties to establish pilot programs under which the county and the state agency jointly provide services and planning for children in protective custody and for continuity of care and case

management. Authorizes state agency to deviate from foster care rate approved by Legislature. Requires report to the Legislature.

NH   *1999 N.H. Laws, Chap. 18*
Removes the prohibition against homosexuals acting as adoptive or foster parents.

        1999 N.H. Laws, Chap. 149
Broadens the definition of children in placement in the statute requiring parents to demonstrate fitness before a child may be returned home.

NC   *1999 N.C. Sess. Laws, Chap. 190*
Sec. 3   Requires that county departments pay, at minimum, the monthly graduated foster care and adoptive assistance payments. Allows counties to pay amounts in excess of such minimums.

ND   *1999 N.D. Sess. Laws, Chap. 34*
Sec. 11   Establishes a moratorium on expansion of residential child care facility bed capacity.

OK   *1999 Okla. Sess. Laws, Chap. 2*
Sec. 4   Requires foster parents and kinship caregivers to participate in behavior management technique training within three months of certification.

        1999 Okla. Sess. Laws, Chap. 233
Redefines "foster family home" in the licensing statutes.

SC   *1999 S.C. Acts, Act 7*
Directs that reports and recommendations regarding foster care policy, procedure and deficiencies be sent to the governor.

        1999 S.C. Acts, Act 104
Requires face-to-face visits by social workers with children in foster care and monthly interviews with foster parents. Requires quarterly interviews with other adults residing in the foster home. Requires more frequent contacts when warranted. Requires foster parents to cooperate with interviews.

Provides standards for determining when disclosure of the child's placement should not be made to the child's parents or guardian.

Requires that foster parents be provided with certain information about the child at the time of placement.

Requires that the state provide the same services and benefits to a licensed relative foster care provider are provided to other licensed providers. Requires that nonlicensed relative caregivers be informed of the procedures for obtaining licensure.

Provides for the issuance of a temporary foster care license after the favorable completion of a state fingerprint review and pending completion of the FBI background check.

Requires local foster care review boards to submit written reports and recommendations to the court following periodic reviews.

Clarifies the rights of children in foster care regarding school attendance.

TN   *1999 Tenn. Pub. Acts, Chap. 493*
Requires that foster parents be provided with certain information with respect to juveniles alleged or adjudicated to have committed certain acts which, if committed by an adult, would constitute murder, rape and certain other crimes.

1999 Tenn. Pub. Acts, Chap. 508
Sec. 6, 10   Requires physical separation of delinquent and dependent children in shelter care. Requires that foster parents be provided with certain information with respect to juveniles alleged to be delinquent.

TX   *1999 Tex. Gen. Laws, Chap. 1087*
Sec. 2   Allows an emergency medical service provider to take possession of a child 30 days old or younger, if the child is voluntarily delivered to the provider. Outlines notification and filing procedures for accepting possession of an abandoned child.

1999 Tex. Gen. Laws, Chap. 1150
Sec. 10   Clarifies the importance of the child's health and safety when determining whether a child should remain in the home.

1999 Tex. Gen. Laws, Chap. 1515
Requires an attorney ad litem to interview a child's foster parents in certain circumstances.

VA   *1999 Va. Acts, Chap. 740*
Requires annual review of variances from licensing regulations. Removes foster homes, child-caring institutions and child-placing agencies from the operation of statute that allows a license applicant to engage in operations if action on the application has not been taken in 60 days. Provides that, when a provisional license expires, the applicant must meet standards or be denied a license.

WA   *1999 Wash. Laws, Chap. 17*
Adds legislative declaration that children who cannot remain with parents should be cared for by relatives. Requires that priority placement for shelter care be with a relative.

1999 Wash. Laws, Chap. 160
Allows waiver of the requirement that foster parents complete first aid/CPR and HIV/AIDS training under certain circumstances. Requires the state to pay for such training.

1999 Wash. Laws, Chap. 188
Requires parental consent for child's admission into a mental health facility and requires placement into closest facility to parents unless health or safety would be jeopardized by such placement. Mandates that state provide minor's mental health treatment records to treating physicians.

1999 Wash. Laws, Chap. 267
Requires Department of Social and Health Services to modify its programs and services to address the needs of homeless children and their families. Requires in dependency cases that judge determine whether the DSHS used reasonable efforts, including housing assistance, to avoid out-of-home placements or shorten the duration of an out-of home placement.

1999 Wash. Laws, Chap. 338
Requires the state to reimburse foster parents for property damage caused by foster children.

WV   *1999 W. Va. Acts, Chap. 45*
Clarifies the definition of legal guardianship.

1999 W. Va. Acts, Chap. 46
Prohibits courts from ordering the placement of a child in a particular facility if such facility has reached its licensed capacity.

WY   *1999 Wyo. Sess. Laws, Chap. 6*
Requires annual review of decrees in which a child is adjudged in need of supervision. Exempts children placed in a state hospital.

1999 Wyo. Sess. Laws, Chap. 72
Extends repeal date of Children in Need of Supervision Act to June 30, 2003.

Permanency Planning

AZ   *1999 Ariz. Sess. Laws, Chap. 198*
Requires that permanency plans specify how the child shall maintain contact with friends, siblings and other relatives.

AR   *1999 Ark. Acts, Act 401*
Secs. 3, 6, 8, 13   Defines "reasonable efforts." Describes circumstances under which reasonable efforts shall not be required, in accordance with ASFA. Defines "aggravated circumstances." Sets forth procedures for "no reunification services" determinations. Requires a permanency hearing within 30 days of such determinations. Lists acceptable permanency goals. Sets forth criteria for continuing to have reunification as the permanency goal.

CA   *1998 Cal. Stats., Chap. 1056*
Shortens time for permanency hearings from 18 months to 12 months, in accordance with ASFA. Requires social workers instead of probation officers to provide reunification services. Requires the safety of the child to be considered in placement decisions.

CT   *1999 Conn. Acts, Act 166*
Requires the state to establish standards for permanency plans. Directs the state to establish a program of concurrent permanency planning.

1999 Conn. Acts, Act 251
Authorizes expansion of subsidized guardianship program to include children who have been in foster care for 12 to 18 months.

FL   *1999 Fla. Laws, Act 517*
Sec. 1   Creates standby guardianship option for chronically ill or near death parents and outlines procedures for executing order of standby guardianship.

HI   *1999 Hawaii Sess. Laws, Act 153*
Expands list of aggravated circumstances under which reasonable efforts to reunify are not required. Requires the court to set a show cause hearing if the child has been in out-of-home placement for 12 consecutive months. Requires a show cause hearing within 30 days after a determination that aggravated circumstances are present. Requires the state to file a motion for a permanency plan hearing if the child has been in foster care for an aggregate of 15 of the most recent 22 months. Specifies exceptions. Shortens from three years to two years the period within which parents have a reasonable time to correct the conditions leading to placement.

IN   *1999 Ind. Acts, PL 96*
Expands the list of factors that a court must consider in determining child custody, defines de facto custodian, and excludes foster parents from the definition.

1999 Ind. Acts, PL 197
Sec. 5   Adds neglect of a dependent to the list of crimes allowing a court to determine that reasonable efforts to reunify shall not be required.

MI   *1998 Mich. Pub. Acts, Act 479*
Shortens time frames for foster care review hearings after termination of parental rights.

MN   *1999 Minn. Laws, Chap. 245*
Art. 8, Secs. 8, 24   Specifies requirements for petitions and permanency plans.

Art. 8, Sec. 22   Requires social service agencies to notify relatives of the need for permanent placement of the child as soon as possible.

Art. 8, Sec. 23   Requires a court hearing to be held within 10 days after the child is removed from a permanent placement.

Art. 8, Sec. 25   Clarifies timing of foster care reviews for children who are developmentally disabled or emotionally handicapped.

Art. 8, Sec. 41   Provides that permanent legal and physical custody of a child by a relative is a permanency option.

Art. 8, Sec. 42   Clarifies procedures when social services may forego reasonable efforts toward family reunification. Requires reasonable efforts to place a child in a permanent home when reunification efforts are not required.

Art. 8, Sec. 62   Clarifies that mandated permanency hearings do not apply to children in placement due solely to handicapping conditions.

MS   *1999 Miss. Laws, Chap. 569*
        Secs. 2, 4   Amends time frames for permanency hearings, in accordance with ASFA. Recites reasonable efforts findings required by youth court.

MT   *1999 Mont. Laws, Chap. 566*
        Secs. 9-12, 18   Provides that child safety and health shall be the paramount concerns in making reasonable efforts. Specifies conditions under which reasonable efforts need not be made, in accordance with ASFA. Requires reasonable efforts to place child in accordance with permanency plan, in accordance with ASFA. Allows concurrent permanency planning. Revises timelines for permanency hearings. Specifies permanency options, including long-term custody for children with severe emotional handicaps. Authorizes subsidized guardianships.

NV   *1999 Nev. Stats., Chap. 435*
        Secs. 8-9, 18, 27   Requires that any search for a relative with whom to place a child must be completed within one year after initial out-of-home placement. Requires reasonable efforts to preserve and reunify family. Makes health and safety of child the paramount concerns. Allows concurrent permanency planning. Requires reasonable efforts to place child in accordance with permanency plan. Specifies circumstances under which reasonable efforts are not required, in accordance with ASFA. Allows courts to consider application for guardianship and to retain jurisdiction or transfer to another court.

NY   *1999 N.Y. Laws, Chap. 7*
        Secs. 4, 6, 19, 22, 28, 30, 33, 37, 39, 43, 48, 50-51   Describes the circumstances under which reasonable efforts to prevent or eliminate need for removing child shall not be required. Defines "aggravated circumstances." Requires permanency hearing within 12 months after child enters foster care, in accordance with ASFA. Specifies permanency options. Requires court to determine reasonable efforts to finalize permanent placement, in accordance with ASFA.

ND   *1999 N.D. Sess. Laws, Chap. 282*
        Secs. 1, 5, 12-14   Defines "permanency hearing." Specifies when reasonable efforts to prevent removal or to reunify are not required, in accordance with ASFA. Specifies time frames for required permanency hearings. Specifies dispositional alternatives after termination of parental rights. Allows juvenile court to appoint a legal guardian for a child. Describes rights of legal guardians.

OH   *1998 Ohio Laws, HB 484*
        Renames "long-term foster care" as a definition of "planned permanent living arrangement." Provides that the child's health and safety are the paramount concerns in development of a case plan. Amends timeline for and purpose of permanency hearings, in accordance with ASFA. Specifies circumstances under which reasonable efforts to reunify are not required. Specifies procedures and required findings related to orders of disposition.

OK   *1999 Okla. Sess. Laws, Chap. 396*
Sec. 6 Requires postadjudication review board to include findings regarding the appropriateness of goals and objectives of permanency plan in six month review report to the court. Expands duties of the board to include reviewing cases of children placed in the state pursuant to the Interstate Compact on the Placement of Children. Outlines procedures.

PA   *1998 Pa. Laws, Act 103*
Clarifies that commencement of standby guardianship does not terminate parental rights. Clarifies duties of standby guardian. Specifies procedures for revocation of a standby guardianship.

SC   *1999 S.C. Acts, Act 104*
Sec. 20 Requires each county clerk of court to make monthly reports to court administration on child protection cases in which a permanency planning order has not been filed. Requires the director of court administration to provide yearly summaries of such reports to the chief justice.

SD   *1999 S.D. Sess. Laws, Chap. 136*
Sec. 1 Defines circumstances under which reunification of a child with a parent is not required.

         1999 S.D. Sess. Laws, Chap. 137
Requires permanency hearing within 30 days after a determination that reasonable efforts are not required, in accordance with ASFA. Adopts ASFA provisions regarding permissible permanency options. Requires that a court determine that a compelling reason exists for long-term foster care.

TX   *1999 Tex. Gen. Laws, Chap. 1150*
Sec. 21 Waives the requirement of a service plan in cases of aggravated circumstances. Adds offenses included in aggravated circumstances.

         Sec. 27 Grants courts the ability to waive service plan requirements in certain circumstances.

UT   *1999 Utah Laws, Chap. 121*
Requires court to establish a primary and a concurrent permanency goal for child. Requires permanency hearing within 30 days if reunification is no longer the primary goal, or 12 months after removal, whichever is sooner.

WV   *1999 W. Va. Acts, Chap. 133* Authorizes the creation of standby guardianships, to take effect upon the death or incompetence of a parent.

WY   *1999 Wyo. Sess. Laws, Chap. 6*
Requires annual review of decrees in which a child is adjudged in need of supervision. Exempts children placed in a state hospital.

Termination of Parental Rights

AR   *1999 Ark. Acts, Act 401*
Secs. 13-14 Describes exceptions to termination of parental rights as a permanency goal, in accordance with ASFA. Adds to grounds for termination of parental rights. Requires court to complete a termination proceeding within 90 days from date of filing petition.

         1999 Ark. Acts, Act 1306
Sec. 1 Establishes deadline and procedures for the withdrawal of consent to the termination of parental rights.

CA   *1998 Cal. Stats., Chap. 572*
Broadens juvenile court authority to terminate parental rights and expedite adoption process if child is likely to be adopted.

1998 Cal. Stats., Chap. 1056
Requires the initiation of termination of parental rights proceedings in certain cases, in accordance with ASFA.

DE   *Vol. 70 Del. Laws, Chap. 179*
Sec. 1   Provides that a felony level crime against any child is a ground for terminating parental rights.

Sec. 2   Adds a felony level offense of endangering the welfare of a child to grounds for termination of parental rights.

GA   *1999 Ga. Laws, Act 159*
Secs. 4, 7-8   Specifies the operation of a surrender of rights to a child when an adoption petition is not filed within a specified time.   Clarifies when surrender or termination of parental rights is not required as a prerequisite to the filing of an adoption petition.   Modifies grounds for termination of parental rights. Modifies the form used for surrender of rights, notice to alleged biological father and mother's affidavit.

ID   *1999 Idaho Sess. Laws, Chap. 314*
Requires the court to accept a termination of parental rights issued in a sister state, including cases where rights of biological father have been terminated based on a failure to claim paternity.   Requires that notice of termination of parental rights and adoption hearings be given to putative father under certain circumstances.

IN   *1999 Ind. Acts, PL 200*
Sec. 26   Specifies circumstances under which a putative father's consent to termination of parental rights is irrevocably implied. Eliminates the requirement to file a motion to dismiss a termination petition if the child is being cared for by a relative.   Adds relative care as an example of a compelling reason that termination is not in the best interest of the child.

LA   *1999 La. Acts, Act 544*
Requires the filing of a petition to terminate parental rights if a child has been in state custody for 17 of the last 22 months, unless a compelling reason for not filing exists.

1999 La. Acts, Act 695
Adds two requirements to a father's consent to termination of parental rights and/or adoption.

1999 La. Acts, Act 754
Provides that custody of a child after termination of parental rights may be granted to a relative who is willing to adopt without a subsidy.

1999 La. Acts, Act 1067
Allows foster parents to file for termination of parental rights when a child has been in state custody under their care for 15 months and the state has failed to file a petition.

MI   *1998 Mich. Pub. Acts, Act 383*
Limits application of statute requiring the state to file a petition to terminate parental rights.

1998 Mich. Pub. Acts, Act 479
Allows parental rights to be terminated if the parent is convicted of certain criminal offenses, including murder and sexual assault, and the court determines that termination is in the child's best interest.   Provides for automatic suspension of parenting time when a petition is filed.   Allows court to order parenting time if the court determines that parenting time will not harm the child.

1999 Mich. Pub. Acts, Act 530
Extends family court jurisdiction in abuse and neglect cases to include authority over nonparent adults in family service plans and termination of parental rights.   Defines "nonparent" adult.

MN   *1999 Minn. Laws, Chap. 245*
States exceptions to the mandated filing of a termination of parental rights petition.

Art. 8, Sec. 52   Outlines the courts' responsibilities in determining, prior to an adjudicatory hearing, whether a petition for termination of parental rights establishes a prima facie case.

Art. 8, Sec. 59   Provides that out-of-home placement for 12 of 22 months gives rise to a presumption regarding failure of reasonable efforts for purposes of terminating parental rights. Reduces period to six months for children under age 8.

Art. 8, Sec. 61   Requires the county attorney to file a termination of parental rights petition within 30 days of the social services agency's determination that the child has been subjected to egregious harm, except in certain circumstances.

MS   *1999 Miss. Laws, Chap. 569*
Sec. 1   Requires the filing of a petition to terminate parental rights with respect to any child who was in foster care before July 1, 1998, and who has been in foster care for 15 of the last 22 months. Specifies exceptions.

1999 Miss. Laws, Chap. 507
Effective July 1, 2000, allows court to determine whether an alleged father in adoption proceedings is unfit to raise a child, within grounds set forth in termination of parental rights.

MT   *1999 Mont. Laws, Chap. 257*
Secs. 2, 4, 5   Requires putative father's registration form to be received by department within 72 hours of child's birth in order for father to be notified of termination of parental rights proceedings.

Clarifies that relinquishment and consent to adopt must specify that relinquishment ends all parental rights and obligations.

Adds determination that putative father has not established or maintained relationship with child to list of grounds for termination of parental rights.

1999 Mont. Laws, Chap. 566
Secs. 14, 17   Specifies when a petition to terminate parental rights must be filed, in accordance with ASFA. Makes corresponding amendments to grounds for termination.

NV   *1999 Nev. Stats., Chap. 435*
Secs. 4, 7   Requires courts to use best efforts to ensure that termination proceedings are completed within six months after petition is filed. Provides that, if a child has been placed out of the home for 14 of any 20 months, termination of parental rights is presumed to be in the child's best interest.

NH   *1999 N.H. Laws, Chap. 133*
Outlines circumstances in which the state is required to file or join a petition for termination of parental rights. Specifies additional grounds under which termination of parental rights may be ordered.

NY   *1998 N.Y. Laws, Chap. 531*
Requires that adoption petitions be filed and heard in the same county that termination of parental rights petition is pending or termination was ordered.

1999 N.Y. Laws, Chap. 7
Secs. 10-11, 21   Describes circumstances under which a petition to terminate parental rights is required to be filed, in accordance with ASFA. Specifies exceptions, including examples of "compelling reasons." Requires that a fact-finding hearing on the petition commence no sooner than one year from the date the child first entered foster care. Allows court to direct authorized agency to file petition in any case in which reasonable efforts are not required.

ND   *1999 N.D. Sess. Laws, Chap. 282*
Sec. 9-10   Adds to grounds for termination of parental rights and specifies when a petition to terminate parental rights must be filed, in accordance with ASFA. Lists exceptions.

OH   *1999 Ohio Laws, HB 484*
Requires that an Agency file a motion for permanent custody if a child has been in placement for 12 months of a consecutive 22-month period or if a court has determined that reunification services are not required. Specifies exceptions. Makes conforming amendments to grounds for permanent custody. Amends grounds for determining that child cannot be placed with either parent within a reasonable time.

OK   *1999 Okla. Sess. Laws, Chap. 396*
Secs. 15, 16, 27-28   Requires the name of person or agency to which a person is relinquishing parental rights to be included in written statement to court relinquishing rights. Specifies that putative father must be at least age 18 to waive rights to a child. Establishes procedures for the relinquishment of rights to children to certain relatives. Outlines requirements for parent to regain custody after relinquishment.

PA   *1998 Pa. Laws, Act 126*
Adds "aggravated circumstances" and "aggravated physical neglect" to definition of dependent child and clarifies how these situations affect revocation of parental rights.

SD   *1999 S.D. Sess. Laws, Chap. 136*
Sec. 2   Adds to grounds for termination of parental rights.

TN   *1999 Tenn. Pub. Acts, Chap. 467*
Requires diligent efforts to verify the death of any parent alleged to be deceased and whose parental rights are proposed to be terminated.

TX   *1999 Tex. Gen. Laws, Chap. 1087*
Sec. 1   Permits the court to order termination of parental rights if a parent voluntarily delivers a child to an emergency medical service provider without expressing intent to return for the child.

WY   *1999 Wyo. Sess. Laws, Chap. 185*
Secs. 1-5, 6   Allows department and guardian ad litem to request the appointment of a guardian as a permanency option in petitions requesting the termination of parental rights.

FAMILY LAW

Custody and Visitation

AL   *1999 Ala. Acts, Act 436*
Allows a grandparent to intervene in an existing action or file an original action for visitation with a minor grandchild if one or both parents are deceased, the marriage of the parents is dissolved, the child has been abandoned, the child was born out of wedlock, or if either or both parents prohibit a relationship between the child and the grandparent. The act requires a court to order visitation if it is in the best interests of the child.

AR   *1999 Ark. Acts, Act 668*
Adopts the Uniform Child Custody Jurisdiction and Enforcement Act (UCCJEA) to deal with interstate child custody and visitation orders.

1999 Ark. Acts, Act 1129 Requires a person claiming visitation interference to present police with a valid court custody or visitation order, creates new misdemeanor penalty for individuals convicted of visitation interference more than twice, and provides defenses to visitation interference under certain circumstances.

CA   *1999 Cal. Stats., Chap. 229*
Broadens the circumstances under which a court may order counseling for parties involved in a custody or visitation dispute and expands the list of factors a court should consider when determining whether to issue such an order.

1998 Cal. Stats., Chap. 390
Allows juvenile courts to issue restraining orders, custody and visitation orders, and paternity orders in delinquency cases.

1998 Cal. Stats., Chap. 704
Prohibits grant of custody or unsupervised visitation to one parent convicted of first degree murder of the other parent unless court finds there is no risk to child's health, safety and welfare.

1998 Cal. Stats., Chap. 981
Establishes one-year pilot program in Los Angeles County and one other county to provide an interpreter at all child custody proceedings where at least one party lacks proficiency in English. Requires the judicial council to evaluate and report its findings to Legislature by Jan. 31, 2001.

1999 Cal. Stats., Chap. 705
Prohibits courts from granting custody or unsupervised visitation to a parent convicted of murdering the child's other parent, except under limited circumstances, and also prohibits any person from taking a child to visit or remain in the custody of the convicted parent without a custody or visitation order or the consent of the child's custodian or guardian.

1999 Cal. Stats., Chap. 721
Creates a pilot project to establish family law information centers to provide legal resources to low-income parties.

CT   *1999 Conn. Acts, PA 137*
Permits courts hearing motions for child custody order modifications to order psychiatric or psychological therapy for the child under certain circumstances before issuing judgment on the modification order.

1999 Conn. Acts, PA 185
Enacts the UCCJEA to govern interstate child custody cases.

GA *1999 Ga. Laws, Act 275*
Sec. 3   Prohibits courts from refusing to consider evidence of family violence in custody determinations simply because there has been no previous finding of family violence, and allows courts to order supervised visitation where there is evidence of family violence.

IN *1999 Ind. Acts, PL 96*
Expands the list of factors that a court must consider in determining child custody, defines de facto custodian, and excludes foster parents from the definition.

1999 Ind. Acts, PL 164
Permits a court in which a paternity or divorce action is filed to modify, under certain circumstances, a child custody order when another court has juvenile jurisdiction over the child.

1999 Ind. Acts, PL 188
Sec. 1   Requires that, if a court finds that a noncustodial parent has been convicted of a domestic battery that was witnessed or heard by the noncustodial parent's child, the court shall limit the noncustodial parent's visitation with the child to supervised visitation for a specified period.

IA *1999 Iowa Acts, Chap. 38*
Prohibits a court from issuing or enforcing a visitation order for a parent convicted of the first degree murder of the other parent of the child, unless it is in the best interests of the child, and provides factors for determining the best interests of the child.

1999 Iowa Acts, Chap. 103
Adopts the UCCJEA to deal with interstate child custody and visitation orders.

1999 Iowa Acts, Chap. 115
Requires order for sibling visitation if siblings are split between parents in custody order.

LA *1999 La. Acts, Act 447*
Prohibits attorneys representing the department to also represent any party involved in custody or visitation disputes where the department is providing support services. Permits either party to raise any issue relating to custody of child and clarifies that custody or visitation matters need not be specifically included in original documents for parties to raise or for courts to decide issue.

1999 La. Acts, Act 790
Sec. 2   Allows a child's name change by the custodial parent without the consent of the noncustodial parent if the noncustodial parent has refused or failed to visit, communicate, or attempt to communicate with the child without just cause for at least 10 years.

1999 La. Acts, Act 974
Grants courts the authority to order parties to a custody or visitation proceeding to submit to a drug test, and directs that test results must be confidential.

1999 La. Acts, Act 1352
Grants visitation rights to grandparents and siblings when the parents have been separated for at least six months, and to grandparents of incarcerated parents.

ME *1999 Me. Public Laws, Chap. 486*
Enacts the UCCJEA to govern interstate child custody cases.

MA *1998 Mass. Acts, Chap. 285*
Sets process for reporting of child's school activities, discipline and achievement to non custodial parents when that parent requests such information.

MA   *1998 Mass. Acts, Chap. 179*
Requires the court to consider evidence of domestic violence and child abuse when issuing a custody order, creates a rebuttable presumption against awarding custody to abusive parent, and outlines factors in setting visitation with abusive parent.

MI   *1998 Mich. Pub. Acts, Act 482*
Allows the court to appoint a lawyer or guardian ad litem to represent the child's best interest in custody disputes.

MO   *1999 Mo. Laws, Chap. 452*
Sec. 452.310   Changes timeline for submitting a parenting plan when filing a motion to modify custody or visitation to within 30 days of filing.

Sec. 452.400   Eliminates additional fee of $25 currently required to file an expedited motion to enforce a visitation order. Also eliminates provisions allowing the fee to be used for alternative dispute resolution programs and the requirement that a hearing be held within 14 days of the date of service if alternative dispute resolution is not available.

MT   *1999 Mont. Laws, Chap. 91*
Replaces the Uniform Child Custody Jurisdiction Act (UCCJA) with the UCCJEA to govern court decisions related to interstate custody disputes.

1999 Mont. Laws, Chap. 414
Permits courts to grant custody or visitation to any person who has established a "child-parent relationship" with a child and defines "child-parent relationship."

1999 Mont. Laws, Chap. 545
Sec. 1   Prohibits the clerk of court from collecting a fee when both parties agree not to contest an amendment of a final parenting plan.

Secs. 3, 5   Allows a summary dissolution of marriage when the parties have children if the parties have a parenting plan and the children have orders for child and medical support, and requires court to seal parenting plans at the request of either party.

NV   *1999 Nev. Stats., Chap. 113*
Extends visitation rights to grandparents and other persons with whom the child has resided and established a meaningful relationship, and expands the factors for courts to consider in determining whether to grant visitation to grandparents and other relatives.

1999 Nev. Stats., Chap. 118
Requires the court to consider the best interest of the child in making a custody determination when it appears that a minor child has been or is likely to be the victim of abduction or concealment by one of his parents or other family members. Deletes section requiring the written consent of the other parent before moving out of state with the child and replaces it with discretion of judge to consider the merits of the move for the child.

1999 Nev. Stats., Chap. 122
Prohibits a court from awarding custody or visitation rights to a person who is convicted of murdering the other parent of the child, except in certain circumstances. Creates a rebuttable presumption that custody of a child by a parent who has engaged in certain acts of domestic violence is not in the best interest of the child and establishes certain requirements for overcoming the presumption.

1999 Nev. Stats., Chap. 569
Prohibits a court from awarding custody or visitation rights to a person who is convicted of murdering the other parent of the child, except in certain circumstances. Creates a rebuttable presumption that custody of a child by a parent who has engaged in certain acts of domestic violence is not in the best interest of the child and establishes certain requirements for overcoming the presumption.

NH   *1999 N.H. Laws, Chap. 294*
Appropriates additional money to expand the child impact program to manage statewide child custody and support impact seminars.

NC   *1999 N.C. Sess. Laws, Chap. 185*
Enacts the Family Law Arbitration Act allowing, by agreement of all parties, binding arbitration of issues arising from separation and divorce, including alimony, child custody and child support. Details the processes and rules for such arbitrations.

1999 N.C. Sess. Laws, Chap. 223
Replaces the UCCJA with the UCCJEA to govern interstate child custody disputes.

ND   *1999 N.D. Sess. Laws, Chap. 146*
Establishes distinct rights of each of the parents to a child involved in a custody order, and permits a court to enforce a visitation order by using any method available for enforcing a child support order that is also appropriate to enforcing a visitation order.

1999 N.D. Sess. Laws, Chap. 147
Replaces the UCCJA with the UCCJEA to govern issues raised in interstate custody cases.

OK   *1999 Okla. Sess. Laws, Chap. 396*
Sec. 27   Requires the parent or parents who wish to reclaim custody of a child who was abandoned or surrendered to have a court order or a release from the relative with current custody.

Clarifies that relatives permitted to accept permanent child custody must be related within the third degree. Requires acknowledgment by one or both parents by a court with jurisdiction before anyone else can accept permanent custody. Allows relatives within the third degree to accept permanent custody if the child has been abandoned by a parent or parents with physical custody.

Secs. 27, 28   Establishes factors for court to consider when determining custody of a child who was abandoned or surrendered by the parent or parents when the parent returns and desires custody. Specifies custody challenge procedures after abandonment or relinquishment do not apply if the child's other parent has permanent custody. Specifies that court must consider duration of abandonment and integration of the child into the relative's home, preference of child if child is mature enough to decide, and the mental and physical health of the child.

1999 Okla. Sess. Laws, Chap. 301
Requires noncustodial parents to pay child support even if the custodial parent interferes with or does not permit visitation with the child, prohibits the custodial parent from interfering with a visitation order, and permits prosecution of individuals who violate a child support or visitation order for civil contempt. Directs courts to apply the best interests of the child standard to custody modifications and permits consideration of interference with a visitation order in that determination. Creates a presumption in favor of shared parenting.

1999 Okla. Sess. Laws, Chap. 383
Extends grandparent visitation rights to great-grandparents and creates sibling visitation rights at the court's discretion based on certain factors.

1999 Okla. Sess. Laws, Chap. 385
Creates the crime of interference with a child custody order.

1999 Okla. Sess. Laws, Chap. 422
Sec. 2   Creates a formula to calculate child support in cases of split custody.

PA   *1998 Pa. Laws, Act 126*
Adds 'aggravated circumstances' and 'aggravated physical neglect' to definitions of dependent child and clarifies how these situations effect revocation of parental rights. Defines sexual violence and rape to

including use of child's likeness for photographing, videotaping, depicting on computer, or filming. Clarifies temporary visitation and permanency hearings as they relate to cases where aggravated circumstances are alleged.

1998 Pa. Laws, Act 127
Sec. 2 Removes provision allowing court to revoke operating licenses for violation of visitation or custody orders.

Sec. 9 Exempts children under 12 years of age from submitting fingerprints for the purpose of a name change.

SD   *1999 S.D. Sess. Laws, Chap. 108*
Appropriates funding for continuation of the Visitation Enforcement Program Implementation Task Force.

TN   *1999 Tenn. Pub. Acts, Chap. 389*
Enacts the UCCJEA.

TX   *1999 Tex. Gen. Laws, Chap. 34*
Replaces the UCCJA with the UCCJEA to govern interstate child custody disputes.

1999 Tex. Gen. Laws, Chap. 556
Sec. 14 Permits a court to modify a custody order so a person with actual physical custody of a child can receive child support payments on behalf of the child if the person with legal custody has voluntarily relinquished care, control and possession of the child for at least six months.

1999 Tex. Gen. Laws, Chap. 774
Includes present or past domestic violence as a determining factor in custody decisions.

1999 Tex. Gen. Laws, Chap. 946
Requires parents participating in certain child custody suits to attend a parent education and family stabilization courses.

1999 Tex. Gen. Laws, Chap. 1034
Provides that makeup visitation awarded after a previous violation of court-ordered visitation must occur within 2 years.

1999 Tex. Gen. Laws, Chap. 1150
Sec. 28 Clarifies the department's responsibility in providing supervision for visitation in a child custody matter.

UT   *1999 Utah Laws, Chap. 6*
Permits judge to interview children privately in custody cases only with consent of both parties.

VA   *1999 Va. Acts, Chap. 574*
Specifies that the goals of mediation may include the development of a proposal addressing the child's residential schedule and care arrangements and how future disputes between the parents will be handled.

1999 Va. Acts, Chap. 634
Requires the court to consider, when issuing custody and visitation orders, each parent's ability to resolve disputes regarding matters affecting the child, and to communicate to the parties, either in writing or orally, the basis for custody or visitation decisions.

WV   *1999 W. Va. Acts, Chap. 10 - 2nd Special Session*
Sec. 48-11-103 Defines parties in custody and visitation cases as the legal parents, an adult with custodial responsibility or decisionmaking responsibility under a parenting plan, and persons who were parties to a prior order establishing custody and visitation. Also allows the court in exceptional cases to grant

permission to other persons or public agencies to intervene if it is in the child's best interest, and specifies that such persons or agencies do not have standing to initiate an action regarding custody or visitation.

Sec. 48-11-104   Requires courts to designate an organization or agency to establish education programs to educate parents about the effects of custody and divorce disputes on children and teach parents how to minimize children's trauma, and directs court to order parents to attend parent education classes if they have filed for a divorce and minor children will be affected, unless the court determines that such attendance is unnecessary.   Also permits courts to order parties to a paternity, maintenance or modification action to attend parent education classes.

Allows the court to charge persons attending parent education classes a fee, unless a party is unable to pay the fee, creates a state fund for collection of such fees, and requires the Supreme Court of Appeals to submit a report on the effectiveness of parent education classes to the legislature within two years of the start of the program.

Sec. 48-11-201   Directs courts to finalize an order when parents agree to a parenting plan, unless the agreement is not knowing or voluntary, or would be harmful to the child, and if the agreement is not accepted by the court, directs the court to allow parents the opportunity to negotiate another agreement. Also requires courts to conduct hearings if there is credible information that child abuse or domestic violence has occurred, and order appropriate protective measures if the court determines that abuse has occurred.

Sec. 48-11-202   Requires the Supreme Court of Appeals to establish rules for pre-mediation screening to determine if mediation would be inappropriate due to domestic violence, child abuse or neglect, acts or threats of duress or coercion, substance abuse, mental illness, or other reasons.

Prohibits a mediator from making a recommendation to the court or revealing confidential information, except information concerning domestic violence or child abuse.

Directs courts to require mediation if parents are unable to reach agreement on a parenting plan, unless mediation would be inappropriate, and specifies that fees for mediation should be appropriate and assessed by a uniform scale. Also prohibits state revenues from being used to pay for the costs of a mediator, except that the Supreme Court of Appeals may use a portion of its budget for administrative costs of mediation programs, and clarifies that grants and gifts specifically to fund mediation are not state revenues.

Sec. 48-11-203   Outlines procedures permitting parents to file amendments of temporary parenting plans, and outlines contents to be included in temporary parenting plans.

Sec. 48-11-204   Lists factors for court to consider in issuing temporary parenting plans, and directs the court to use expedited procedures to facilitate the prompt issuance of a temporary parenting plan.

Sec. 48-11-205   Directs a parent seeking custodial responsibility or decisionmaking responsibility to file a proposed parenting plan with the court, and allows parties to file a joint plan. Specifies information to be contained in the proposed parenting plan. Also directs the court to develop a process to identify cases where there is credible information that child abuse or neglect, or domestic or family violence has occurred, to include assistance and referral to appropriate resources.

Secs. 48-11-206, 48-11-207   Requires the court to allocate custodial responsibility and significant decisionmaking responsibility for a child according to specific objectives.

Sec. 48-11-208   Directs the court to order a method of dispute resolution when parents are unable to agree on provisions of a parenting plan that serves the children's best interest, and specifies criteria to consider in ordering dispute resolution.

Sec. 48-11-209   Directs the court, if either parent requests or upon receipt of credible information, to determine if a parent who would otherwise receive responsibility under a parenting plan has abused, neglected or abandoned a child, has sexually assaulted or abused a child, has committed domestic violence, has interfered with the other parent's access to the child, or has repeatedly made fraudulent reports of domestic violence or child abuse. In such circumstances, directs the court to impose reasonable limits to protect the child or child's parent from harm, and lists some of the limits that the court may impose.

Sec. 48-11-302   Allows the court to appoint an attorney or guardian ad litem to represent the child, and requires the court to order an investigation when substantial allegations of domestic abuse have been made. Also allows the court to require the parents to provide necessary information to the investigator, and specifies that both the guardian ad litem and an investigator are subject to cross-examination. Directs that these services will be provided at no cost to the parties.

Sec. 48-11-303   Permits the court to interview a child privately or direct another person to interview a child.

Secs. 48-11-401, 48-11-402   Requires the court to modify a parenting plan due to a substantial change in circumstances of the child or the parents, and allows a modification in exceptional circumstances if the plan is not working as anticipated and is manifestly harmful to the child. Also specifies situations that do not qualify as a substantial change in circumstance, and when a court may modify a parenting plan without showing a change in circumstances.

Sec. 48-11-403   Clarifies that the relocation of a parent constitutes a substantial change in circumstances, requires a parent planning a relocation to provide notice to the other parent, and specifies procedures and conditions for determining and a change in the parenting plan based on a parental relocation.

Sec. 48-11-501   Directs the court to enforce remedies for violation of provisions of a parenting plan, specifies remedies that may be applied, and clarifies that a parent may not claim as a defense that the other parent violated provisions of the parenting plan or a support order.

Sec. 48-11-601   Specifies each parent's right to access a child's records.

Sec. 48-11-602   Directs that parenting plans to specify a custodial parent solely for purposes of other state and federal statutes which require determination of custody.

Sec. 48-11-604   Allows parents in certain circumstances to request a modification of visitation orders, and prohibits a formerly noncustodial parent from receiving more than 50 percent of custodial responsibility in a modification.

Sec. 48A-4-9   Requires that a scheduled final hearing on a support order cannot be continued without agreement of the parties or a review of the temporary parenting plan and support order. Also directs the family law master, if a party claims inability to pay fees and costs, to determine whether either party is able to pay, and if so, to assess payment as part of a recommended order.

Sec. 48A-4-20   Specifies standards for a circuit court review of the family law master recommendation in a case.

Secs. 51-2A-1 through 51-2A-11   Creates new family law division of county circuit courts, specifies procedures for appointment and election, qualifications, responsibilities, and allocation of family law masters in the state. Also outlines procedures for removal, suspension or discipline of family law masters, and sets rules for compensation. Specifies rules of practice and procedure, matters to be heard, and contempt powers for family law masters.

Sec. 51-3-14   Removes outdated language regarding the court security fund, and directs that beginning in 2000, certain fees and costs received for the court security fund be transmitted to the family court fund.

Sec. 59-1-11, 59-1-28a   Sets fees for filing domestic relations actions.

Domestic Abuse and Miscellaneous

CO   *1999 Colo. Sess. Laws, Chap. 291*
Exempts persons who are seeking a name change from the statutory publication requirement if those persons are victims of domestic violence-related crimes, child abuse or domestic abuse. Appropriates funds for domestic violence programs from the general fund. Defines "family violence."

FL   *1999 Fla. Laws, Chap. 168*
Creates exception to child abuse reporting requirements for individuals whom the court has determined are victims of domestic violence and are living in the same house as a child abuse victim.

1999 Fla. Laws, Chap. 193
Permits a parent or legal guardian of a minor child who is living at home to seek an injunction for protection against repeat violence on behalf of that child if parent or guardian was an eyewitness or has other physical evidence of the violence.

1999 Fla. Laws, Chap. 375
Sec. 1   Requires parties to provide full names, dates of birth, and Social Security numbers of minor children in dissolution of marriage pleadings.

Sec. 8 Clarifies that a family violence indicator must be placed on record in the state case registry when the party believes that release of the information to the Federal Case Registry may result in harm to the party or the child, and requires that a protected person be notified with an opportunity for a hearing before the family violence indicator can be removed,

MN   *1999 Minn. Laws, Chap. 245*
Art. 8, Sec. 80   Requires that a member of a county multidisciplinary child protection team be designated as a lead person responsible for the planning process to develop standards for battered women's programs and services.

MS   *1999 Miss. Laws, Chap. 512*
Sec. 14   Establishes confidentiality safeguards in child support cases where there is domestic violence, and specifies that any unauthorized disclosure of information made in good faith shall not be considered a violation of confidentiality safeguards.

MT   *1999 Mont. Laws, Chap. 386*
Raises fees for certain district court filings on domestic matters, designates that money collected from court filing fees must be deposited in several state funds benefiting children and victims of domestic violence, and establishes a civil legal assistance fund for indigent victims of domestic violence.

OK   *1999 Okla. Sess. Laws, Chap. 97*
Amends procedures for protective orders to create fixed periods and notice requirements.

1999 Okla. Sess. Laws, Chap. 34
Permits the conversion of temporary protective order to a permanent one if the subject of the order does not appear at the hearing.   .

1999 Okla. Sess. Laws, Chap. 309
Creates a minimum sentence of at least 6 months for any person convicted of domestic abuse that was committed in the presence of a child; subsequent convictions for the same violation to receive at least one year in jail.

SC   *1999 S.C. Acts, Act 80*
Sec. 43-1-205 Requires an agency, organization, or entity receiving funds from the Department of Social Services for the treatment of perpetrators of domestic violence to comply with program standards contained in the department's annual Battered Spouse State Plan, these standards including treatment services

---

and supervision provided by a person with a master's degree in social work, counseling, or another related field.

TX   *1999 Tex. Gen. Laws, Chap. 949*
Authorizes a nonparent, licensed child placement agency, or another agency appointed as a child's managing conservator to have access to the child's medical records, unless limited by court order.

VA   *1999 Va. Acts, Chap. 54*
Requires a juvenile and domestic relations district court intake officer to accept and file a petition when family abuse is alleged and a protective order is sought.

       1999 Va. Acts, Chap. 665
Broadens the definition of "family abuse" to apply to situations beyond "acts of violence," as previously defined.

       1999 Va. Acts, Chap. 807
Amends section that requires the issuance of an emergency protective order when a warrant is issued for assault and battery against a family or household member to make the issuance of a protective order discretionary when the defendant is a minor.

       1999 Va. Acts, Chap. 868
Grants localities the authority to establish a team to examine fatal family violence incidents and to create a clearinghouse of information to help prevent future family violence fatalities.

WV   *1999 W. Va. Acts, Chap. 10 - 2nd Special Session*
Sec. 48-11-201   Directs courts to finalize an order when parents agree to a parenting plan, unless the agreement is not knowing or voluntary, or would be harmful to the child, and if the agreement is not accepted by the court, directs the court to allow parents the opportunity to negotiate another agreement. Also requires courts to conduct hearings if there is credible information that child abuse or domestic violence has occurred, and order appropriate protective measures if the court determines that abuse has occurred.

Sec. 48-11-202   Requires the Supreme Court of Appeals to establish rules for pre-mediation screening to determine if mediation would be inappropriate due to domestic violence, child abuse or neglect, acts or threats of duress or coercion, substance abuse, mental illness, or other reasons.

Prohibits a mediator from making a recommendation to the court or revealing confidential information, except information concerning domestic violence or child abuse.

Sec. 48-11-205   Directs a parent seeking custodial responsibility or decisionmaking responsibility to file a proposed parenting plan with the court, and allows parties to file a joint plan. Specifies information to be contained in the proposed parenting plan. Also directs the court to develop a process to identify cases where there is credible information that child abuse or neglect, or domestic or family violence has occurred, to include assistance and referral to appropriate resources.

Sec. 48-11-209   Directs the court, if either parent requests, or upon receipt of credible information, to determine if a parent who would otherwise receive responsibility under a parenting plan, has abused, neglected or abandoned a child, has sexually assaulted or abused a child, has committed domestic violence, has interfered with the other parent's access to the child, or has repeatedly made fraudulent reports of domestic violence or child abuse. In such circumstances, directs the court to impose reasonable limits to protect the child or child's parent from harm, and lists some of the limits that the court may impose.

Sec. 48-11-301   Permits the court to order an investigation and a report to assist in determining custodial responsibility arrangements, and specifies who may conduct such an investigation, and the parameters, limitations, and procedures of the investigation.

Sec. 48-11-302   Allows the court to appoint an attorney or guardian ad litem to represent the child, and requires the court to order an investigation when substantial allegations of domestic abuse have been made. Also allows the court to require the parents to provide necessary information to the investigator, and specifies that both the guardian ad litem and an investigator are subject to cross-examination. Directs that these services will be provided at no cost to the parties.

Sec. 48-2A-3   Directs that full hearings in which a protective order is sought be heard before a circuit judge or family law master.

Sec. 48-2A-6   Requires the court to a charge a fee to a person against whom a protective order is issued after a full hearing.

GENERAL HUMAN SERVICES

Administration/Reorganization

DE   *Vol. 70 Del. Laws, Chap. 149*
        Gives the Department of Corrections responsibility for treatment and evaluation for youth transferred or
        remanded to the department. Removes all authority of the department of Services for Children, Youth and
        Families.

FL   *1999 Fla. Laws, Chap. 219*
        Secs. 1-2 Waives certain provisions so that the Department of Children and Family Services (DCFS) may
        organize program, districts and functions to achieve a more effective service delivery system and to
        improve accountability. Requires that the secretary of the DCFS submit a comprehensive reorganization
        plan to the governor and the Legislature. Directs DCFS to develop, with the Office of the State Court
        Administrator, a proposed plan to realign the districts of the department so that the district boundaries are
        consistent with the boundaries of the judicial circuits.

GA   *1999 Ga. Laws, Act 316*
        Extends the Children's Trust Fund and the Children's Trust Fund Commission until 2010.

IA   *1999 Iowa Acts, Chap. 190*
        Sec. 3 Revises the membership of the Iowa Empowerment Board, created in 1998, to facilitate state and
        community efforts and requires the board to have membership representation of education, health, human
        services, business, faith and public interest.

MI   *1998 Mich. Pub. Acts, Act 517*
        Extends the authority currently held by the child welfare agency to newly created county juvenile justice
        agencies.

MO   *1999 Mo. Laws, Chaps. 210, 660*
        Expands membership on the Children's Trust Fund Board.

NV   *1999 Nev. Stats., LR 53*
        Requires an interim study and a report to the Legislature on the integration of state and local child welfare
        systems in Nevada.

UT   *1999 Utah Laws, Chap. 104*
        Expands membership and modifies other aspects of the Families, Agencies and Communities Together
        State Council.

VT   *1999 Vt. Acts, Act 62*
        Sec. 100 Requires Department of Human Services and Department of Education to file a report regarding
        the state and regional partnerships, the status of outcomes at the local level, the findings of research, and
        any recommendations for improving partnerships based on the outcome research.

Coordination/Collaboration

FL   *1999 Fla. Laws, Chap. 357*
        Establishes the Florida Partnership for School Readiness in the governor's office to coordinate program-
        matic, administrative and fiscal policies, and standards for school readiness programs.

IN   *1999 Ind. Acts, PL 121*
        Sec. 6 Adds two members to the Interagency Coordinating Council for Children with Disabilities, includ-
        ing a Head Start agency representative and a state child care agency representative.

IA   *1999 Iowa Acts, Chap. 190*
        Secs. 2, 16   States that the purpose of the Community Empowerment Initiative is to facilitate collabora-
        tion amongst individuals, governments and agencies within communities. Requires these collaborations
        to identify and implement the best means for attaining the desired results for local communities. Requires
        the Community Empowerment Board to coordinate planning and budgeting with the governing board of
        any child welfare decategorization project in the empowerment area.

MD   *1999 Md. Laws, Chap. 363*
        Creates a Joint Committee on Children, Youth and Families that identifies state policies and actions that
        work to achieve conditions of well-being for children, youth and families.

MN   *1999 Minn. Laws, Chap. 245*
        Art 8, Sec. 80   Requires that a member of a county multidisciplinary child protection team be designated
        as a lead person responsible for the planning process to develop standards for battered women's programs
        and services.

OH   *1999 Ohio Laws, HB 484*
        Requires the Department of Alcohol and Drug Addiction Services and the Department of Human Services
        to develop a joint state plan to improve accessibility and timeliness of addiction services for parents of at-
        risk children. Adds reasonable efforts to prevent or eliminate the need to remove a child from home to the
        responsibilities of a public childrens' services agency.

SC   *1999 S.C. Acts, Act 99*
        Secs. 2-3, 5-7   Establishes the state First Steps to School Readiness Office and requires it to provide
        information on successful strategies; review, support and provide technical assistance to county partner-
        ships; implement a standard fiscal accountability system; and coordinate the program with all related
        state programs. Establishes membership for county partnerships. Establishes county partnership require-
        ments and duties, including an annual report that includes an evaluation and estimate of cost savings.
        Establishes a board of trustees to evaluate the partnerships. Requires legislatively appointed and board-
        appointed committee members to oversee the evaluator's work. Requires the board to develop a compre-
        hensive, long-range improvement initiative, including recommendations for coordination and results-ori-
        ented measures and objectives. Requires specific state agencies to support the initiative.

TN   *1999 Tenn. Pub. Acts, Chap. 508*
        Directs the state to implement the recommendations of the Child Welfare League of America regarding
        staffing, training, foster care, adoption services, resolution of interagency issues related to TennCare, and
        review of the role of children's services agencies.

TX   *1999 Tex. Gen. Laws, Chap. 33*
        Requires the Interagency Council on Early Childhood Intervention to seek funding that maximizes federal,
        private and local sources.

VT   *1999 Vt. Acts, Act 62*
        Sec. 100   Supports and encourages collaboration between DHS, DoE, the University of Vermont and
        community partners to improve the well-being of all state citizens. Creates a research partnership among
        the parties and allows research to be cooperatively funded.

WA   *1999 Wash. Laws, Chap. 267*
        Sec. 2   Designates the Department of Community Trade and Economic Development (DCTED) to be the
        principal state agency responsible for the state's activities for developing a coordinated and comprehen-
        sive plan to serve homeless children and their families. Requires the Department of Social and Health
        Services to coordinate with the DCTED on the plan to serve homeless children and their families and must
        modify its programs and services to address the needs of homeless children and their families.

WV   *1999 W. Va. Acts, Act 5 - 1st Special Session*
        Requires the Department of Health and Human Services and the Division of Juvenile Services to present
        a coordinated plan of child welfare and juvenile justice services to a designated legislative task force.

Family Support

IA   *1999 Iowa Acts, Chap. 189*
Defines a children's center as a privately-funded facility that serves seven or more children at once, is not under the custody or authority of a government agency, and offers certain services, including child care and family support services. Requires the state to establish and review certification and licensing standards for the protection of children. Prohibits the state from establishing program standards for the centers.

1999 Iowa Acts, Chap. 190
Sec. 8 Authorizes the Iowa Empowerment Board to identify core functions for home visitation, parent support and preschool services provided under the school ready children grants.

LA   *1999 La. Acts, Act 799*
Requires the Louisiana Children's Trust Board to develop a pilot program for community-based family centers to assist families in providing optimum learning environments for the children, especially those from birth to age 4. Requires the board to establish and implement a pilot program for a community-based family center in at least one parish where there are high rates of teen pregnancy, people on public assistance and juvenile delinquency.

ME   *1999 Me. Public Laws, Chap. 79*
Renames the Task Force to Study Strategies to Support Parents as Children's First Teachers to the Task Force on Early Care and Education. Expands the membership to two additional legislators. Requires two reports to the Legislature.

NM   *1999 N.M. Laws, Chap. 12*
Appropriates state welfare funds for early childhood and family support and education training programs to include before- and after-school programs for children ages 5 to 8 and classes to develop job skills and leadership skills for parents.

Financing—Pooled/Blended Funding

IA   *1999 Iowa Acts, Chap. 190*
Sec. 12 Allows a public agency, community action agency or nonprofit corporation to be the fiscal agent for the grant and other funds administered by a community empowerment board. Requires a five- and 10-year plan for consolidating, blending and redistributing state-administered funding streams and describes the funding streams. Clarifies that the state Empowerment Board is to develop and annually update a five-year plan for blending of state funding directed to children from birth to age 5 through community empowerment areas and a 10-year plan for similar purposes directed to other age groups.

MT   *1999 Mont. Laws, Chap. 356*
Removes the limitation on the amount of money that may be deposited in the Endowment for Children.

Local Planning and Governance

FL   *1999 Fla. Laws, Chap. 357*
Requires the establishment of county or multicounty school readiness coalitions and requires them to make plans to address all eligible children.

IA   *1999 Iowa Acts, Chap. 190*
Sec. 3 Revises the membership of the Iowa Empowerment Board to have membership of education, health, human services, business, faith and public interest representation who are appointed by the governor.

MI   *1998 Mich. Pub. Acts, Act 516*
Defines "county juvenile agency services" to include services for youths under court control for delinquent acts and status offenses. Specifies county formula for block grant eligibility. Changes Social Welfare Act to maintain consistency with the newly enacted County Juvenile Agency Act. Defines "county

juvenile agency services" to include services for youths under court control for delinquent acts and status offenses. Specifies county formula for block grant eligibility. Changes Social Welfare Act to maintain consistency with the newly enacted statutes associated with the County Juvenile Agency Act.

1998 Mich. Pub. Acts, Act 518
Creates the County Juvenile Agency Act, permitting a county to accept full responsibility, including costs, for delinquent juveniles.

NV   *1999 Nev. Stats., Chap. 435*
Secs. 12-15   Creates rural and local advisory boards to expedite proceedings for placement of children. Specifies membership and duties.

SC   *1999 S.C. Acts, Act 99*
Establishes county partnership requirements and duties to the Office of First Steps to School Readiness, including an annual report that includes an evaluation and estimate of cost savings. Establishes a board of trustees to evaluate the partnerships.

Oversight/Results-Based Evaluation

CA   *1998 Cal. Stats., Chap. 311*
Sec. 71   Authorizes any county to enter into performance agreements with private, nonprofit agencies to encourage innovation in the delivery of children's services, to develop services not available in the community and to promote change in the child welfare system.

IA   *1999 Iowa Acts, Chap. 190*
Sec. 2   Requires that every community in Iowa will have achieved the following results—healthy children, children ready to succeed in school, safe and supportive communities, secure and nurturing families and child care environments—through the community empowerment initiative, by June 2005.

VT   *1999 Vt. Acts, Act 62*
Sec. 100   Defines the outcomes to be studied to include that pregnant women and infants thrive, children are ready and successful in school, children live in stable and supported families, youth choose healthy behaviors and successfully make the transition to adulthood, individuals contribute to community decisions and activities, safe and supportive communities and elders, and people with disabilities live with dignity and independence.

WA   *1999 Wash. Laws, Chap. 267*
Requires the Washington Institute for Public Policy to determine measurable outcomes, evaluate and report to the Legislature on the HOPE Centers, and evaluate procedures used by Department of Social and Health Services to link with the missing children's clearinghouse.

Policy

WA   *1999 Wash. Laws, Chap. 390*
Clarifies confidentiality and good faith policies for the Children's Ombudsman. Guardians ad litem, contracting agencies and service providers may release confidential information to the Children's Ombudsman.

Results-Based Planning and Budgeting

AR   *1999 Ark. Acts, Act 324*
Specifies that the Early Childhood Education Commission examine recommendations of groups producing scientifically proven and cost effective results of child care and early childhood services.

IA *1999 Iowa Acts, Chap. 190*
Sec. 2 Requires that the community empowerment initiative, by June 2005, will have achieved the following set of results: healthy children, children ready to succeed in school, safe and supportive communities, secure and nurturing families, and child care environments in every community in Iowa.

ME *1999 Me. Public Laws, Chap. 529*
Includes quality child care as part of the state's overall statewide goal to prevent child abuse and expands the definition of prevention programs to include the promotion of high-quality child care.

SC *1999 S.C. Acts, Act 99*
Requires the First Steps to School Readiness Office to implement a standard of fiscal accountability system and the board to develop results-oriented measures and objectives.

JUVENILE JUSTICE

Administration/Organization

AR   *1999 Ark. Acts, Act 469*
Increases training and education requirements for youth service workers and security officers employed by the division of youth services.

1999 Ark. Acts, Act 1580
Creates an ombudsman function within the Public Defenders Commission to provide for independent oversight of juveniles placed secure facilities. Requires an evaluation and report.

DE   *Vol. 70 Del. Laws, Chap. 149*
Gives the department of corrections responsibility for treatment and evaluation for youth transferred or remanded to the department. Removes all authority of the Department of Services for Children, Youth and Families.

ID   *1999 Idaho Sess. Laws, Chap. 155*
Increases the charge for a petition filed against a juvenile to fund training for juvenile detention officers.

IN   *1999 Ind. Acts, PL 250*
Allows the Legislative Council to determine whether to establish the Juvenile and Restorative Justice Study Commission to study issues related to juvenile laws and make recommendations for revision and improvement. Requires the commission to focus on modifying the juvenile code to effectively address the rising juvenile crime rate and to examine the delivery of juvenile services.

KS   *1999 Kan. Sess. Laws, Chap. 156*
Sec. 1   Transfers all powers and duties of the Kansas Youth Authority to the Advisory Group on Juvenile Justice and Delinquency Prevention.

Secs. 21, 28   Extends the Joint Committee on Corrections and Juvenile Justice Oversight to Dec. 31, 2003. Authorizes the Advisory Group on Juvenile Justice and Delinquency Prevention to review and make recommendations about the administration of the Juvenile Detention Facilities Fund.

MI   *1998 Mich. Pub. Acts, Act 516*
Defines "county juvenile agency services" to include services for youths under court control for delinquent acts and status offenses. Specifies county formula for block grant eligibility. Sets preference for placement in state Family Independence Agency beds rather than out-of-state beds when county juvenile agencies are over capacity. Changes Social Welfare Act to maintain consistency with the newly enacted statutes associated with the County Juvenile Agency Act. Defines 'county juvenile agency services' to include services for youths under court control for delinquent acts and status offenses. Specifies county formula for block-grant eligibility. Changes Social Welfare Act to maintain consistency with the newly enacted County Juvenile Agency Act.

1998 Mich. Pub. Acts, Act 517
Extends the authority currently held by the child welfare agency to newly created county juvenile justice agencies.

1998 Mich. Pub. Acts, Act 518
Applies solely to counties eligible for state Title IV-E (foster care) funds under a 1997 federal waiver (in present case only Wayne County and Detroit). Specifies types of services that must be provided by counties under arrangement, including training, halfway houses, detention and diagnostic centers, contracting for services and funding for capital improvements.

NC   *1999 N.C. Sess. Laws, Chap. 423*
Sec. 10   Changes the number and composition of the Governor's Crime Commission.

Sec. 15 Changes terms of appointment and frequency of meetings of the Juvenile Crime Prevention Council.

TN   *1999 Tenn. Pub. Acts, Chap. 393*
Replaces "civil service regulations of the county" from a statute section relating to juvenile court referees with language permitting appeals.

VT   *1999 Vt. Acts, Act 62*
Sec. 138 (c) Transfers the youthful offender coordinator position from the Human Services Department to the Department of Social and Rehabilitative Services and requires the youthful offender coordinator to be a classified social worker.

WV   *1999 W. Va. Acts, Act 5 - 1st Special Session*
Repeals the 1997 Child Placement Alternatives Act. Incorporates certain repealed sections into larger purpose stated in a coordinated system of child welfare and juvenile justice of this act. Requires Departments of Health and Human Services and Division of Juvenile Services to present a coordinated plan of child welfare and juvenile justice to a designated legislative task force. Requires Division of Juvenile Services to develop and annually update its comprehensive plan to establish a unified system for social and rehabilitative programming and treatment of juveniles. Sets Division of Juvenile Services responsibilities, which were previously performed by Department of Health and Human Services.

Disposition/Penalties/Offenses

AR   *1999 Ark. Acts, Act 1149*
Makes parents guilty of a Class B misdemeanor if they know that a minor illegally possesses a firearm on school property or at school events and fail to prevent possession or report possession.

       1999 Ark. Acts, Act 1331
Makes it unlawful for anyone under age 18 to possess, purchase or use cigarettes or other tobacco products. Establishes penalties for violations.

CA   *1998 Cal. Stats., Chap. 390*
Allows juvenile court to issue restraining orders, make custody and visitation orders and paternity findings in delinquency cases.

       1998 Cal. Stats., Chap. 761
Expands some victim juvenile justice offender punishment programs.

CO   *1999 Colo. Sess. Laws, Chap. 13*
Sec. 1 Allows the state to petition the court for an order authorizing the juvenile parole board to release a juvenile any time after he or she has served the minimum mandatory period of commitment or three years, whichever is sooner. Requires the juvenile court to commit a juvenile adjudicated an aggravated juvenile offender for an offense that would constitute a class 1 or 2 felony if committed by an adult to the state for a determinate period of at least three but not more than five years.

       1999 Colo. Sess. Laws, Chap. 133
Creates the mandatory penalty of revoking a juvenile's driver's license if convicted of defacing property.

       1999 Colo. Sess. Laws, Chap. 332
Secs. 4, 5 Requires adjudicated repeat offenders to be placed or committed out of the home for a minimum of one year, unless the juvenile court finds that an alternative sentence would be more appropriate. Permits the court to sentence a repeat juvenile offender to up to two years in jail or a community corrections facility if the offender is 18 years or older at time of sentencing.

FL   *1999 Fla. Laws, Chap. 267*
Authorizes law enforcement and school districts to establish prearrest diversion programs that require a juvenile who is alleged to have committed a delinquent act to surrender or refrain from applying for his or her driver's license.

FL   *1999 Fla. Laws, Chap. 284*
Sec. 40 Adds carjacking, home invasion robbery, and burglary with an assault or battery to the list of crimes under which a youth at least age 13 may be committed to a physically secure residential commitment program.

KS   *1999 Kan. Sess. Laws, Chap. 156*
Sec. 2 Requires a hearing if a disposition departs from what is specified in the sentencing matrix. Provides for victim impact statements and appellate review.

Sec. 11 Allows a juvenile to be taken directly to a sanction house for verifiable probation violation. Defines sanction house as a facility that is operated or structured to ensure that entrances and exits are under the exclusive control of the staff.

Sec. 12 Allows continued placement of an adjudicated delinquent in a child welfare placement unless the offender was adjudicated for a felony or a second or subsequent misdemeanor.

Sec. 24 Allows the intake and assessment works to make recommendations to prosecutors regarding the immediate intervention programs that may benefit the juvenile.

LA   *1999 La. Acts, Act 1356*
Prohibits a juvenile who committed a felony-grade or misdemeanor-grade delinquent act from being placed in a shelter care facility under any circumstances.

ME   *1999 Me. Public Laws, Chap. 463*
Allows the court to commit an adjudicated delinquent to the Maine Youth Center.

MD   *1999 Md. Laws, Chap. 329*
Authorizes parental restitution and the suspension or restriction of juvenile driving privileges if a juvenile has committed a destructive device offense, including bomb threats.

MI   *1998 Mich. Pub. Acts, Act 478*
Specifies court responsibilities in committing a juvenile to either the Child Welfare Agency or to an appropriate county juvenile justice agency. Permits county juvenile justice agencies to place a minor in a juvenile boot camp program.

MN   *1999 Minn. Laws, Chap 139*
Art. 2, Sec. 3, Sub 16 Includes in the definition of juvenile petty offense a juvenile alcohol offense, juvenile controlled substance offense, or a violation of a local ordinance.

Art. 2, Sec. 30, Sub 1 Requires the court to order certain dispositions necessary to rehabilitate a delinquent child.

Art. 2, Sec. 30, Sub 4 Allows the court, prior to a postadjudication placement of a juvenile in a secure treatment facility to 1) consider whether the juvenile was adjudicated for a felony offense, failed to appear in court or ran away from home; 2) assess whether the child is a danger to himself or herself or others, would abscond from a nonsecure facility, or if the child's health or welfare would be endangered if not placed in a secure facility; 3) conduct a psychological evaluation; and 4) conduct an educational and physical assessment of the juvenile.

1999 Minn. Laws, Chap. 216
Art. 6, Secs. 8, 9, 11-13 Requires courts, when ordering a delinquency disposition exceeding 30 days, to prepare a written case plan.

MT   *1999 Mont. Laws, Chap. 523*
Abolishes the death penalty for offenders younger than age 18.

1999 Mont. Laws, Chap. 537
Prohibits a juvenile who is prosecuted in a juvenile court and later transferred to a district court from being sentenced to an adult facility. Requires that the combined time of sentence under an extended jurisdiction prosecution may not exceed the time of imprisonment that an adult could receive under an adult prosecution.

NV   *1999 Nev. Stats., Chap. 15*
Allows the juvenile courts to place juvenile offenders in restitution programs that include instruction in employment skills and work ethics.

1999 Nev. Stats., Chap. 16
Allows a juvenile court to place nonviolent delinquents in a supervised program for the arts.

1999 Nev. Stats., Chap. 111
Sec. 3   Requires a juvenile court to order counseling or other psychological treatment for a youth who commits an offense involving cruelty to animals. Requires the parents or guardian to pay the costs of counseling or psychological treatment.

1999 Nev. Stats., Chap. 123
Authorizes the juvenile court to place offenders in a cognitive training and human development program.

NH   *1999 N.H. Laws, Chap. 266*
Emphasizes parental responsibility and allows the court to order substance abuse evaluations of child, parents, guardian or custodian. Prohibits more than one continuation of a dispositional hearing, for good cause or more than 14 days, where the child is placed outside the home.

NJ   *1999 N.J. Laws, Chap. 102*
Makes it an offense for an adult to employ a juvenile in the commission of a crime.

NC   *1999 N.C. Sess. Laws, Chap. 423*
Sec. 13   Requires the court to consider the best interest of the child before placing a juvenile with a relative.

OK   *1999 Okla. Sess. Laws, Chap. 99*
Makes assault and battery against employees of a juvenile facility a felony.

TX   *1999 Tex. Gen. Laws, Chap. 48*
Requires the county juvenile board to adopt guidelines for informal disposition of a juvenile offender.

1999 Tex. Gen. Laws, Chap. 76
Prohibits confinement of a juvenile for contempt of a justice or municipal court order. Allows justice and municipal courts to require juveniles over age 16 to take high school equivalency test.

1999 Tex. Gen. Laws, Chap. 174
Requires juvenile court to impose a graffiti eradication fee upon the child, parent or guardian when the child is adjudicated delinquent for violating the state graffiti statute.

1999 Tex. Gen. Laws, Chap. 1448
Authorizes commitment of juvenile offenders to the Texas Youth Commission for misdemeanor offenses under certain circumstances when the child committed the same act previously. Articulates circumstances under which felony or misdemeanor dispositions may be modified.

VA   *1999 Va. Acts, Chap. 21*
Establishes Class I misdemeanors for committing specific offenses while detained in a secure juvenile facility or detention home.

1999 Va. Acts, Chap. 350
Allows the court to require a juvenile found delinquent based on certain crimes to participate in a gang-activity prevention program.

1999 Va. Acts, Chap. 508
Allows juvenile offenders who are being supervised by the Serious or Habitual Offender Comprehensive Action Program (SHOCAP) on their 18 birthday to continue under the program until they reach age 21.

1999 Va. Acts, Chap. 622
Requires the court to order juveniles found delinquent of certain offenses to make restitution or reparation to victims and gives the court discretion to assign community service hours to offenders.

1999 Va. Acts, Chap 997
Sec. 16.1-356   Requires the court to order treatment services in three-month intervals for juveniles determined to be incompetent. Requires the juvenile's treatment provider to notify the court upon determination of competency or to provide recommendations for long-term care if competency is not restored.

WV   *1999 W. Va. Acts, Act 5 - 1st Special Session*
Authorizes Juvenile Services director to modify a juvenile's dispositional order.

WY   *1999 Wyo. Sess. Laws, Chap. 8*
Requires annual review of case of each child adjudicated delinquent. Exempts placements at boys' school, girls' school and state hospital from this requirement.

Financing

CA   *1998 Cal. Stats., Chap. 339*
Specifies that funds received from the federal Violent Offender/Truth-in-Sentencing Grant Program be allocated for local detention and correctional facilities.

1998 Cal. Stats., Chap. 502
Appropriates $50 million to supplement Juvenile Crime Enforcement and Accountability Challenge Grant Program (see 1998 Cal. Stats., Chap. 325) and for implementation of better strategies to curb juvenile crime.

FL   *1999 Fla. Laws, Chap. 327*
Creates the Welfare Trust Fund to which money allocated to the Department of Juvenile Justice will be deposited. Appropriates such funds for the benefit, education, and general welfare of youth in a state program under the department.

MI   *1998 Mich. Pub. Acts, Act 516*
Specifies county formula for block grant eligibility.

MN   *1999 Minn. Laws, Chap. 139*
Art. 2, Sec. 25, Sub 5   Allows detaining a child at a state correctional institution for juveniles if the commissioner of corrections consents and the county agrees to pay the costs of the child's detention.

1999 Minn. Laws, Chap. 216
Art. 1, Sec 13, subd. 3 and 4   Appropriates nearly $27 million for juvenile services over two years, including specific earmarks for facility repair, educational programming, and expanded aftercare and transitional services. Earmarks $1.25 million over two years for weekend juvenile camp programming. Provides $1 million over two years for Asian-American juvenile crime intervention and prevention grants.

MS   *1999 Miss. Laws, Chap. 554*
        Creates the Juvenile Detention Fund to provide grants to local governmental units to construct, renovate and maintain detention facilities.

NV   *1999 Nev. Stats., Chap. 216*
        Provides a mechanism to fund regional facilities that provide for the temporary care, custody, control and treatment of a delinquent child under the jurisdiction of a juvenile court.

VA   *1999 Va. Acts, Chap. 50*
        Sec. 2   Allows Crater Youth Care Commission to borrow funds and issue bonds to cover the local share of the cost of constructing new or expanded juvenile detention facilities.

Institutions/Programs/Services

AR   *1999 Ark. Acts, Act 1030*
        Requires juvenile offenders committed to the state to be separated by age and seriousness of the offense.

        1999 Ark. Acts, Act 1318
        Appropriates funds for the reimbursement of educational services in juvenile detention facilities.

        1999 Ark. Acts, Act 1353
        Defines offender, sex or child offender, and sexually violent predator to include an adjudicated delinquent when ordered to register by the juvenile court judge. Sets registry requirements, procedures, and notification of adjudicated delinquents. Creates the Sex Offender Assessment Committee to determine whether an adjudicated delinquent should be registered.

CA   *1998 Cal. Stats., Chap. 327*
        Established the Repeat Offender Prevention Project as a three-year demonstration project in selected counties to provide a comprehensive intervention program to reduce juvenile recidivism rates.

        1998 Cal. Stats., Chap. 375
        Permits, under certain conditions, placement of more than 125 minors in juvenile ranch or forestry camps.

        1998 Cal. Stats., Chap. 496
        Requires notification within 24 hours of parents or guardians if detained minor has suffered serious injury or become a victim of a serious offense.

        1998 Cal. Stats., Chap. 499
        Appropriates $100 million for competitive grants to counties for renovation, construction, repair and replacement of county juvenile facilities. Appropriates another $25 million for the Juvenile and Gang Violence Prevention, Detention and Public Protection Act for grants to nonprofit organizations for the acquisition, renovation and construction of defined youth centers.

CO   *1999 Colo. Sess. Laws, Chap. 17*
        Extends the Youthful Offender System for five years and requires an evaluation that includes tracking offenders for five years after release.

        1999 Colo. Sess. Laws, Chap. 24
        Allows the juvenile parole board to require, as a condition of parole, a juvenile committed to the Department of Human Services to work toward attainment of a high school diploma or general equivalency degree (GED). Permits the court to require a defendant under age 18 at the time of sentencing to work to attain a high school diploma or GED.

        1999 Colo. Sess. Laws, Chap. 28
        Sec. 1   Authorizes the Department of Public Safety to use funds or grants to provide restorative justice programs.

1999 Colo. Sess. Laws, Chap. 39
Reduces the minimum percentage of capital construction appropriations for juvenile facilities that must be used for art.

CT   *1999 Conn. Acts, Act 26*
Authorizes $27.5 million for the development and construction of a new 240-bed juvenile training school and to take the place of the existing Long Lane juvenile facility.

FL   *1999 Fla. Laws, Chap. 267*
Permits law enforcement agencies or school districts to create a juvenile diversion program for at-risk youth. Allows a youth's driver's license to be suspended for failure to successfully complete this program.

1999 Fla. Laws, Chap. 284
Sec. 17   Requires that aftercare services may be delivered to a youth after release from a residential commitment program through either minimum-risk nonresidential commitment restrictiveness programs or postcommitment community control.

Sec. 32   Requires the Juvenile Justice Accountability Board to conduct a study regarding the types of effective juvenile vocational and work programs across the country; and the status of such programs in juvenile facilities across the state.

Sec. 41   Requires the school year for schools that provide educational services in the Department of Juvenile Justice to include 250 days of instruction over 12 months.

Sec. 48   Requires the Education Department to serve as the lead agency for juvenile justice education programs to ensure that curriculum, support services and resources are provided. Requires the state to designate a coordinator for juvenile justice education programs.

1999 Fla. Laws, Chap. 327
Makes the Department of Corrections responsible for all aspects of custody-including treatment and evaluation-of youth offenders who are sentenced as adults or transferred to the department.

1999 Fla. Laws, Chap. 328
Requires the Department of Juvenile Justice to administer and maintain the Care and Maintenance Trust Fund for juvenile offenders.

ID   *1999 Idaho Sess. Laws, Chap. 390*
Allows a juvenile prosecuted in adult court to be sentenced under the juvenile sentencing options if adult sentencing measures are inappropriate.

KS   *1999 Kan. Sess. Laws, Chap. 156*
Sec. 11   Allows a juvenile to be taken directly to a sanction house for verifiable probation violation. Defines sanction house as a facility that is operated or structured to ensure that entrances and exits are under the exclusive control of the staff.

Sec. 13   Permits court services or juvenile community corrections officer to arrest a juvenile without a warrant and place him or her in a juvenile detention center.

Sec. 15   Permits a court to place a juvenile offender in a detention facility if the juvenile has been arrested by any court service or juvenile correction officer.

Sec. 18   Requires the state to consider recommendations of the juvenile corrections office prior to release from a juvenile correctional facility.

Sec. 24   Permits the commissioner to adopt rules and regulations that allow local juvenile intake and assessment programs to create a risk assessment tool.

1999 Kan. Sess. Laws, Chap. 164
Sec. 8   Expands the crime of unlawful sexual relations to include offenses against juveniles, age 16 or older, who are confined to custody in a juvenile facility.

LA   *1999 La. Acts, Act 810*
Establishes a school district to provide education for youths who are placed in the custody of the Department of Public Safety and Corrections and assigned for confinement in a privately operated correctional center for youth. Requires the state to annually appropriate sufficient money to fund such schools.

ME   *1999 Me. Public Laws, Chap. 260*
Changes the requirement that a hearing must be held within 48 hours after a juvenile is placed in a secure detention to 24 hours. Requires prosecutors to make detention placement within 12 hours of arrest. Permits juvenile caseworkers to review conditions imposed upon a juvenile and eliminate or lessen the conditions if an accompanying law enforcement report is not filed within 15 days of confinement. Allows caseworkers to suspend ongoing supervision of a minor. Eliminates age restriction on minors held at Northern Maine Regional Juvenile Detention Facility so that younger youths may be detained when no alternatives exist. Establishes the State Bureau of Identification as the repository for juvenile crime information.

MD   *1999 Md. Laws, Chap. 432*
Requires the state to conduct a study and develop standards for certain juvenile detention facilities. Requires a report to the governor and the legislature.

1999 Md. Laws, Chap. 446
Requires a juvenile intake officer to discuss with a child and the child's parent information regarding a voluntary referral for a mental health and substance abuse assessment.

MI   *1998 Mich. Pub. Acts, Act 516*
Defines 'county juvenile agency services' to include services for youths under court control for delinquent acts and status offenses. Specifies county formula for block-grant eligibility. Sets preference for placement in state rather than out-of-state beds when county juvenile agencies are over capacity. Defines "county juvenile agency services" to include services for youths under court control for delinquent acts and status offenses. Specifies county formula for block-grant eligibility. Sets preference for placement in state Family Independence Agency beds rather than out-of-state beds when county juvenile agencies are over capacity. Changes Social Welfare Act to maintain consistency with the newly enacted statutes associated with the County Juvenile Agency Act.

1998 Mich. Pub. Acts, Act 517
Raises misdemeanor penalties and fines for inducing or assisting juveniles in custody to leave residential placement.

1998 Mich. Pub. Acts, Act 518
Creates the County Juvenile Agency Act permitting a county to accept full responsibility, including costs, for delinquent juveniles. Applies solely to counties eligible for state Title IV-E (foster care) funds under a 1997 federal waiver (in present case only Wayne County, and Detroit). Specifies types of services which must be provided by counties under arrangement including training, halfway houses, detention and diagnostic centers, contracting for services and funding for capital improvements. Creates the County Juvenile Agency Act, permitting a county to accept full responsibility, including costs, for delinquent juveniles.

MN   *1999 Minn. Laws, Chap. 139*
Art. 2, Sec. 7   Allows county boards to purchase, lease, erect, equip, and maintain a detention home for boys and girls, or separate detention homes.

Art. 2, Sec. 18   Allows the local social services agency to establish a multidisciplinary juvenile treatment screening team to conduct screenings and prepare case plans.

Art. 2, Sec. 18, Sub 2 Prohibits holding a child taken into custody and placed in a shelter care facility or relative's home for longer than 72 hours unless a petition has been filed that the judge or referee determines that the child must remain in custody.

1999 Minn. Laws, Chap. 216
Art. 4, Secs. 12, 14 Requires Department of Correction's Excellence Task Force to seek a private vendor to operate educational program at Red Wing juvenile facility. Authorizes RFPs from private vendors to provide female juvenile programming.

Art. 6, Secs. 20-24 Requires state Supreme Court chief justice to convene a juvenile out-of-home placement task force. Sets membership and responsibilities and requires report to the Legislature. Requires corrections and human services commissioners to find ways to collect comprehensive information on juvenile out-of-home placement spending and placements. Requires aforementioned commissioners to convene a task force to adopt uniform definitions for measuring juvenile residential program completion rates and to study issues regarding culturally appropriate screening, assessment, case management and direct services. Requires Department of Human Services to identify and correct errors to ensure accuracy of its juvenile out-of-home placement database.

Art. 6, Secs. 8, 9, 11-13 Requires all counties to establish juvenile treatment screening team and develop a written classification system for juvenile offenders. Requires courts, when ordering a delinquency disposition exceeding 30 days, to prepare a written case plan. Requires counties to monitor transitional service plans when a child is placed in residential treatment for more than 30 days. Requires the state to report to the Legislature on outcomes related to court-ordered out-of-home placements.

MT   *1999 Mont. Laws, Chap. 469*
Permits detention facilities to supply their own in-house training of juvenile detention officers through June 2001.

NE   *1999 Neb. Laws, LB 878*
Appropriates funds to develop a facilities master plan for youth rehabilitation and treatment centers.

NV   *1999 Nev. Stats., Chap 442*
Requires that a juvenile who is taken into custody for domestic violence be detained for at least 12 hours.

NH   *1999 N.H. Laws, Chap. 219*
Permits Department of Youth Development Services to file a motion to extend jurisdiction for any minor in its custody. Lowers to 17 the age for the department's control over a minor's parole. Permits juvenile parole boards access to all Health and Human Services and Youth Development Services records concerning juveniles.

OK   *1999 Okla. Sess. Laws, Chap. 365*
Sec. 2   Defines a municipal juvenile facility as a temporary detention facility other than a community intervention center that accepts a child under age 18 charged with violating a municipal ordinance, that is entirely separate from any jail, adult lockup or other adult facility.

Sec. 3   Requires the community intervention center to serve as a short-term reception facility to receive and hold juveniles who have been taken into custody by law enforcement agencies for the alleged violation of a municipal ordinance or state law and for whom detention is inappropriate or unavailable. Prohibits isolating juveniles other than for short-term protective holding for combative or self-destructive behavior. Prohibits holding juveniles in a community intervention center for more than 24 hours.

Sec. 5   Prohibits no more than one-third of the juveniles in the regimented training program to be from other states. Prohibits placement of sex offenders in the program.

1999 Okla. Sess. Laws, Chap. 99
Makes assault and battery against employees of a juvenile facility a felony.

1999 Okla. Sess. Laws, Chap. 177
Modifies eligibility and costs under victim compensation fund.

OR *1999 Or. Laws, S 341*
Requires the state to conduct intake assessments when youth offenders are initially placed in a youth correction facility. The assessment must include a psychological evaluation, if one has not been done in the six months prior to commitment, and an education evaluation.

1999 Or. Laws, S 75
Requires a citizen review board to review cases of youth offenders in state custody placed in substitute care. Requires the board to focus on public safety, youth offender accountability, and reformation in conducting reviews.

TN *1999 Tenn. Pub. Acts, Chap. 508*
Sec. 6-8 Requires physical separation of delinquent and dependent children in shelter care. Requires the provision of necessary services to children in shelter care.

TX *1999 Tex. Gen. Laws, Chap. 162*
Sec. 1 Authorizes the Texas Youth Commission to establish infant care and parenting programs for minor parents. Describes conditions under which minor parents in residential care may retain custody of an infant.

1999 Tex. Gen. Laws, Chap. 232
Requires detention of a juvenile upon allegation of any offense involving a firearm. Provides for juvenile detention in county jail and requires a detention hearing within 24 hours.

1999 Tex. Gen. Laws, Chap. 1477
Sec. 26 Authorizes examination of juvenile justice programs and facilities upon reports of abuse or neglect. Regulates provision of educational services by a school district to juveniles in detention within its parameters.

VA *1999 Va. Acts, Chap. 997*
Sec. 16.1-356 Requires the commissioner of mental health, mental retardation and substance abuse services to determine the appropriate hospital for a juvenile evaluation, to approve the training and qualifications of individuals authorized to conduct juvenile competency evaluations and provide treatment services. Limits juvenile hospitalization for a competency evaluation to a maximum of 10 days from the date of admission. Requires juvenile competency evaluations to be performed on an outpatient basis at a specified location unless the juvenile is currently in a psychiatric hospital or if the court determines the juvenile should be hospitalized during the evaluation.

WV *1999 W. Va. Acts, Act 5 - 1st Special Session*
Repeals the 1997 Child Placement Alternatives Act. Incorporates certain repealed sections into larger purpose stated in a coordinated system of child welfare and juvenile justice of this act. Requires Departments of Health and Human Services and Division of Juvenile Services to present a coordinated plan of child welfare and juvenile justice to a designated legislative task force. Requires Division of Juvenile Services to develop and annually update its comprehensive plan to establish a unified system for social and rehabilitative programming and treatment of juveniles. Requires several cabinet-level members and other officials to develop and agree to criteria for construction, renovation, acquisition or repair of juvenile facilities. Authorizes Juvenile Services director to modify a juvenile's dispositional order. Clarifies purpose for state plan for predispositional juvenile detention centers. Sets Division of Juvenile Services responsibilities which were previously performed by Department of Health and Human Services. Sets priority for hiring at juvenile detention and correction facilities. Prioritizes medical treatment choices for juveniles under state care. Adds division of juvenile services to agencies required to keep juvenile records confidential except in specified circumstances.

Juvenile Court/Legal Procedures

AR *1999 Ark. Acts, Act 1340*
Sec. 31 (a) (1)   Permits a judge during juvenile proceedings to take a child into protective custody.

CA *1998 Cal. Stats., Chap. 761*
Requires juvenile probation officer to inform victims of certain rights.

CO *1999 Colo. Sess. Laws, Chap. 233*
Applies federal reasonable efforts requirement to juvenile delinquents in community placement.

1999 Colo. Sess. Laws, Chap. 258
Makes statements made by a juvenile during a custodial interrogation inadmissible into evidence when made in the absence of a parent or guardian.

1999 Colo. Sess. Laws, Chap. 332
Sec. 6   Allows a parent or guardian who is responsible for a juvenile released on bond to request that the court revoke it if he or she cannot control the juvenile.

Sec. 7 Permits the court to order a change of venue if necessary to ensure the juvenile receives a fair trial.

Sec. 8 Clarifies that a juvenile may be released on bond if he or she appears on a summons.

Sec. 9   Clarifies that service of a summons on a juvenile's parent or guardian is sufficient to compel attendance of the juvenile and parent or guardian in court.

Sec. 10   Specifies that a statement made by a juvenile in the course of interrogation, in the absence of a parent or guardian, may be admissible if the juvenile misrepresented his or her age as age 18 or older.

Sec. 11   Corrects certain statutory references regarding juvenile appointments and authority of magistrates.

IN *1999 Ind. Acts, PL 188*
Reduces legal requirements for detaining a juvenile when the juvenile will be on probation and/or detained in the home of a parent or guardian. Removes the time limitation for a delinquency hearing when the juvenile is on probation or detained in the home of a parent or guardian.

KS *1999 Kan. Sess. Laws, Chap. 51*
Establishes a change of venue for purposes of sentencing an adjudicated delinquent.

1999 Kan. Sess. Laws, Chap. 156
Secs. 2, 13   Requires a hearing if a disposition departs from what is specified in the sentencing matrix. Provides for victim impact statements and appellate review. Permits court services or juvenile community corrections officer to arrest a juvenile without a warrant.

ME *1999 Me. Public Laws, Chap. 260*
Changes the requirement that a hearing must be held within 48 hours after a juvenile is placed in a secure detention to 24 hours. Requires prosecutors to make detention placement within 12 hours of arrest. Permits juvenile caseworkers to review conditions imposed upon a juvenile and eliminate or lessen the conditions if an accompanying law enforcement report is not filed within 15 days of confinement. Allows caseworkers to suspend ongoing supervision of a minor.

1999 Me. Public Laws, Chap. 266
Permits law enforcement officers to summon a minor to court.

MD   *1999 Md. Laws, Chap. 619*
Allows victims of juvenile violence to submit an impact statement to juvenile or adult court to determine whether a case should be transferred.

MI   *1998 Mich. Pub. Acts, Act 478*
Specifies the family division of the circuit court responsibilities in committing a juvenile to either the Child Welfare Agency or to an appropriate county juvenile justice agency. Allows family court to enter into agreements with any other courts to waive jurisdiction over juvenile civil cases.

      1998 Mich. Pub. Acts, Act 520
Changes Code of Criminal Procedure to maintain consistency with the newly enacted statutes associated with the County Juvenile Agency Act.

MN   *1999 Minn. Laws, Chap. 139*
Art 2, Sec. 9, Sub 1   Requires a court (other than a juvenile court) to transfer to the juvenile court a minor who appears before it for violating a state or local law or ordinance and who was under age 18 at the time of the alleged offense.

Art. 2, Sec. 17, Sub 3   Authorizes a peace officer who takes a child into custody to perform a protective pat-down search of the child in order to protect the officer's safety.

Art. 2, Sec. 18, Sub 2   Prohibits holding a child taken into custody and placed in a shelter care facility or relative's home for longer than 72 hours unless a petition has been filed that the judge or referee determines that the child must remain in custody.

Art. 2, Sec. 25, Sub 1   Requires a court to hold a detention hearing within a certain amount of time, depending on where the child is held, and that a child who has been detained in an adult jail or municipal lockup and for whom continued detention is ordered to be transferred to a secure juvenile detention or shelter care facility, unless a motion is pending to refer a child for adult prosecution.

Art. 2, Sec. 29, Sub 4   Allows the court to dismiss a petition or terminate its jurisdiction. Specifies the court jurisdiction must continue until the individual becomes age 19 if it is in the best interest of the individual. Gives the juvenile court jurisdiction over a person who was adjudicated delinquent until age 21 if the person fails to appear at any juvenile court hearing or placement under a juvenile court order. Also involves such court jurisdiction over a convicted extended jurisdiction juvenile who fails to appear at any juvenile court hearing or fails to appear at or absconds from any placement.

MO   *1999 Mo. Laws, Chap. 211*
Requires a juvenile court judge to refer an individual who is age 17 or older to the prosecutor for endangering the welfare of a child.

NE   *1999 Neb. Laws, LB 522*
Expands the number of people who may issue detainers for the apprehension and detention of juveniles.

NV   *1999 Nev. Stats., Chap. 112*
Requires parental notification when a juvenile is taken into custody or is detained. Changes notification language from" immediate" to "without undue delay."

NH   *1999 N.H. Laws, Chap. 266*
Sec. Chap 266   Prohibits more than one continuation of a dispositional hearing, for good cause or more than 14 days, where the child is placed outside the home.

NC   *1999 N.C. Sess. Laws, Chap. 423*
Secs. 1, 13   Removes a specific prohibition against appearing before the court of appeals to appeal a court order transferring jurisdiction in a juvenile case. Requires a determination that a juvenile is within the jurisdiction of the juvenile court before a predisposition report or risk and needs assessment is made.

PA   *1998 Pa. Laws, Act 3*
Allows an extradited juvenile to request a new trial upon return to the United States, provided a conviction was obtained in the child's absence.

TN   *1999 Tenn. Pub. Acts, Chap. 508*
Specifies guidelines for compensation of guardians ad litem for juveniles accused of being delinquent.

TX   *1999 Tex. Gen. Laws, Chap. 76*
Expands the jurisdiction of justice and municipal courts to include parents or guardians of juvenile offenders, and allows such courts to require juveniles over age 16 to take the high school equivalency examination. Prohibits confinement of a juvenile for contempt of a justice or municipal court order.

1999 Tex. Gen. Laws, Chap. 232
Requires detention of a juvenile upon allegation of any offense involving a firearm. Provides for juvenile detention in county jail and requires a detention hearing within 24 hours.

1999 Tex. Gen. Laws, Chap. 982
Declares statements of a child admissible if made while in custody or during or after interrogation. Does not preclude admissibility of voluntary statements made under different circumstances.

1999 Tex. Gen. Laws, Chap. 1446
Requires a child placed on probation for an offense involving a handgun to inform the probation officer of the manner in which the child acquired the gun and requires the probation officer to relay such information to local law enforcement agency. Declares information regarding acquisition of handguns inadmissible as evidence against the child in any juvenile or criminal proceeding.

1999 Tex. Gen. Laws, Chap. 1477
Sec. 1   Allows an authorized referee to perform the duties of a magistrate in juvenile cases without the approval of the juvenile court.

Sec. 6   Authorizes the prosecuting attorney to refer juvenile offenses to a grand jury.

Sec. 14   Authorizes the examination of juveniles for mental illness or disability and authorizes the juvenile court to determine unfitness to proceed or lack of responsibility. Outlines procedures for juvenile court to initiate commitment proceedings and requires any mental examination records to be transferred to the appropriate court.

VA   *1999 Va. Acts, Chap 58*
Requires time limitations for certain juvenile hearings to be applied in cases where the child is missing, has escaped from custody or fails to appear in court.

1999 Va. Acts, Chap. 952
Sec. 4   Requires that only one parent, rather than both, be notified when a civil or criminal petition is filed concerning a juvenile.

1999 Va. Acts, Chap. 997
Sec. 16.1-356   Establishes court and mental health procedures for determining whether a juvenile is competent to stand trial and requires restoration services.

WV   *1999 W. Va. Acts, Chap. 64*
Limits age and disposition of certain youthful offenders whose sentences can be suspended.

WY   *1999 Wyo. Sess. Laws, Chap. 185*
Allows judge to issue contempt warrant for parental failure to ensure minor's appearance for certain proceedings.

Prevention/Intervention

AR   *1999 Ark. Acts, Act 628*
Establishes a state program to provide mediation services and training assistance to youth.

CA   *1998 Cal. Stats., Chap. 325*
Reduces to $25 million funds available for Juvenile Crime Enforcement and Accountability Challenge Grant Program and revises criteria and evaluation for awarding counties such grants. Requires Board of Corrections to evaluate this program and report findings by March 1, 2003.

        1998 Cal. Stats., Chap. 327
Established the Repeat Offender Prevention Project as a three-year demonstration in selected counties to provide a comprehensive intervention program to reduce juvenile recidivism rates.

        1998 Cal. Stats., Chap. 502
Appropriates $50 million to supplement Juvenile Crime Enforcement and Accountability Challenge Grant Program (see 1998 Cal. Stats., Chap. 325) and for implementation of better strategies to curb juvenile crime.

FL   *1999 Fla. Laws, Chap. 267*
Permits law enforcement agencies or school districts to create a prearrest diversion programs. Allows a youth's driver's license to be suspended for failure to successfully complete this program.

ID   *1999 Idaho Sess. Laws, Chap. 77*
Provides that a portion of the youth license plate fee is used to provide prevention and early intervention programs for at-risk youth.

IL   *1999 Ill. Laws, PA 10*
Creates Safe to Learn Program for support and funding of school-based safety and violence prevention programs. Funds demonstration, technical assistance and evaluation of three pilot prekindergarten through 12th grade school-based violence prevention programs.

IN   *1999 Ind. Acts, PL 101*
Authorizes Project IMPACT USA Inc. to develop programs for provision of delinquency prevention services in five sites throughout the state. Specifies objectives of programs.

KS   *1999 Kan. Sess. Laws, Chaps. 132,160*
Appropriates funds for the new Experimental Wraparound Kansas Project administered by the State Board of Education. Requires the state board to make awards to applicant school districts in collaboration with community mental health centers to implement mental health support services in the school setting that focus on violence prevention.

MA   *1999 Mass. Acts, Chap. 422*
Requires elementary and high schools to implement violence prevention programs.

MN   *1999 Minn. Laws, Chap. 216*
Art. 1, Sec. 13, subd. 3 and 4   Provides $1 million over two years for Asian-American juvenile crime intervention and prevention grants.

NC   *1999 N.C. Sess. Laws, Chap. 423*
Sec. 15   Changes terms of appointment and frequency of meetings of the Juvenile Crime Prevention Council.

TX   *1999 Tex. Gen. Laws, Chap. 489*
Secs. 1, 2   Requires the Department of Protective and Regulatory Services to implement and manage programs that provide prevention and intervention services for at-risk youth. Establishes the Division of

Prevention and Early Intervention Services under the Department of Protective and Regulatory Services to manage the delivery of services to at-risk youth.

VA   *1999 Va. Acts, Chap. 350*
Allows the court to require a juvenile found delinquent based on certain crimes to participate in a gang-activity prevention program.

Records

AK   *1999 Alaska Sess. Laws, Chap. 36*
Requires school districts to provide certain criminal record information to new district when student transfers.

AR   *1999 Ark. Acts, Act 954*
Permits the exchange of confidential information regarding the arrest or detention of a juvenile for the purposes of obtaining services for the juvenile or to ensure public safety. Provides a list of people who may obtain confidential information.

        1999 Ark. Acts, Act 1451
Permits the Arkansas Crime Information Center access to records of delinquency adjudications where violence or a weapon was involved.

CA   *1998 Cal. Stats., Chap. 374*
Permits use of certain juvenile records for three-strikes law and enhanced sentencing.

CT   *1999 Conn. Acts, Act 247*
Requires the state to notify school superintendents when a serious juvenile offender may return to school and the department believes, in good faith, that the offender is a risk to self or others.

FL   *1999 Fla. Laws, Chap. 284*
Secs. 2, 6   Requires fingerprinting a minor who has committed unlawful possession or discharge of a weapon or firearm at a school-sponsored event or on school property. Requires the Criminal Justice Information Program to retain the criminal history record of a minor who is committed to a juvenile correctional facility or juvenile prison for five years after the offender reaches age 21.

ID   *1999 Idaho Sess. Laws, Chap. 248*
Creates a list of offenses that may not be expunged from a juvenile's record.

IA   *1999 Iowa Acts, Chap. 37*
Requires fingerprinting of juveniles who have been arrested or taken into custody and charged with an offense greater than a simple misdemeanor. Allows a juvenile court officer to submit juvenile dispositions to the state for the purpose of generating criminal statistics.

        1999 Iowa Acts, Chap. 112
Sec. 13   Adds that police departments may disclose information to juvenile justice agencies for law enforcement or prosecution purposes. Specifies that the Department of Public Safety or a juvenile court may disclose information to government agencies for confidential background investigations.

Sec. 19   Permits a juvenile court officer to conduct risk assessment for juvenile sex offenders and to disclose the information to government agencies that are conducting confidential background investigations. Requires the Department of Public Safety to disclose the assessment of risk that offenders required to register pose of reoffending with the juvenile courts. Requires the juvenile court to share information with other departments to develop procedures for the assessment of risk for the juveniles who qualify for the sex offender registry.

LA   *1999 La. Acts, Act 515*
Mandates court to notify school within 24 hours after a minor registered in that school has been adjudicated delinquent for a felony offense. Permits principals to use such orders in disciplinary actions.

1999 La. Acts, Act 976
Opens records for minors age 14 and older who have been adjudicated delinquent with an intent to distribute violation of the Uniform Controlled Dangerous Substances Act.

ME   *1999 Me. Public Laws, Chap. 96*
Protects access to juvenile information gathered by a municipality in administration of recreational or nonmandatory educational programs, if that municipality has enacted an ordinance preventing such disclosure.

ME   *1999 Me. Public Laws, Chap. 198*
Allows superintendent, instead of school board, to notify local law enforcement agency that minor has been declared habitually truant.

1999 Me. Public Laws, Chap. 260
Establishes the State Bureau of Identification as the repository for juvenile crime information.

1999 Me. Public Laws, Chap. 345
Sets information that district attorney must convey to school superintendent when a minor is charged with certain acts. Establishes that the superintendent must convene a school notification team within 10 days of receipt of such information.

MI   *1999 Mich. Pub. Acts, Act 86*
Revises juvenile code to maintain consistency with the Sex Offenders Registration Act, including conditions under which fingerprints of the juvenile should be recorded.

MN   *1999 Minn. Laws, Chap. 139*
Art. 2, Sec. 16   Requires that a person who receives access to juvenile court or peace officer records of children that are not accessible to the public may not release or disclose the records except as authorized by law.

Art. 2, Sec. 19   Requires the court to open the hearings to the public in delinquency or extended jurisdiction juvenile proceedings where the child committed or allegedly committed an offense that would be a felony if committed by an adult and was at least age 16 at the time of the offense. The court may exclude the public from portions of the hearing to discuss psychological material or other evidence that would not be accessible to the public in an adult proceeding.

Art. 2, Sec. 21(a)   Requires the court to keep and maintain records pertaining to delinquent adjudications until the person reaches age 28 and release the records on an individual to another juvenile court that has jurisdiction of the juvenile, to a requesting adult court for sentencing, or to an adult or juvenile court.

Art. 2, Sec. 21 Sub 4   Makes records of the juvenile court and appeals from a nonpublic juvenile court proceeding open to public inspection. Allows the victim of an alleged delinquent, upon the victim's request, to obtain certain information about the juvenile. Provides exceptions.

Art. 2, Sec. 21 Sub 5   Requires a law enforcement agency to notify the principal or chief administrative officer of a juvenile's school of an incident within the agency's jurisdiction if 1) the agency believes that juvenile committed an offense that would be a crime if committed as an adult that the victim is a student or school staff member and that notice to the school is necessary to protect the victim, or 2) the agency believes that the juvenile committed an offense that would be a crime if committed by an adult, regardless of whether the victim is a student or school staff member.

MT   *1999 Mont. Laws, Chap. 106*
Lists exceptions when youth court records may be inspected. Requires the state to separate the offense and disposition information from the name of the youth in the management information system for purposes of research and evaluation.

        1999 Mont. Laws, Chap. 564
Requires the court to notify school districts of a youth's suspected criminal activity or drug use under certain circumstances. Permits the school district to disclose educational records that pertain to violations of juvenile or criminal laws.

NH   *1999 N.H. Laws, Chap. 219*
Permits juvenile parole boards access to all health and human services and youth development services records concerning juveniles. Also, permits commissioner of youth development services to access to all health and human services records concerning juveniles.

OK   *1999 Okla. Sess. Laws, Chap. 415*
Requires the Office of Juvenile Affairs to provide the Oklahoma State Bureau of Investigation direct access to records in order to check applicants of concealed handgun licenses. Requires the bureau to deny any applicant who was adjudicated a delinquent for an offense that would constitute a felony if committed by an adult.

        1999 Okla. Sess. Laws, Chap. 365
Sec. 3   Allows fingerprinting at community intervention center of a juvenile who allegedly committed an offense that would be a felony if committed by an adult.

PA   *1998 Pa. Laws, Act 3*
Assigns responsibility for fingerprinting and photographing of adjudicated delinquents to the charging law enforcement agency or probation department.

TX   *1999 Tex. Gen. Laws, Chap. 1368*
Requires creation of a DNA record for juveniles convicted of, or adjudicated for, committing certain violent offenses.

        1999 Tex. Gen. Laws, Chap. 217
Authorizes interagency sharing of juvenile records upon agreement between the district school superintendent and juvenile probation officer.

        1999 Tex. Gen. Laws, Chap. 1477
Secs. 18, 19   Authorizes the juvenile court to inform the public regarding juvenile offenders at-large.

        1999 Tex. Gen. Laws, Chap. 407
Authorizes release of information to the public regarding juvenile offenders who flee after committing a felony.

VA   *1999 Va. Acts, Chap. 350*
Requires juvenile transfer reports and social history reports to include a gang affiliation assessment.

        1999 Va. Acts, Chap. 710
Allows a judge to release information to the public whenever a juvenile age 14 or older is charged with an offense that would be a felony involving a weapon if committed by an adult.

        1999 Va. Acts, Chap. 952
Sec. 1   Expands the list of offenses committed by a juvenile requiring immediate notification of the school superintendent where the juvenile is or should be enrolled.

1999 W. Va. Acts, Act 5 - 1st Special Session
Adds Division of Juvenile Services to agencies required to keep juvenile records confidential except in specified circumstances.

Waiver/Certification to Adult Court

AR   *1999 Ark. Acts, Act 717*
Permits the judge to reduce the sentence of a juvenile convicted as an adult for committing certain crimes.

FL   *1999 Fla. Laws, Chap. 257*
Permits the state to charge juveniles, age 14 or 15, as adults for auto theft if the juvenile has been previously adjudicated of this crime. Requires the state to utilize a waiver hearing procedure in order to transfer a juvenile, age 14 or 15, to adult court on a charge of auto theft.

1999 Fla. Laws, Chap. 284
Sec. 35   Specifies that, when a case is transferred for an offense that is punishable by death or life imprisonment, all other felony cases pending in juvenile court be transferred as well. Specifies that if the juvenile is acquitted of the charge(s) in the original case, the juvenile is subject to juvenile court sanctions.

Sec. 37   Requires mandatory waiver of a child age 14 or older who is adjudicated for certain felonies.

1999 Fla. Laws, S 1648
Makes the Department of Corrections responsible for all aspects of custody, including treatment and evaluation, of youth offenders who are sentenced as adults or transferred to the department.

ID   *1999 Idaho Sess. Laws, Chap. 390*
Allows a juvenile prosecuted in adult court to be sentenced under the juvenile sentencing options if adult sentencing measures are inappropriate.

KS   *1999 Kan. Sess. Laws, Chap. 156*
Secs. 11, 14   Modifies the definition of juvenile offender to exclude juveniles who previously have been convicted as an adult. Requires a due process hearing for juveniles who are prosecuted in adult court or subject to extended juvenile jurisdiction.

MD   *1999 Md. Laws, Chap. 619*
Allows victims of juvenile violence to submit an impact statement to juvenile or adult court in order to determine whether a case should be transferred.

MN   *1999 Minn. Laws, Chap. 139*
Art. 2, Sec. 9, Sub 1   Requires a court (other than a juvenile court) to transfer to the juvenile court a minor who appears before it for violating a state or local law or ordinance and was under age 18 at the time of the alleged offense.

Art. 2, Sec. 12   Makes a proceeding involving a child who allegedly committed a felony an extended jurisdiction juvenile prosecution under certain circumstances.

Art. 2, Sec. 19   Gives a child who is prosecuted as an extended jurisdiction juvenile the right to a jury trial on the issue of guilt.

Art. 2, Sec. 29, Sub 4   Requires that the court jurisdiction over an extended jurisdiction juvenile extends until age 21, unless the court terminates jurisdiction before that date.

MT   *1999 Mont. Laws, Chap. 390*
Allows the court to impose a jail or prison sentence or a department commitment over five years on a youth transferred to district court and found guilty of certain offenses that are considered unlawful if committed by an adult.

1999 Mont. Laws, Chap. 523
Requires that the district court hold a hearing to determine whether a case, that involves a youth age 17, must be filed in district court or should be transferred to the jurisdiction of juvenile court.

1999 Mont. Laws, Chap. 537
Prohibits a juvenile who is prosecuted in a juvenile court and later transferred to a district court from being sentenced to an adult facility. Requires that the combined time of sentence under an extended jurisdiction prosecution may not exceed the time of imprisonment that an adult could receive under an adult prosecution.

TX   *1999 Tex. Gen. Laws, Chap. 1477*
Sec. 8   Authorizes waiver of juveniles between the ages of 10 and 17 for capital felonies and certain other offenses. Requires a detention hearing prior to discretionary transfer with certain exceptions. Authorizes the juvenile court to set or deny bond when a juvenile is detained in an adult county facility.

Sec. 12   Authorizes the juvenile court to transfer a case for criminal proceedings if the alleged perpetrator is age 18 or older and was 10 and 17 at the time of the murder or capital murder offense.

Weapons Offenses

AR   *1999 Ark. Acts, Act 1451*
Permits the Arkansas Crime Information Center access to records of delinquency adjudications where violence or a weapon was involved.

FL   *1999 Fla. Laws, Chap. 284*
Sec. 1   Requires that a minor who commits possession of firearms must serve up to 15 days in a secure detention facility.

Sec. 3   Requires detaining in secure detention a minor under age 18 who is charged with possessing or discharging a firearm on school property, unless the state attorney authorizes release. Also requires a probable cause hearing, where the court may order holding the minor in detention for 21 days and older that the minor receive examinations.

Sec. 38   Requires that a delinquency adjudication for a felony disqualifies a person from lawfully possessing a firearm until the person reaches age 24.

GA   *1999 Ga. Laws, Chap. 282*
Adds razor blade in definition of weapon.

ID   *1999 Idaho Sess. Laws, Chap. 389*
Removes exemption for carrying a concealed weapon on school property from the Juvenile Corrections Act.

LA   *1999 La. Acts, Act 1218*
Prohibits any one under age 17 from carrying a handgun with certain limited exceptions. Sets penalties and fines for such violations.

NV   *1999 Nev. Stats., Chap. 111*
Sec. 2   Requires a mental health evaluation for youths who are taken into custody for allegedly committing an offense involving a firearm.

OK   *1999 Okla. Sess. Laws, Chap. 415*
      Requires the state to deny a license for a concealed handgun to any applicant who was adjudicated delinquent for an offense that would constitute a felony if committed by an adult.

TX   *1999 Tex. Gen. Laws, Chap. 232*
      Requires detention of a juvenile upon allegation of any offense involving a firearm.

      1999 Tex. Gen. Laws, Chap. 1446
      Requires a child placed on probation for an offense involving a handgun to inform the probation officer of the manner in which the child acquired the gun and requires the probation officer to relay such information to local law enforcement. Declares information regarding acquisition of handguns inadmissible as evidence against the child in any juvenile or criminal proceeding.

VA   *1999 Va. Acts, Chap. 710*
      Allows a judge to release information to the public whenever a juvenile 14 years or older is charged with an offense that would be a felony involving a weapon if committed by an adult.

WA   *1999 Wash. Laws, Chap. 167*
      Sec. 1   Allows youths between the ages of 12 and 21 to be detained and requires them to undergo a mental health examination for possessing a firearm on school grounds.

WELFARE REFORM AND PUBLIC ASSISTANCE

Family Assistance—Administration

AR   *1999 Ark. Acts, Act 1217*

Secs. 5, 6, 8, 11, 12   Requires an annual report on the individual development account program. Specifies expenditures of funds for Individual Development Account (IDA) by nonprofit organizations. Specifies responsibilities including enforcement of penalties for withdrawing money under false circumstances or using money for non-approved purposes.

1999 Ark. Acts, Act 1567

Sec. 10   Expands the department's duties and powers to include developing and implementing a training program on TEA program requirements and the skills and knowledge required for caseworker and manager positions. Other new duties include administering grants, developing performance standards and bonus awards for program staff, working with local TEA coalitions to develop a statewide local transportation assistance policy and coordinating with planning organizations that receive federal assistance under the Job Access and Reverse Commute Program.

Secs. 10, 12   Outlines department actions and decisions that require state TEA board approval.

Sec. 12   Requires state TEA board approval of criteria to exempt or defer participants from work activity requirements.

Sec. 13   Requires an annual plan be submitted to the state TEA board that includes strategies for monitoring and protecting the safety and well being of children in families whose assistance was terminated for reasons other than obtaining employment and reaching self-sufficiency.

Sec. 19   Requires the department to establish a monitoring system to ensure participants are receiving support services needed to find and retain jobs with advancement opportunities. Specifies the system shall include an evaluation of outcome measures and financial activities. Requires state TEA board review and approval. Requires reports to the state TEA board.

Sec. 21   Requires the development of a process to review case closures closed due to noncompliance. Specifies the review process shall include a determination of whether the caseworkers followed state policy and attempted to contact former recipients to consider the family's version of the reasons for case closure. Specifies the information required for the reports to the governor and legislature. Allows the state TEA board or the legislature to request corrective action by the department for cases determined to be closed mistakenly. Requires the department to develop and implement a plan for correcting any problems due to mistaken case closures.

Sec. 3   Adds the Department of Workforce Education to the group of organizations and agencies working with the department to provide services.

Sec. 6   Establishes a 10-member Agency Advisory Council to advise the state TEA board pertaining to collaborative efforts among agencies involved in the TEA program, periodically report to the board on local coalition activities and advise the board on how to address outcomes. Establishes specific TEA program outcomes for assisting recipients and other poor families that are focused on ensuring needy families get assistance, information and services needed to become self-sufficient.

Secs. 6-7   Replaces the Transitional Employment Assistance Program Advisory Council with the Arkansas Transitional Employment Board. Establishes specific responsibilities of the board. Requires state TEA board annual implementation plan to include performance standards and measurement criteria for state and county department offices and expands guidelines to be followed by local TEA coalitions. Modifies the board's membership. Establishes membership requirements. Increases the term for membership from three to four years. Sets meeting and report timeframes.

Sec. 7   Expands the information to be included in the quarterly TEA program progress reports. Specifies the reports submitted by the board address all information requested by legislative committees. Requires the board to distribute the report to each employment opportunity district and each county.

1999 Ark. Acts, Act 1567
Sec. 8   Shifts responsibility for contracting with consultants for an independent evaluation of the TEA program and program development from the governor to the state TEA board. Expands required information for the consultant's biannual report to include TEA program effectiveness in addressing outcomes and any performance improvement measures. Expands list of required criteria for consultants to use in determining the effects of the TEA program on recipients and children. Requires evaluation to include a survey of former recipients using professionally recognized research techniques. Specifies information to be included in the survey. Removes the number of individuals placed in jobs as a measure of training effectiveness.

Sec. 9   Requires local TEA coalition boards to work with the department to develop a local, cost-effective, long-term transportation plan to assist current and former recipients and other low-income families. Specifies that transportation policies may include subsidized public transit, van-pooling and subsidized vehicle purchase and maintenance plans.

Requires local TEA coalitions to establish a board consisting of new members or existing coalition members. Specifies the board must have an 11-member minimum. Establishes guidelines for selecting new or replacement board members. Limits terms to three years. Establishes local coalition board's role and responsibilities.

CA   *1998 Cal. Stats., Chap. 329*
Modifies the composition and duties of the Emergency Food Assistance Program Advisory Board. Requires the department to provide legal immigrants who lose supplemental security income and state supplemental payments with the same level of assistance. Allows counties to continue reducing the level of general assistance beyond the time limit if the county meets specific requirements.

Sec. 4   Requires county welfare department to administer and manage a child care subsidy program for participants. Allows counties to contract with public or private child care providers for any or all services.

Secs. 5-6   Specifies department of education will administer child care assistance and services for employed participants or participants transitioning off of assistance. Allows department of education to contract with a county welfare department or other agencies to provide services.

CO   *1999 Colo. Sess. Laws, Chap. 12*
Secs. 1, 2   Requires state board to define rules related to cash assistance based on federal regulations.

1999 Colo. Sess. Laws, Chap. 105
Sec. 1   Requires board of county commissioners to create written policies for assistance and services including descriptions of services and eligibility. Requires policies to be made available to applicants and participants.

FL   *1999 Fla. Laws, Chap. 241*
Secs. 17, 19   Requires Work and Gain Economic Self-Sufficiency (WAGES) Program State Board of Directors to determine lump sum payment amount for domestic violence victims and individuals with mental illness or substance abuse problems.

1999 Fla. Laws, Chap. 241
Sec. 3   Establishes matching grant program for donations and expenditures by charitable organizations. Allows WAGES board to define program specifics, including funding, accountability and the value of donations.

Sec. 4   Requires WAGES board to submit an annual plan detailing performance measures, caseload trends, work participation and a description of agreements and partnerships with community agencies and non-profits. Also requires information on efforts of local WAGES coalitions to provide program information to recipients and former recipients.

Sec. 5   Allows state WAGES board of directors to disband local assistance coalitions. Allows state WAGES board of directors to contract with service providers until a new coalition is established.

Requires at least 25 percent of funds appropriated to local assistance coalitions to be used to contract with local public or private agencies with local residents on their boards.   Requires local assistance offices that fail to achieve performance requirements to provide an analysis of the problem and a plan for corrective action. Plan must be approved by state WAGES board.

Sec. 6   Limits funds for economic development projects to $5,000 per new job created. Allows local WAGES coalitions to provide for administrative costs.   Requires contracts for employment projects to be performance-based and fixed unit price. Requires a three-year commitment to employ participants and provide health care benefits.

Expands possible number of WAGES employment projects needing extraordinary state and local assistance. Removes three-project limit for Dade County.

Sec. 8   Establishes reporting criteria for cash assistance cases.

Sec. 9   Shifts responsibility for assigning approved work activities at career centers from Department of Labor and Economic Security to local assistance coalition.

Sec. 25   Allows WAGES program state board of directors, the Workforce Development Board, regional workforce development boards and WAGES coalitions to collaborate and create a list of programs and courses at postsecondary institutions that promote job retention and advancement.

IL   *1999 Ill. Laws, PA 331*
Sec. 9A-8.1   Requires department to annually review procedures and written materials for informing applicants and recipients of available services and benefits, all applicable eligibility requirements and participants' rights and responsibilities. Requires report to Family Self-Sufficiency Council. Specifies new or revised procedures and materials will be produced each year.

Sec. 11-20.1   Reduces recipient reporting from monthly to quarterly.

1999 Ill. Laws, SB 680
Sec. 9A-14   Requires department to contract for training services provided under job skills enhancement pilot program and maintain a database of vendors. Requires department to manage each pilot program participant's training plan and produce necessary fiscal reports.

IA   *1999 Iowa Acts, Chap. 100*
Sec. 4-5   Requires department to adopt rules to conform Iowa requirements with federal provisions for IDAs.

ME   *1999 Me. Public Laws, Chap. 461*
Sec. 1   Requires legislative report comparing state's TANF benefits to other New England states and to nonfarm income poverty line if department has not increased benefits to low-income families with children by at least 5 percent by Jan. 1, 2001. Report must identify amount of funding required to raise benefit levels over a three-year and five-year period to the average maximum benefit amount for a family of three in all other New England states.

MI   *1999 Mich. Pub. Acts, Act 26*

Sec. 57a Requires implementation of automated finger imaging system by Oct. 1, 2001. Allows contracting with a state or federal government entity for implementation and administration. Specifies all image records will be confidential and used only for purposes of reducing fraud.

MN   *1999 Minn. Laws, Chap. 205*

Art. 1, Sec. 66 Requires commissioner of finance to determine if a portion of authorized fiscal year 2000-01 expenditures can be used to provide a state match in order to obtain federal Welfare-to-Work funds without compromising maintenance of effort funds.

Art. 4, Sec. 9 Requires a quarterly review of participants' IDAs to ensure accounts contain the required amount for matching funds. Allows TANF to be used for matches.

Art. 4, Sec. 10 Requires a quarterly report from the fiscal agent managing the IDAs and requires the report to identify participants with accounts. Requires establishment of a task force to review adult basic education services.

1999 Minn. Laws, Chap. 245

Sec. 49 Requires the department to recover 3 percent of the standard of need or the amount of the monthly assistance payment, whichever is less, for overpayment of benefits not related to fraud.

Sec. 81 Requires regular review of county expenditures and allows unspent county funds to be reallocated to needy counties.

Art. 6, Sec. 1 Requires department to reimburse counties and their service providers for actual costs of benefits and services up to $400 per participant, including administrative costs, based on available resources. Allows counties to expend funds above limits without state reimbursement.

Art. 6, Sec. 1, 72 (2a), 81 (2) Specifies method of allocating funds to counties and eligible tribal providers. Requires $1 million set aside for emergency situations. Permits unspent funds to be reallocated to needy counties and tribes.

Art. 6, Sec. 34 (5) Requires notice of adverse action must be mailed at least four working days before the end of the month. Specifies adverse action notices will be mailed when county receives information that includes reasons for payment reduction, suspension or termination. Specifies valid reasons for reducing, suspending or terminating assistance payments.

Art. 6, Sec. 80 Requires department to report to counties quarterly on percent of caseload in paid employment, percent of caseload only receiving fraud assistance, cases that left assistance, federal participation requirements and median placement wage rate. Requires department to work with counties to develop additional performance measures, including measure for cases that leave assistance due to employment, job retention of former recipients and earnings of former participants at a designated follow-up point.

Requires state pay 88 percent of cost for federal sanctions for failure to meet specified performance standards and counties to pay for 12 percent. Specifies the county portion shall be distributed across all counties in proportion to the average monthly caseload for sanction period.

1999 Minn. Laws, Chap. 245

Art. 6, Sec. 80 Requires department to organize joint state and county technical assistance team to help counties that fail to meet performance standards.

Art. 6, Sec. 81 (4) Requires proposal for county performance incentive bonus program.

Art. 6, Sec. 81 (4) Requires department to report to legislature the number of participants who have received 60 months of cash assistance by January 15, 2000.

MO *1999 Mo. Laws, Chap. 208*
Sec. 6   Outlines a grievance procedure to address complaints related to wage supplementation.

Sec. 10   Requires the development of an evaluation and review process for the IDA program to ensure account holder compliance with spending requirements. Requires organizations administering the program to provide the department with an annual list of all contributors and amounts distributed. Requires the forfeiture of any matching funds if the money is spent on non-authorized purposes. Allows funds to be transferred to a contingent beneficiary upon account holder's death.

Sec. 208.040   Requires department to accept all assistance applications. Applicants can request assistance in person at county offices, by telephone or by mail. Establishes department requirements for providing applicants with complete, accurate information on the application process and of all available benefits and services and the consequences of accepting benefits or services. Requires notification of other services for applicants who are denied benefits. Requires eligibility determination with 45 days.

1999 Mo. Laws, Chap. 620
Creates a committee to develop caseload standards based on actual duties of caseworkers in each program area and consistent with professional caseload standards. Standards will be included in annual personnel request to the governor.

MT *1999 Mont. Laws, Chap. 341*
Sec. 1   Requires department payment for salaries, travel expenses and some administrative costs for certain personnel working with county boards. Requires board to reimburse department 50 percent of costs related to cash & emergency assistance programs, and requires board to reimburse department for unrelated costs not reimbursed by the federal government. Any other administrative costs to be paid by county funds.

Sec. 2   Changes state maintenance of effort level to 77 percent.

Sec. 3   Specifies reimbursement for non-enrolled tribal members, not including federal medical assistance percentage. Caps reimbursement at 1996 levels.

1999 Mont. Laws, Chap. 458
Sec. 2   Requires department to conduct a study, as part of current evaluation efforts, on sanction impacts. Outlines contents. Requires legislative report.

1999 Mont. Laws, Chap. 509
Sec. 1   Directs state funding for tribes federally approved for tribal family assistance plans. Specifies eligibility for MOE funding and creates allocation. Allows tribes and department to form funding partnerships for special projects. Requires limited technical assistance to the tribes and allows tribes to contract with department for additional services.

NE *1999 Neb. Laws, LB 475*
Sec. 2   Requires department make state funds available for tribes who choose to operate separate welfare reform programs.

NY *1998 N.Y. Laws, Chap. 204*
Sec. 1   Requires notification of possible assistance eligibility to former homeless individuals or couples who have obtained a permanent residence. Requires benefits to eligible participants be provided for at least six months, beginning the first day of the month after permanent housing is secured.

NC *1999 N.C. Sess. Laws, Chap. 234*
Sec. 2   Requires department to monitor and evaluate impact of the Work First program on job retention and advancement and other related factors. Requires all monitoring and evaluating efforts to be based on both aggregated and disaggregated data.

Sec. 3   Specifies state funds for county demonstration projects and cash assistance payments shall not count in determining county block grant amounts.

Sec. 4   Requires counties that fail to meet maintenance of effort requirement (MOE) and performance indicators for reducing MOE to submit a corrective action plan. Allows department to reduce block grant allocation, withhold funds or reallocate funds to other counties.

Requires department to work with counties to assist in maximizing flexibility in the expenditure of TANF and MOE funds. Requires counties to spend 100 percent of county funds budgeted in 1996-97 for welfare-related programs. Allows a county to request a reduction in block grant and maintenance of effort if it can demonstrate its clients' needs are met without spending all of grant, as defined by department performance indicators. Allows department to reallocate state or federal funds released from a county that reduced its maintenance of effort or from counties not spending grant. Requires county match for funds reallocated to counties.

ND   *1999 N.D. Sess. Laws, Chap. 421*
Sec. 1   Eliminates costs associated with achieving caseload ratio goals from being part of administrative costs.

Sec. 3   Allows department to work with Indian tribes to establish pilot project for tribal assistance funded with federal and state money. Requires department administration of program. Specifies participants must be eligible for TANF and an enrolled tribal member or married to an enrolled member. Specifies participants must be living in Indian Country or on reservation lands. Allows withdrawal of state funding upon breach of negotiated agreement. Requires legislative report.

OK   *1999 Okla. Sess. Laws, Chap. 17*
Sec. 241   Shifts responsibility for food stamp program from counties to state department.

1999 Okla. Sess. Laws, SJR 9
Creates task force to review worker-to-caseload ratio and other staffing issues. Requires legislative report.

TX   *1999 Tex. Gen. Laws, Chap. 32*
Sec. 1   Requires the department to notify a parent or caretaker of medical assistance benefits for children at a scheduled eligibility renewal review or at the time financial assistance is terminated. Requires department to revise recipient education and notification policies relating to child's eligibility for medical assistance.

WV   *1999 W. Va. Acts, Chap. 141*
Art. 9, Sec. 9-9-7   Requires department to work with college and university systems to develop plan to utilize programs at postsecondary institutions to assist participants in two or four-year programs in meeting work requirement. Requires legislative report.

Family Assistance—Electronic Benefit Transfer

CA   *1998 Cal. Stats., Chap. 329*
Shifts responsibility for implementation, management and operation of a statewide EBT system from the counties to the state. Specifies the state is responsible for finding and contracting for statewide EBT system. Requires the Health and Welfare Agency Data Center to manage the EBT system.

OK   *1999 Okla. Sess. Laws, Chap. 17*
Sec. 241   Requires programs distributing food stamp benefits to provide access to EBT.

Family Assistance—Eligibility and Benefits

AR   *1999 Ark. Acts, Act 1217*
Sec. 15   Exempts funds in IDAs from being counted as income, assets or resources in determining financial eligibility.

        1999 Ark. Acts, Act 1567
Sec. 3   Allows participants eligible for cash assistance to receive extended support services, including those who have obtained jobs.

Sec. 11   Allows qualified aliens with legal immigrant status for at least five years to apply for assistance. Specifies individuals must have been physically in the United States on or after Aug. 22, 1996.

Sec. 13   Expands home visits to families with children who were terminated from assistance from a minimum of one visit within 30 days of termination to a three-visit minimum within six months. Specifies the first visit shall occur in the first 30 days, the second visit three months after assistance termination and the third at six months. Requires home visits to include information on available support services.

Sec. 15   Expands the maximum age for continuing assistance to children in sanctioned families from 16 to 18.

CO   *1999 Colo. Sess. Laws, Chap. 20*
Sec. 1   Denies assistance to drug felons. Requires referral to other services for recipients declared ineligible for cash assistance.

CT   *1999 Conn. Acts, PA 279*
Sec. 17b-104   Authorizes cash assistance increase for fiscal years 2000 and 2001, but not exceeding five percent .

Secs. 17b-112c   Extends assistance eligibility to July 1, 2001, for qualified aliens or legal immigrants determined eligible before July 1, 1997.

FL   *1999 Fla. Laws, Chap. 241*
Sec. 10   Clarifies sanction policies for noncompliance, including providing recipients with information regarding consequences and referral to necessary services. Allows for good cause exemption.

Secs. 15, 17, 18, 19, 20, 21   Allows employed recipients to access $1,000 lump sum payment in lieu of receiving ongoing assistance.

Sec. 16   Removes six-month application waiting period for cash assistance for non-domestic violence related relocation assistance recipients. Removes eight-month time limit for assistance payback payments. Requires WAGES state board of directors to define waiting period for assistance applicants after receiving relocation assistance.

Sec. 17   Allows eligible domestic violence victims to access a one-time lump sum payment and victim services through a certified shelter.

Sec. 19   Allows eligible individuals with mental illness or substance abuse problems to access a one-time lump sum payment and services in lieu of ongoing cash assistance.

Sec. 26   Expands transitional transportation benefits to include a vehicle used for training, education or employment purposes valued at $8,500.

IL   *1999 Ill. Laws, PA 331*
Sec. 11-20.1   Requires department to notify participants of rules for disregarding earned income tax credit when determining eligibility.

Requires notification to applicants and recipients that cash assistance amounts for newly employed recipients is adjusted based on estimated income. Specifies recipient must notify department of actual income.

Requires department to notify recipient of eligibility requirements and availability of cash assistance if recipient loses earned income or experiences a decrease during a calendar quarter in which assistance was previously based on a higher income.

ME   *1999 Me. Public Laws, Chap. 461*
Sec. 1   Authorizes department to use unspent federal or state funds to increase maximum levels of assistance by at least 5 percent.

MI   *1999 Mich. Pub. Acts, Act 26*
Sec. 57a Requires finger imaging as a condition of eligibility. Exempts senior citizens, children, homebound individuals or nursing home patients.

1999 Mich. Pub. Acts, HB 4090
Sec. 57i   Establishes drug testing pilot program in specific counties for applicants and recipients as a condition of eligibility. Exempts individuals 65 or older and those currently participating in court-ordered substance abuse treatment. Requires second drug test for individuals who have tested positive and sanctions or penalties for individuals who test positive twice and refuse to participate in assessment and comply with required substance abuse treatment plan.

MN   *1999 Minn. Laws, Chap. 205*
Art. 1, Sec. 24   Allows participants in compliance with work activities or those eligible for or receiving child care assistance under the basic sliding fee program to receive a subsidy in lieu of receiving assistance.

1999 Minn. Laws, Chap. 245
Secs. 20, 23   Clarifies household composition and income guidelines for eligibility determination.

Sec. 30   Requires applicants and participants to accept any non-welfare benefits offered that will supplement assistance payments.

Art. 6, Sec. 5   Specifies state and federal assistance funds must be used to assist families with children who have income below 200 percent of federal poverty guidelines.

Art. 6, Sec. 15 (3)   Requires legal adult noncitizens under age 70 living in United States for four years or more to be lawful permanent residents and meet eligibility requirements in order to receive state-funded benefits.

Art. 6, Sec. 16 (1a)   Requires 30 consecutive days of residency as a condition of eligibility.

Art. 6, Sec. 23 (8)   Allows payments for shelter to be made directly to participant if nonparent caregiver is not included in assistance unit.

Art. 6, Sec. 23 (8)   Excludes individuals who provide child care to a child receiving assistance from shared household standard when determining eligibility.

Art. 6, Sec. 34 (12)   Allows certain recipients to stop receiving cash and retain eligibility for other services. Grants one month of child care and medical assistance eligibility for each month recipient does not receive cash.

Art. 6, Sec. 52 (1)   Specifies procedure for calculating benefits for applicants who have not met residency requirements.

Art. 6, Sec. 58 (4)   Requires use of standard of need to determine number of days a participant is ineligible for emergency assistance after receiving diversionary assistance. Excludes sanctioned and disqualified participants from emergency assistance eligibility.

Art. 6, Sec. 59 (3)   Specifies payment standard for emergency needs.

MS   *1999 Miss. Laws, Chap. 390*
        Sec. 1   Increases maximum monthly cash benefit amount from $60 to $110 for caretaker relative of dependent child.

MO   *1999 Mo. Laws, Chap. 208*
        Sec. 7   Specifies that public assistance recipients cannot be sanctioned for refusing a job offer in a direct placement program if certain circumstances exist, such as travel time being over two hours round trip.

        Specifies that cash benefits will be paid with maintenance of effort funds for eligible grandparents in the Grandparents as Foster Parents Program, or close relative who is age 50 or older and is child's legal guardian. Reimbursement and assistance for ineligible grandparents will be paid with TANF funds and will be subject to work participation and time limit requirements.

        Sec. 208.040   Requires that work history requirements and definition of unemployed are not applicable when considering eligibility for parents under 21.

NM   *1999 N.M. Laws, SB 115*
        Sec. 1   Reduces the maximum age of a dependent child for benefit purposes from 18 to 17, unless the dependent is 18 and has not graduated from high school.

TX   *1999 Tex. Gen. Laws, Chap. 32*
        Sec. 1   Requires department to establish procedures for automatically reviewing a child's eligibility for medical assistance for children receiving cash assistance or when cash assistance ends. Specifies the department can allow provisional eligibility for children who do not meet requirements.

VA   *1999 Va. Acts, Chap. 638*
        Sec. 1   Requires assistance be provided to two-parent families on same terms and conditions as to single-parent families. Eliminates requirement that a child be deprived of one parent as a eligibility criteria for assistance.

WA   *1999 Wash. Laws, Chap. 120*
        When determining eligibility for TANF, the state standard of need is not considered and the earned income of a dependent child who is a full-time student is not disregarded. Qualified families are not prohibited from receiving welfare if the adult is involved in a strike. Children between the ages of 18 and 21 who have disabilities and are full-time students may receive TANF assistance. The department is also authorized to grant eligibility exceptions to children between the ages of 18 and 21, on a discretionary basis, if the department determines that the exception will enable the child to complete his or her high school education, GED or vocational education.

WV   *1999 W. Va. Acts, Chap. 141*
        Art. 9, Sec. 9-9-3   Excludes SSI from assistance eligibility determination. Excludes earned income of minor children in school from assistance eligibility determination.

Family Assistance—Employment-Related Policies

AR   *1999 Ark. Acts, Act 1567*
        Sec. 12   Removes requirement that participants in job skills training have a written agreement from an employer offering employment upon successful completion of the program. Eliminates requirement that recipients complete an entrance assessment or test before entering a job skills training program if such tests are required for employment upon completion of the program.

Changes community service definition to time spent in an approved activity at a government entity or community-based, charitable organization. Defines work experience as job-training experience linked to education or training that improves a recipient's employability at a supervised public or private nonprofit agency or organization with a private, for-profit employer. Defines on-the-job training as training and work experience at a public or private nonprofit agency or organization or private for-profit employers that provide an opportunity for job training and employment upon successful completion of training. Specifies activities such as work study, training-related practicums and internships are considered work experience.

Allows the department to exempt parents or caregivers over 60 and child only cases from work activity requirements.

Specifies occupational training services must meet one of four requirements to be considered an allowable work activity.

Sec. 14   Modifies the required minimum hours for self-employment to be considered an allowable work activity.

Sec. 18   Allows the department to implement regulations for requiring applicants who have been determined to be job ready during the application process to immediately begin a job search. Requires state TEA board approval. Prevents the department from requiring a job search if it has been determined that the participant has one or more barriers to finding long-term employment with advancement opportunities.

Requires the department to conduct an assessment of the functional education and skill levels, prior work experience and employability within 30 days of an application approval. Requires participant assessments to identify barriers to immediate employment and barriers that may prevent participants from increasing earnings and job advancement. Establishes specific barriers to be assessed.

Requires the department to work with participants to develop an individual employment plan. Requires the department to review employment plan progress and meet with participants to review and revise the plan as necessary. Requires the department to notify participants of time remaining in lifetime assistance limit and reassess needs for support services based on months remaining. Specifies information to be included in employment plan.

Requires the department to ask applicants if child care or transportation is needed for the applicant to perform a job search. Exempts applicants without available child care or transportation from required job search activities.

AR   *1999 Ark. Acts, Act 1567*
Secs. 3, 12, 22   Requires the department to allow recipients to obtain education and training needed to get and retain jobs with advancement opportunities. Expands approved work activities to include vocational education training. Defines vocational education training as post secondary education, including two-, four- or five-year programs at a college, university, technical institute, vocational school or job-related training. Expands the definition of education and training to include elementary and secondary education to obtain a high school diploma equivalent and ESL courses. Sets eligibility requirements for participating in basic remedial education or adult education. Allows participants in education and training activities access to available support services.

Sec. 20   Requires the department to establish a post-employment referral program to provide information on transitional support services and education and training opportunities for employed participants and participants with closed cases due to employment.

Sec. 22   Authorizes the department to require participants in an education or training activity to participate in internships, work experience or employment for up to 15 hours per week. Allow the department to increase or decrease required work activity hours based on whether or not the state is meeting its federal work participation requirement. Requires the department to allow at least 700 participants in vocational education activities and at least 400 in postsecondary education activities.

CT   *1999 Conn. Acts, PA 279*
      Sec. 17b-694   Expands eligibility for local employment services for Medicaid recipients ages 18 to 20.

DE   *Vol. 70 Del. Laws, SB 101*
      Sec. 523   Allows postsecondary education, adult basic education or vocational training to count as a work activity and requires the department to inform applicants and recipients of this option. Allows work study, internships, externships or work as research assistant to count towards work requirement. Allows participants in education or training programs to continue to receive support services.

FL   *1999 Fla. Laws, Chap. 241*
      Sec. 10   Allows local WAGES coalitions to include educational activities that do not meet federal work participation requirements as work activities. Allows adjustment of regional participation requirement not exceeding federal adjustment for caseload decline.

      Shifts responsibility for screening, requiring work participation and other responsibilities from Department of Labor and Employment to local WAGES coalitions.

      Redefines job skills training to include literacy instruction, language proficiency classes and removes requirement that participants in job skills training have a written commitment from employers that offer employment upon completion. Allows English as a second language courses to count as a primary work activity for more than 12 months if necessary.

      Requires participants with a verified medical limitation to be assigned activities suited to the limitation. Requires vocational assessment or work evaluation as part of work activity plan. Allows department or local assistance coalition to require medical or vocational assessment to evaluate participant's ability to participate in work activity.

      Sec. 11   Allows recipients who need residential care for substance abuse or mental illness to be exempted from work activities. Requires participation in treatment program.

      Sec. 22   Establishes special needs dependent care program for eligible families with children age 13 to 17 to allow parent to comply with work requirement. Requires financial guidelines for subsidized child care eligibility be used. Allows special needs dependent care to continue as transitional service up to two years after assistance eligibility ends.

      Sec. 25   Allows TANF funds to be used to develop Retention Incentive Training Accounts to fund tuition, fees, educational material, coaching and mentoring, performance incentives, transportation and child care necessary for job retention and advancement. Requires legislative report.

FL   *1999 Fla. Laws, Chap. 241*
      Sec. 4   Defines benefits and services that local WAGES coalitions are to provide.

IL   *1999 Ill. Laws, PA 331*
      Sec. 11-20.1   Requires department to notify recipients participating in a work activity if additional activities are necessary to meet monthly requirement. Specifies department provide a list of approved activities and notify recipient if the employment allows months of continued cash assistance to not count towards lifetime limit.

      Requires notification to recipients participating in a work activity if additional activities are necessary to meet monthly requirement. Requires a list of approved activities and notification if the employment allows months of continued cash assistance to not count towards lifetime limit.

      1999 Ill. Laws, SB 680
      Sec. 9A-14   Establishes job skills enhancement pilot program in three counties. Allows eligible, newly employed current and former recipients who lack skills or are semiskilled in entry level positions with limited advancement opportunities to participate in training. Specifies the training is to enhance existing

---

job skills, gain additional or alternative skills or learn interpersonal communication or other skills. Specifies participation is voluntary and participants must sign a training agreement with the department.

ME   *1999 Me. Public Laws, Chap. 407*
Sec. 1 Allows the department to make reasonable adjustments to the work participation requirements for Parents as Scholars participants who show good cause. Defines good cause.

Removes the requirement that after 24 months in an educational program Parents as Scholars participants perform a minimum of 20 hours per week of worksite experience in addition to time spent in education, training or study. Gives participants the option of completing 15 hours per week of worksite experience or a total of 40 hours per week of education, training, study or worksite experience. Requires the department to notify Parents as Scholars participants of work requirement options after being in the program for 24 months. Requires department to adopt rules defining satisfactory academic progress and specifies an educational plan cannot be denied because of extended duration.

MN   *1999 Minn. Laws, Chap. 205*
Art. 1, Sec. 24 Waives the one-year work exemption requirement for individuals who participate in the at-home infant care program.

Art. 1, Sec. 31 Reduces the work requirement for full-time students receiving child care assistance from 20 hours per week to 10. Allows work study programs to be considered as employment.

1999 Minn. Laws, Chap. 245
Art. 6, Sec. 5 Authorizes use of state and federal assistance funds for welfare-to-work extended employment services for recipients with severe employment barriers.

Art. 6, Sec. 62 Sanctions participants who fail to attend employment and training orientation.

Art. 6, Sec. 64 Allows basic education activities to be included in job search or employment plan for participants with an education level lower than eighth grade.

1999 Minn. Laws, Chap. 245
Art. 6, Sec. 64 (3) Allows participant and job counselor to develop a job search support plan that limits job search to jobs within participants' employment goals. Allows job search support plan to include adult basic education and ESL classes towards required job search hours.

Art. 6, Sec. 64 (4) Requires job counselors to notify participants of available training and employment resources.

Allows job counselor to require substance abuse assessment or psychological assessment if caseworker believes recipient cannot secure employment because of substance abuse or other medical condition. Requires transportation or child care if necessary.

Sanctions recipients who fail to complete a requested secondary education assessment.

Art. 6, Sec. 69 (4) Requires both parents in a two-parent family to receive services from the same employment and training provider unless one parent has a special identified need not available at that service provider.

MO   *1999 Mo. Laws, Chap. 208*
Sec. 4 Creates Welfare to Work Protection Act. Requires all adults receiving Work First Program benefits and employed or assigned to a work activity be considered same as other employees for purpose of being covered by all state and federal labor laws. Requires participants receive same paid sick, holiday, vacation and other leave as other employees.

Sec. 7 Specifies that public assistance recipients cannot be sanctioned for refusing a job offer in a direct placement program in certain situations, for instance if travel time is over two hours round trip.

Sec. 8   Requires quarterly reports that include a list of employers participating in supplemental wage assistance, direct placement and community work experience programs and will also include the number of clients placed with each employer.

Sec. 208.040   Allows subsidized employment for up to 48 months.

MT   *1999 Mont. Laws, Chap. 124*
Sec. 1   Requires department to provide worker's compensation coverage for participants of training projects placed at public or private worksites. Specifies coverage limits.

NM   *1999 N.M. Laws, HB 228*
Sec. 1   Allows self-employment to count as work activity.

1999 N.M. Laws, Chap. 12
Sec. 1   Appropriates MOE funds to Commission on the Status of Women to develop and operate job placement programs for participants. Requires department approval for programs and measurable performance standards, identification of target clients and tracking and reporting.

Appropriates MOE funds to department of human services in cooperation with the Martin Luther King Jr. commission for work-first focused services. Requires measurable performance standards, identification of target clients and tracking and reporting.

Appropriates MOE funds to regents of western New Mexico University for job training and placement of participants referred by department. Requires measurable performance standards, identification of target clients and tracking and reporting. Grants MOE funds to New Mexico University to continue operating a child development center.

Makes TANF block grant appropriation to department for training participants to become licensed day care providers.

Appropriates MOE funds for early childhood and family support and education training programs to include before and after school programs for children ages 5-8 and classes to develop job skills and leadership skills for parents. Requires programs to be offered in areas lacking certified child care. Requires measurable performance standards, identification of target clients and tracking and reporting.

NC   *1999 N.C. Sess. Laws, Chap. 234*
Sec. 1.2   Expands work activities to include part-time enrollment in postsecondary education programs for up to 20 percent of recipients. Allows extension of benefits up to three years for recipients enrolled at least part-time in a postsecondary education program and maintaining a minimum 2.5 GPA.

Sec. 2   Allows two-parent families to receive cash assistance for three months during a one-year period after qualifying and not be subject to work requirements during that period.

1999 N.C. Sess. Laws, Chap. 421
Sec. 1   Eliminates payment of unemployment insurance premium if employer fires recipient within 100 days for failure to perform job duties.

VA   *1999 Va. Acts, Chap. 759*
Sec. 1   Allows placement in a vocational education program and specifies exemption criteria for job search requirements. Requires work of eight hours per week and training for minimum of 30 hours. Requires agreement with an employer to place participant at end of program if qualified and the employer has an opening.

WA   *1999 Wash. Laws, Chap. 1936*
Sec. 1   Requires TANF recipients to receive employability screening prior to job search and referral and requires more intensive screening for unemployable recipient to determine barriers.

WV   *1999 W. Va. Acts, Chap. 141*
      Art. 9, Sec. 9-9-7   Requires department to work with college and university systems to develop plan to utilize programs at postsecondary institutions to assist participants in two or four-year programs in meeting work requirement.   Requires legislative report.

WY   *1999 Wyo. Sess. Laws, Act 66*
      Sec. 1   Expands obligations for recipients of welfare employment services program to include cooperation with establishment and modification of child support orders.

Family Assistance—Fraud

IL   *1999 Ill. Laws, SB 1116*
      Sec. 11-6.2   Requires department conduct periodic audits of fingerprint program.   Establishes a statewide electronic finger imaging program for all applicants and recipients.   Specifies that fingerprint information shall only be used to prevent multiple enrollments for assistance.   Requires department to investigate suspected fraud before sanctioning recipients.

MI   *1999 Mich. Pub. Acts, Act 26*
      Sec. 57a   Requires finger imaging as a condition of eligibility.   Exempts senior citizens, children, homebound individuals or nursing home patients.

      Requires implementation of automated finger imaging system by Oct. 1, 2001.   Allows contracting with a state or federal government entity for implementation and administration.   Specifies all image records will be confidential and used only for purposes of reducing fraud.

MN   *1999 Minn. Laws, Chap. 205*
      Art. 1, Sec. 54   Includes wrongfully obtained child care assistance as theft.   Defines theft of child care assistance as wrongful receipt of assistance payments or providing a false claim for assistance.

      Art. 1, Sec. 57   Requires recipients to authorize the release of information necessary for fraud investigation.

      Art. 1, Sec. 58   Requires reimbursement to counties for child care assistance program fraud investigations and program compliance expenses.

      1999 Minn. Laws, Chap. 245
      Sec. 49   Requires the department to recover 10 percent of the applicable standard for overpayment of benefits due to fraud.

      Art. 6, Sec. 49 (4)   Specifies fraud recovery procedures.

OK   *1999 Okla. Sess. Laws, Chap. 77*
      Sec. 185   Requires fine or jail time for anyone who commits fraud.   Penalty based on amount of fraud.

TN   *1999 Tenn. Pub. Acts, Chap. 248*
      Sec. 1   Defines felony fraud as obtaining unauthorized public assistance benefits valued at $100 or more, including food assistance benefits.   Specifies possible penalties, including disqualification from future assistance, and jail.   Requires department to notify all recipients of fraud penalties.

Family Assistance—General

CA   *1998 Cal. Stats., Chap. 329*
      Requires the department to provide legal immigrants who lose SSI and state supplemental payments with the same level of assistance.   Revises dates of annual benefits adjustments and suspends adjustments in fiscal years in which there is no increase in taxes.

Sec. 2 Excludes income from SSI and state supplemental payments (SSP) when determining child care eligibility.

Sec. 3 Allows eligibility for all child care services while receiving aid and requires fee determination be based on family size and income.

Sec. 32 Allows income, resources and deductible expenses of household members determined to be ineligible for food stamp benefits to be excluded when determining federal food stamp benefits. Specifies households with members ineligible for food stamps shall not received higher food stamp benefits than other households.

Sec. 33 Expands food assistance program for legal immigrants to include individuals of any age. Specifies immigrants must have legally been in the United Street before Aug. 22, 1996, and must meet eligibility requirements.

Sec. 38 Specifies eligibility requirements for a state-funded cash assistance program to older, blind or disabled legal immigrants not eligible for federal assistance due to immigration status be based on SSI requirements for aged, blind and disabled. Extends eligibility to legal immigrants who arrived in the United States after Aug. 22, 1996, if certain conditions are met. Specifies benefits will be similar to SSI benefits.

Establishes a state funded program administered by the counties to provide cash assistance to aged, blind and disabled legal noncitizens not eligible for TANF due to immigration status. Sunsets assistance program on July 1, 2000. Requires department to review all disabled individuals' applications. Requires reimbursement to counties for administrative and actual costs of administering the program. Allows department to contract with the federal government to administer the program. Specifies state funds will be transferred to pay for costs of contracting with the federal government.

CO   *1999 Colo. Sess. Laws, Chap. 331*
Sec. 2 Establishes family planning pilot program for individuals below 150 percent of federal poverty level. Dependent on federal waiver. Requires legislative report.

FL   *1999 Fla. Laws, Chap. 241*
Sec. 20 Establishes services to reduce and prevent teen pregnancy, including assisting teens in completing educational programs.

MN   *1999 Minn. Laws, Chap. 245*
Secs. 3, 15 Allows state funds to be used for noncitizen benefits when federal food stamp funds cannot be used.

Reduces eligibility for state food assistance for legal immigrants to individuals age 50 years or older.

Art. 6, Sec. 5 Authorizes use of state and federal funds for a health care and human services training and retention program, rent assistance and homeless prevention.

Art. 6, Sec. 71 Includes work schedules or court proceedings as good cause exceptions for missing department appointments. Requires job counselor to work with participant to reschedule mandatory meetings.

MO   *1999 Mo. Laws, Chaps. 210, 660*
Sec. 208.029 Lowers the age of eligible grandparents in the Grandparents as Foster Parents Program from 55 to 50. Authorizes the state to allow other relatives of a child to participate in the program if there are no grandparents willing to do so. Authorizes the provision of support services. Provides that funding for cash assistance and other services shall be funded from state MOE funds. Reimbursement and assistance for non-eligible grandparents will be funded with TANF.

NC   *1999 N.C. Sess. Laws, Chap. 234*
      Sec. 5   Requires counties to establish an emergency assistance program for eligible families at or below 200 percent of federal poverty level.

VA   *1999 Va. Acts, Chap. 910*
      Sec. 1   Allows department to purchase or receive donated vehicles from the state motor vehicle fleet to sell or transfer to recipients. Exempts department from consideration as a motor vehicle dealer.

      1999 Va. Acts, Chap. 911
      Sec. 1   Allows surplus motor vehicles in the state motor vehicle fleet to be sold to local departments before being offered in a public sale or auction. Specifies the vehicles are to be transferred or sold to recipients.

Family Assistance—Income and Assets

AR   *1999 Ark. Acts, Act 1217*
      Secs. 2, 6-7   Requires the establishment of IDAs. Sets eligibility guidelines and allows funds to be used for buying or repairing a home, starting a business, postsecondary education, retirement or buying or repairing a vehicle. Specifies state matching funds must be used for retirement or vehicle purchase or repairs. IDA's must not be used exclusively for vehicle related costs. Grants a $3 matching contribution up to $2,000 per year per account holder or $4,000 per household for individuals that have incomes below 185 percent of the poverty level.

      Sec. 9   Allows individuals, businesses or organizations to make a tax deductible contributions for matching funds in individual development accounts. Requires funds to be distributed proportionately among account holders.

      1999 Ark. Acts, Act 1567
      Sec. 12   Specifies contracts between the department and private or public sector employers receiving a subsidy or incentive may include provisions addressing contributions to a recipient's IDA.

CT   *1999 Conn. Acts, PA 279*
      Sec. 17b-112   Expands earned income disregard to include previously ineligible families who become temporarily ineligible because a family member temporarily receives worker's compensation and returns to work immediately after benefits end.

FL   *1999 Fla. Laws, Chap. 241*
      Sec. 12   Excludes incentive payments as income.

IL   *1999 Ill. Laws, PA 331*
      Sec. 11-20.1   Requires department to notify participants of rules for disregarding earned income tax credit when determining eligibility.

IA   *1999 Iowa Acts, Chap. 100*
      Sec. 5   Provides matching funds from self-employment loan program for IDAs. Restricts use of funds to starting new businesses, obtaining job-related training or postsecondary education, or buying permanent residence. Allows funding to be distributed as loans or grants.   Permits department to contract with a nationally known, experienced nonprofit corporation for help administering program.

LA   *1999 La. Acts, HCR 94*
      Authorizes the department to develop initiatives to promote use of IDAs. Requests department study feasibility of providing tax incentives to individuals and corporate IDA contributors and the viability of matching contributions.

MD   *1999 Md. Laws, Chap. 469*
      Increases income disregard from 26 percent to 35 percent.

MI   *1998 Mich. Pub. Acts, Act 361*
        Sec. 57k   Requires establishment of IDAs. Sets eligibility guidelines and allows funds to be used for buying a home. Disregards funds and interest in determining eligibility.

MN   *1999 Minn. Laws, Chap. 205*
        Sec. 20   Clarifies income guidelines for eligibility determination.

        Art. 1, Sec. 6   Excludes grants that provide reimbursement for tuition, fees and other education expenses, foster care assistance and child care assistance from earned income. Clarifies that state and federal tax earned income credits are excluded from income. Includes at-home infant care subsidy payments as earned income.

        Art. 4, Sec. 8 Reduces the household income eligibility requirement for assistance recipients from income at 200 percent of the poverty level to 185 percent and maximum assets of $25,000 to assets of $15,000.

        Art. 4, Sec. 9   Allows TANF funds to be used as match for IDAs and reduces the matching contribution from $2 for every $1 to $1.50.

        1999 Minn. Laws, Chap. 245
        Art. 6, Secs. 7, 28   Requires department to determine income disregard amount for FY 00/01 to ensure participants do not lose assistance eligibility until income reaches at least 120 percent of federal poverty level.

        Art. 6, Sec. 19 (3)   Excludes value of special equipment and one vehicle per physically disabled person from eligibility determination when vehicle is needed to transport the disabled individual. Excludes value of vehicle used for long-distance travel for employment when determining eligibility or the value of any motor vehicles used at least 50 percent of the time for self-employment business. Also excludes the value of a vehicle from eligibility determination when used as an applicant or recipient's primary residence.

        Art. 6, Sec. 20 (2)   Disregards income from both of minor parent applicant's parents and stepparents in determining eligibility.

        Excludes income received from reimbursement for employment-related carpool expenses from family's earned income for eligibility purposes.

        Art. 6, Sec. 39 (4)   Specifies supplemental assistance payments for significant change in income shall not be paid when income change results from receipt of lump sum payment, extra paycheck, business fluctuation in self-employment income or participant of recipient in strike or other labor action.

        Art. 6, Sec. 47 (9)   Defines housing assistance as unearned income until 2001. Expands time limit for consideration of $100 or less of housing assistance as unearned income to January 1, 2001. Specifies exemptions.

        Sec. 256.20 (3) Excludes value of special equipment and one vehicle per physically disabled person from eligibility determination when vehicle is needed to transport the disabled individual. Excludes value of vehicle used for long-distance travel for employment when determining eligibility.

MO   *1999 Mo. Laws, Chap. 208*
        Sec. 10   Requires the establishment of family development accounts limited to $50,000. Sets eligibility guidelines. Allows funds to be expended on education, buying a home or starting a small business. Grants a matching fund contribution for families with incomes below 200 percent of the poverty level. Limits deposits to $2,000 per year. Specifies that funds in account shall be disregarded for eligibility purposes. Provides state income tax credit against liability up to $50,000 per contributor and up to 50 percent of contributed amount. Limits total tax credits to $4 million per fiscal year.

Sec. 208.040   Disregards income up to 100 percent of federal poverty level for minor parents who live with parent or in an adult-supervised setting.

Increases earned income disregard to two-thirds of income by Oct. 1, 1999, only for unemployed cash assistance recipients who find jobs. Maintains the same level of income disregard for new applicants who are already working. Specifies that recipients can only receive disregards for 12 months while receiving cash benefits. Eligible again after not receiving cash assistance for 12 consecutive months.

ND   *1999 N.D. Sess. Laws, Chap. 421*
Sec. 2   Allows department to determine asset limits. Allows department to consider exempting funds in IDA's for eligibility determination.   •

UT   *1999 Utah Laws, Chap. 70*
Sec. 1 Disregards $50 of vehicle insurance payment and $100 of purchase or lease payment for applicant's primary vehicle in determining eligibility.

WV   *1999 W. Va. Acts, Chap. 141*
Art. 9, Sec. 9-9-3   Excludes SSI from assistance eligibility determination. Excludes earned income of minor children in school from assistance eligibility determination.

Family Assistance—Minor Parents

MN   *1999 Minn. Laws, Chap. 245*
Art. 6, Sec. 18   Requires assistance payment for minor parent and minor child to be paid in protective payment whenever possible.

Requires county agency to notify minor parent applicants of eligibility requirements, rights and obligations and applicable orientation information.

Art. 6, Sec. 36 (4)   Eliminates county requirement to verify anticipated graduation date for 18-year-olds.

Art. 6, Sec. 68 (2)   Allows participants without a high school diploma or equivalent upon reaching age 18 or 19 to choose to continue receiving services under their current plan with social services or participants can choose to use an employment and training services provider.

MO   *1999 Mo. Laws, Chap. 208*
Sec. 208.040   Disregards income up to 100 percent of federal poverty level for minor parents who live with parent or in an adult-supervised setting.

Requires minor parents to live with parent or in an adult-supervised setting.

Family Assistance—Responsibility Contracts

AR   *1999 Ark. Acts, Act 1567*
Secs. 7, 18   Requires applicants and the department to sign a responsibility contract upon submitting an application. Specifies that skills and employability assessments be used in developing a responsibility contract and that the responsibility contract addresses a participant's strengths and barriers in obtaining a job and the support services to be provided.

CO   *1999 Colo. Sess. Laws, Chap. 191*
Secs. 1, 2   Requires responsibility contracts notify participants that public assistance is not a legal entitlement. Signing the contract indicates agreement with terms. Noncompliance with contract can result in sanctions. Allows recipient to request a review of responsibility contract if they believe contract is unreasonable.

IL   *1999 Ill. Laws, PA 331*
Sec. 9A-8   Allows changes in responsibility contract to reflect enrollment in education, training and employment programs and participation in substance abuse or mental health treatment, activities to escape or prevent domestic violence and dependent care for disabled family members.

IA   *1999 Iowa Acts, Chap. 100*
Sec. 1   Requires applicants to sign statement committing to self-sufficiency as a condition of eligibility. Allows statement to become responsibility contract if applicant is accepted for assistance. Reduces benefits for noncompliance.

MN   *1999 Minn. Laws, Chap. 245*
Art. 6, Sec. 64   Allows basic education activities to be included in job search or employment plan for participants with an education level lower than eighth grade.

MT   *1999 Mont. Laws, Chap. 458*
Sec. 1   Exempts termination of food stamps and Medicaid from a sanction for noncompliance with responsibility contract. Allows child care benefits for work activities specified in the responsibility contract.

ND   *1999 N.D. Sess. Laws, Chap. 421*
Sec. 2   Sanctions household for not developing a responsibility contract.

Family Assistance—School Attendance Requirements

ND   *1999 N.D. Sess. Laws, Chap. 421*
Sec. 2   Eliminates sanction for parents who do not ensure minor children attend school.

Family Assistance—Substance Abuse

CO   *1999 Colo. Sess. Laws, Chap. 20*
Sec. 1, 2   Denies assistance to drug felons.

FL   *1999 Fla. Laws, Chap. 241*
Sec. 11   Allows recipients who need residential care for substance abuse or mental illness to be exempted from work activities. Recipients must participate in treatment program.

Sec. 31   Requires substance abuse screening for recipients in substance abuse demonstration. Allows drug testing. Subjects recipients who do not comply to work activity requirements.

IL   *1999 Ill. Laws, PA 331*
Sec. 9A-8   Requires all applicants and recipients be notified of substance abuse treatment programs.

MI   *1999 Mich. Pub. Acts, HB 4090*
Sec. 57i   Establishes drug testing pilot program for applicants and recipients as a condition of eligibility, including random drug testing. Exempts individuals age 65 or older and those currently participating in court-ordered substance abuse treatment. Requires second drug test for individuals who have tested positive. Sanctions individuals who test positive twice and refuse to participate in assessment and comply with required substance abuse treatment plan.

MN   *1999 Minn. Laws, Chap. 245*
Art. 6, Sec. 24 (1)   Allows assistance to drug felons.

Art. 6, Sec. 29 (1)   Imposes grant reduction for failing a drug test.

Requires applicants or recipients with a drug conviction for offenses committed after July 1, 1997, requesting only food stamps to submit to random drug testing for continued eligibility. Specifies that individuals who test positive are subject to sanctions.

Art. 6, Sec. 81 (4)   Requires department to work with agencies, organizations and providers to develop policy for implementing substance abuse assessment.

NJ   *1999 N.J. Laws, SB 1493*
Requires cash benefits for drug felons to be paid to drug treatment provider while in treatment, less a personal needs allowance. Drug felons convicted of distribution can receive food stamp benefits upon completion of drug treatment program. Requires termination for drug felons who complete treatment and test positive for illegal substances within 60 days of completing treatment.

NM   *1999 N.M. Laws, Chap. 8*
Sec. 1   Establishes substance abuse treatment pilot program in two northern counties. Requires legislative report.

        1999 N.M. Laws, Chap. 12
Sec. 1   Appropriates a Welfare-to-Work match to department of health for substance abuse counseling. Appropriates Welfare-to-Work match for substance abuse counseling of Native American participants.

Family Assistance—Support Services

AR   *1999 Ark. Acts, Act 1567*
Secs. 3, 22   Allows participants eligible for cash assistance to receive extended support services, including those who have obtained jobs. Allows participants in education and training activities access to available support services.

Sec. 9   Specifies that transportation policies may include subsidized public transit, van-pooling and subsidized vehicle purchase and maintenance plans.

Secs. 13, 18   Requires notification to participants of available supportive services for removing employment barriers and increasing long-term earnings and advancement opportunities. Requires the department to make effort to deliver support services for individuals with barriers.

Sec. 18   Requires the department to notify participants of time remaining in lifetime assistance limit and reassess needs for support services based on months remaining.

Sec. 19   Requires the department to establish a monitoring system to ensure participants are receiving support services needed to find and retain jobs with advancement opportunities. Specifies the system shall include an evaluation of outcome measures and financial activities. Requires state TEA board review and approval. Requires reports to the state TEA board.

Sec. 20   Requires the department to establish a post-employment referral program to provide information on transitional support services and education and training opportunities for employed participants and participants with closed cases due to employment.

CA   *1998 Cal. Stats., Chap. 329*
Secs. 5-6   Specifies department of education will administer child care assistance and services for employed participants or participants transitioning off of assistance. Allows department of education to contract with a county welfare department or other agency to provide services.

FL   *1999 Fla. Laws, Chap. 241*
Sec. 10   Requires caseworkers to inform newly-employed recipients about their eligibility for transitional benefits.

Sec. 12   Requires the development of procedures to notify and provide transitional benefits and services to recipients leaving cash assistance due to sanctions or noncompliance.

Sec. 16   Specifies that relocation program participants are eligible for transitional benefits. Removes four-month cash assistance limit for relocation assistance.

Sec. 26   Allows direct payment by cash or voucher for transitional transportation expenses.

IL   *1999 Ill. Laws, PA 331*
Sec. 9A-8   Requires notification to applicants and recipients of available support services including child care assistance, transportation, assistance with initial employment expenses and books and fees assistance, including eligibility requirements. Also requires notification of sanction, termination and appeal processes.

Removes department requirement to notify sanctioned or ineligible participants of education, training and employment programs. Requires notification to applicants and recipients of education, training and employment program opportunities including eligibility requirements. Specifies that applicants receive a complete list of services including substance abuse or mental health treatment, activities to escape or prevent domestic violence and dependent care for disabled family members. Allows changes in responsibility contract to reflect enrollment in programs.

Sec. 11-20.1   Requires notification to recipients of eligibility requirements and availability of supportive services for those participating in education and training programs while working.

Requires department to notify recipients of the availability of 12 months of child care and medical assistance after cash assistance is canceled due to an earned income increase.

ME   *1999 Me. Public Laws, Chap. 383*
Allows the state to provide transitional child care to families who request to discontinue receiving TANF benefits but who are still eligible.

MN   *1999 Minn. Laws, Chap. 205*
Art. 1, Sec. 9   Allows participants receiving transitional assistance to received child care services that support employment or job search activities.

Art. 1, Sec. 22   Expands eligibility for child care assistance to families participating in tribal assistance programs.

Art. 1, Sec. 24   Removes requirement that a family must be a two-parent family to receive the at-home infant child care subsidy. Expands the definition of parent to include birth or adoptive parent or stepparent for the purposes of this program. Requires the determination of the amount of the at-home infant child care subsidy to include family size. Specifies that receipt of at-home infant care assistance does not establish an employer-employee relationship between any member of the family and the county or state.

Art. 1, Sec. 25   Removes exemption from child care assistance time limit for high school students participating in a postsecondary program while pursuing a high school diploma. Eliminates automatic eligibility for child care assistance for financially eligible students who have received assistance for one academic year.

1999 Minn. Laws, Chap. 245
Art. 6, Sec. 71 (9)   Extends transitional supportive services for 12 months after eligibility termination for participants who achieve employment goals.

NM   *1999 N.M. Laws, Chap. 12*
Sec. 1   Appropriates a Welfare-to-Work match to department of health for substance abuse counseling. Appropriates Welfare-to-Work match for substance abuse counseling of Native American participants.

NY   *1998 N.Y. Laws, Chap. 564*
Sec. 131-z   Allows participants who become ineligible for cash assistance due to increased employment earnings to remain eligible for medical assistance for up to 12 months. Dependent on receipt of federal waiver.

Family Assistance—Time Limits

AR   *1999 Ark. Acts, Act 1567*
Sec. 13   Specifies there are no limits on the length and number of time limit deferrals or exemptions as long as the individual is meeting program requirements.

Requires periodic department review of all cases exempted or deferred from the 24-month assistance limit. Requires department to review all cases six months before the time limit expiration and consider granting a six-month an extension at the time of the review if participants meet the criteria. Specifies the review will include an assessment of the remaining barriers and available support services. Requires the department to make effort to deliver support services for individuals with barriers.

Allows the department to defer or exempt individuals participating in education and training activities from the 24-month cumulative assistance limit. Specifies the individual must be in compliance with program requirements, making satisfactory academic progress and expected to complete the education program within a reasonable timeframe.

Sec. 18   Requires the department to notify participants of time remaining in lifetime assistance limit.

IL   *1999 Ill. Laws, PA 331*
Sec. 9A-8   Requires department to notify applicants and recipients of lifetime eligibility limit, including current months of remaining eligibility. Specifies notification include situations when a month will not count towards limit and situations for allowable receipt of benefits beyond lifetime limit.

LA   *1999 La. Acts, Act 572*
Sec. 1   Exempts the months a recipient receives the earned income disregards from the state 24-month time limit.

MN   *1999 Minn. Laws, Chap. 245*
Art. 6, Sec. 50 (1)   Expands 60-month cash assistance time limit to include participants in a tribal TANF program.

Art. 6, Sec. 81 (4)   Requires report on the number of participants who have received 60 months of cash assistance by Jan. 15, 2000.

NC   *1999 N.C. Sess. Laws, Chap. 234*
Secs. 1, 2   Allows up to a three-year assistance extension for recipients enrolled at least part-time in a postsecondary education program and maintaining a minimum 2.5 GPA.

Sec. 5   Requires counties to conduct client reviews at least three months before time limit and to assist recipients with transition off of assistance to employment. Specifies families must be informed in writing of available noncash benefits. Allows counties to provide cash assistance extensions for qualified families.

Specifies families must be informed in writing of available noncash benefits once cash assistance time limit has expired. Allows counties to provide cash assistance extensions for qualified families.

ND   *1999 N.D. Sess. Laws, Chap. 421*
Sec. 2   Allows department to define hardship exemptions.

YOUTH AT RISK

Administration—General

ID   *1999 Idaho Sess. Laws, Chap. 77*
Provides that a portion of the youth license plate fee is used to provide prevention and early intervention programs for at-risk youth.

IN   *1999 Ind. Acts, PL 211*
Sec. 7   Establishes the Indiana youth development charter committee. Specifies membership, terms and duties, and requires it to consider problems affecting youth, recommend solutions, promote youth development activities and perform related tasks.

ME   *1999 Me. Public Laws, Chap. 87*
Establishes the Commission to Study Children in Need of Services to study truancy, runaways, emancipation and related issues. Requires a report to the Legislature.

NY   *1999 N.Y. Laws, SB 6289*
Requires an agent of the Department of Environmental Conservation to conduct courses in responsible hunting practices and supervise juveniles ages 12 to 16 at shooting ranges.

TX   *1999 Tex. Gen. Laws, Chap. 489*
Sec. 1   Requires the Department of Protective and Regulatory Services to implement and manage programs that provide prevention and intervention services for at-risk youth. Establishes the Division of Prevention and Early Intervention Services under the Department of Protective and Regulatory Services to manage the delivery of services to at-risk youth.

Missing/Runaway

CA   *1998 Cal. Stats., Chap. 1065*
Creates a pilot project to provide private, nonprofit temporary shelters, family crisis resolution and transitional-living services for runaway youths and their families.

ID   *1999 Idaho Sess. Laws, Chap. 12*
Establishes a permanent missing persons clearinghouse. Requires law enforcement officials to immediately enter information on missing and runaway children into the National Crime Information Center.

LA   *1999 La. Acts, Act 1087*
Shifts responsibility for licensing and certification of approved runaway facilities from Department of Health and Hospitals to Department of Social Services. Permits runaway youths over age 11 to remain in a facility for up to 72 hours before being returned to the home environment and requires the state to provide 72 hours of safe harbor to that runaway regardless of who maintains custody over the minor.

ME   *1999 Me. Public Laws, Chap. 55*
·Creates the Homeless Youth Demonstration Project to develop and deliver innovative and collaborative nontraditional services to unaccompanied youths aged 14 to 17 at two pilot sites. Requires project to report to Legislature, with evaluation of project, including measurable outcomes and recommended legislation, by Feb. 1, 2001.

MI   *1998 Mich. Pub. Acts, Act 516*
Defines 'county juvenile agency services' to include services for youths under court control for criminal acts, but also running away from home and truancy. Specifies county formula for block-grant eligibility. Sets preference for placement in state Family Independence Agency beds rather than out-of-state beds when county juvenile agencies are over capacity. Changes Social Welfare Act to maintain consistency with the newly enacted statutes associated with the County Juvenile Agency Act.

VA   *1999 Va. Acts, Chap. 453*
          Sec. 1   Requires juveniles who have run away or deserted their parents or legal custodians to have done
          so on more than one occasion in order to be characterized as a "child in need of supervision."

WA   *1999 Wash. Laws, Chap. 267*
          Directs Department of Social and Health Services to license and establish beds for short-term crisis resi-
          dential services, and dependent youth. Requires coordination with the Missing Children's Clearinghouse
          and make sure that efforts are made to reunify runaway youth served in its programs with parents who are
          looking for them.

          Sec. 11   Requires the state to establish HOPE centers that provide transitional living services to street
          youth and a therapeutic model of service delivery.

School Safety Policies/Truancy

AK   *1999 Alaska Sess. Laws, Chap. 36*
          Requires school districts to provide certain criminal record information to new district when student trans-
          fers.

AR   *1999 Ark. Acts, Act 628*
          Establishes a youth mediation program to provide conflict resolution training and assistance to schools and
          juvenile courts.

          1999 Ark. Acts, Act 1149
          Makes parent guilty of a Class B misdemeanor if they know that a minor illegally possesses a firearm on
          school property or at school events and fails to prevent possession or report possession.

CA   *1998 Cal. Stats., Chap. 317*
          Creates the School Community Policing Partnership Act and accompanying grant program to last at least
           three years. Requires grant recipients to demonstrate a collaborative and integrated approach for imple-
          menting a system of providing safe and secure environments through community policing. Mandates
          biennial evaluation and legislative reports.

CO   *1999 Colo. Sess. Laws, Chap. 134*
          Permits school districts to prohibit certain expelled students from enrolling in the same school as their
          victims.

CT   *1999 Conn. Acts, Act 247*
          Requires the state to notify school superintendents when a serious juvenile offender may return to school
          and the department believes, in good faith, that the offender is a risk to self or others.

FL   *1999 Fla. Laws, Chap. 284*
          Sec. 2   Requires fingerprinting and secure detention of a minor who has committed unlawful possession
          or discharge of a weapon or firearm at a school-sponsored event or on school property. Requires detaining
          in secure detention a minor under age 18 who is charged with possessing or discharging a firearm on
          school property, unless the state attorney authorizes release.

GA   *1999 Ga. Laws, Chap. 282*
          Requires the character education program to include methods of discouraging bullying and violent acts
          against fellow students. Adds razor blade in definition of weapon.

ID   *1999 Idaho Sess. Laws, Chap. 389*
          Removes exemption for carrying a concealed weapon on school property from the Juvenile Corrections
          Act.